One Another's Equals

One Another's Equals

THE BASIS OF HUMAN EQUALITY

JEREMY WALDRON

The Belknap Press of Harvard University Press

Cambridge, Massachusetts

London, England   2017

First printing

Library of Congress Cataloging-in-Publication Data

Names: Waldron, Jeremy, author.

Title: One another's equals : the basis of human equality / Jeremy Waldron.

Description: Cambridge, Massachusetts : The Belknap Press of Harvard University Press, 2017. | Includes bibliographical references and index.

Identifiers: LCCN 2016047874 | ISBN 9780674659766 (alk. paper)

Subjects: LCSH: Equality. | Civilization, Western.

Classification: LCC JC575 .W335 2017 | DDC 320.01/1—dc23

LC record available at https://lccn.loc.gov/2016047874

FOR THE MEMORY OF

Bob Hargrave
1949–2012

with love

Contents

Preface

One Another's Equals presents revised versions of the Gifford Lectures that I delivered at the University of Edinburgh at the end of January and the beginning of February 2015. It was a pleasure to spend two weeks in Scotland. I had taught in Edinburgh for almost five years, from 1983 until 1987. They were some of the best years of my life, and it was great to revisit old friends and old haunts in Auld Reekie.

The lectures were delivered in the elegant surroundings of the Playfair Library in Edinburgh University's Old College. I am most grateful to the audience, who sat through six lectures on an abstruse theme; it was more punishment than any of them deserved. Their interest and their unabated enthusiasm were a delight, and their questions challenged me, in a good way, at the end of each session.

For hospitality and support, I owe a particular debt to old friends and new. They include Michael Adler, Kenneth Amaeshi, Malcolm Anderson, Zenon Bankowski, Alice Brown, Gordon Brown, Stewart Brown, Rev. Frances Burberry, Rowan Cruft, Tom Daly, David Fergusson, Alexander Forsyth, Sue Fyvel, Nuala Gormley and her colleagues in the Scottish government, Elizabeth Grant, Vinit Haksar, Larry Hurtado, Charles Jeffrey, Bonnie and Tomas Kennedy-Grant,

Peter Kravitz, Sir Timothy O'Shea (rector of the university), Charles Raab, Jo Shaw, Mona Siddiqui, the Rt. Rev. Brian Smith, Neil Walker, and the Honorable Sarah Wolf. I am especially grateful to Anna Conroy and Alistair Lauder (for the Gifford Foundation) for organizational and administrative support.

Back in New York, in Oxford, and elsewhere: over the years, I have benefited from conversations about equality with Richard Arneson, Victor Austin, Charles Beitz, Patrick Brennan, Ian Carter, Jack Coons, the late Ronald Dworkin, Kent Greenawalt, Moshe Halbertal, George Kateb, Desmond King, Nikolas Kirby, Lewis Kornhauser, Nicola Lacey, Yair Lorberbaum, Robin Lovin, Trevor Morrison, Liam Murphy, Thomas Nagel, Marcia Pally, Thomas Pogge, Joseph Raz, Michael Rosen, Adam Samaha, Carol Sanger, Samuel Scheffler, Ian Shapiro, David Soskice, William Storrar, Jeffrey Stout, and John Tasioulas. I am grateful to them all.

I am happy to acknowledge the support of the Filomen D'Agostino and Max E. Greenberg Research Fund at New York University Law School for the final stages of developing these lectures for publication in 2015 and 2016. Ian Malcolm of Harvard University Press was a tower of confidence during that process and, as always, a model of patience.

One Another's Equals

1

"More Than Merely Equal Consideration"?

My theme is equality. Human equality: the principle that holds that we humans, despite all our differences, are to be regarded as one another's equals. Created equal, as it says in Thomas Jefferson's opening claim in the Declaration of Independence. Or, even if not *created*—and I take the "Creator" aspect quite seriously in some of these lectures— then equal anyway, by nature perhaps or by fixed and fundamental convention.

1.

My lectures do not address particular policy positions, like the policy that requires us to reduce the economic inequality of our society or the policy that requires us to change our education system so that it better secures equality of opportunity. The lectures are not about the various disparities and inequalities of wealth, income, power, and opportunity that disfigure our social and economic arrangements. Those are tremendously important matters. But I shall address an underlying concern—one that asks whether people are being treated and respected as equals, whatever disparities (justified or unjustified) may exist between them in wealth, income, power, and opportunity. I am interested in basic moral equality, our status as one another's equals. Sometimes this is called "deep" equality, sometimes "abstract" equality,[1] sometimes "moral equality."[2]

There are many ways of characterizing basic equality. We can present it as a principle of "equal worth,"[3] so that these lectures are about the equal worth of human beings—perhaps their equal worth in the eyes of God, or just *their equal worth* (if one does not want to talk in religious terms). Human worth we often contrast with merit. We have different merits—all of us—different skills, different achievements, different deserts or deservings, different ways in which we can be useful to each other and to the community, different prices that people are willing to pay for our abilities and services. All this is in the realm of merit. Human worth is what is left over when you take merit away or set it aside. Some think that inherent human worth is an empty concept; I guess they think that merit is everything.[4] Others—I am among them—believe that each human life and the living of each human life has a high worth that is important and equal in the case of each person.

1. Both terms—"deep" and "abstract"—may be attributed to Ronald Dworkin: see respectively his book A *Matter of Principle* (Harvard University Press, 1985), 271–273, and his article "Comment on Narveson: In Defense of Equality," *Social Philosophy and Policy* 1 (1983): 24–40.

2. See, for example, Lansing Pollock, "Moral Equality," *Public Affairs Quarterly* 15 (2001): 241–260.

3. See Christopher Nathan, "What Is Basic Equality?," in *Do All Persons Have Equal Moral Worth? On Basic Equality and Equal Respect and Concern*, ed. Uwe Steinhoff (Oxford University Press, 2015), 1.

4. See, for example, Héctor Wittwer, "The Irrelevance of the Concept of Worth to the Debate between Egalitarianism and Non-Egalitarianism," in Steinhoff, *Do All Persons Have Equal Moral Worth?*, 76–95. Wittwer distinguishes inherent human worth from acquired human worth. The former idea is the one he is criticizing; the latter he associates with what I have been calling merit.

Another concept invoked in these discussions is that of human dignity. Dignity, I believe, is best understood as a status term: it refers to the standing of human beings in the great scheme of things, their status as persons who command a high level of concern and respect. The basis of our equal dignity as humans is supposed to be something fundamental about us that makes it important for us to accord equal moral consideration to one another and to respect each other in the same way. In part it is a legal idea, requiring us to attribute to each other the same human rights, to respect and uphold those rights, and to offer each other the protection and consideration of the same laws—"equal protection," as the Americans put it in the Fourteenth Amendment to the U.S. Constitution.

These terms—"basic equality," "equal worth," "equal concern and respect," and "human dignity"—are not synonyms. But they cluster together to form a powerful body of principle. Each of them does two jobs, one vertical and one horizontal: vertically, it identifies a particular value or set of requirements that attend our dealings with each human person; horizontally, it asserts an equality of that value or a sameness of those requirements across all human persons. In each case, the user of the term promises to explain the content of the idea: what our worth or dignity, for example, requires, what it is supposed to be based on, and why it is the same for everyone. As we will see in Lecture 3, different theorists do this in different ways. In each case, too, the user of the term in question promises to explain the range of its application: does it apply to all humans, all persons, all rational agents, all sentient beings, or what?

I use all of these terms from time to time in what follows. I hope the context will make clear why I am using one of them and not another. I do, however, largely confine my use of "human dignity" to conceptions that attribute a high *and distinctive* status to humans, a status that is supposed to contrast with the moral considerability of non-human animals. As we shall see, theories of basic human equality need not do this. One can maintain the position that humans are all one another's equals without necessarily committing oneself to or against the position that humans stand higher in the scheme of things than the highest of the other animals. Human dignity presupposes an equality of worth or standing among humans, but it adds to that an additional stronger thesis—by which I mean a claim that requires further defense—about distinctive human worth.

2.

These all sound like abstruse philosophical ideals. But I hope they will resonate—and that the challenge of clarifying them will resonate—with ordinary lives as well. When I delivered the Gifford Lectures in Edinburgh at the beginning of 2015, I asked those attending to look around and consider the differences among members of the audience: some were old, some quite young; some men, some women; there were evident differences of race and ethnicity (perhaps not as many as there should have been). There were differences of appearance—some people were fit, some like me were not so fit and not so thin either. Some showed in their faces that they were healthy, while others were struggling to conceal illness and infirmity. Yet despite these differences, we might look around the hundred or so people in the room and tell ourselves that we all respect one another as equals. That basic equality, we might say, matters more than our organic differences. Still we have to ask, "Matters how? Matters why? Matters in what respects and for what purposes?" That is what these lectures are about.

There are also differences between us that are not physically apparent. Differences of ability, certainly—different skills, experiences, and levels of creativity. There are differences of virtue, moral differences. Some of us shamefaced have to hide our moral shortcomings, while others have the good fortune to be able to be entirely open about their character and actions. Different kinds of merit, too. Yet, despite these differences, do we not also say that all of us, the skilled and the unskilled, the good and the bad, are equal as human persons? I do not mean that no one is ever allowed to consider moral or merito-cratic differences. On the contrary, those are among the most impor-tant things about us. The challenge of basic equality is to reconcile the importance of these differences with the principle that nevertheless we are one another's equals.

I asked the members of the audience to look around yet again, and this time to focus on differences of income and power: some were rich, some were poor students beginning to groan under the burden of educational debt; some were powerful and successful (and some aspired to that, while some had tried and failed). In principle, basic equality can be reconciled with differences of wealth and power, cer-tainly if those differences are calculated to serve the interests of all. But basic equality also provides a platform for the scrutiny of social and economic inequality; it provides a basis for arguing about that in-equality as well as a ground for more direct concern when the extent of the inequality begins to affect people's ability to see themselves in the lives of others.

The last thing I asked the Edinburgh audience to consider as they looked across at one another was difference of status. Obviously, dif-ferences of status connected to differences of wealth and power, but status can also have a life of its own. There are differences of profes-sional status: the rector of the university, the professors, the lecturers, the graduate students, and the undergraduates. There are differences of status in the eyes of the law: most members of the audience were citizens of the United Kingdom, but I am a New Zealander living in the United States as a resident alien; I was in Edinburgh to give these lectures under a temporary U.K. visa. And again different status in the eyes of the law: maybe there were soldiers in the audience as well as civilians. Perhaps there were fugitives and convicts as well as law-abiding citizens; homeless people as well as property owners; bankrupts, infants, and lunatics. All these are statuses that differentiate us in the eyes of the law, and yet they too are supposed to be reconcilable with the fact that fundamentally there is just one sort of human being, just one rank of humanity, a special status (I call it human dignity) that we all bear.

In my Tanner Lectures at Berkeley a few years ago, I distinguished two kinds of legal status: I called them *sortal* status and *conditional* status.[5] (In the Anglican liturgy, there is a prayer for "all sorts and conditions of men," so I stole that terminology from the Prayer Book.)[6] Most of the status distinctions that obtain these days apply to individuals in virtue of certain conditions they are in: bankruptcy, minority, alienage, membership in the armed forces. These are occupations or vicissitudes that people have gotten themselves into for the time being, and they attract distinctive rights, powers, and disabilities. Marriage is a status—for most of us, a desirable status, as is shown by the urgent demand for the legal availability of same-sex marriage. A conditional status like marriage, minority, alienage, or bankruptcy is important in the lives of those to whom it applies. But such statuses do not tell us anything about the underlying personhood of the individual who has them.

5. Jeremy Waldron, with Wai-Chee Dimmock, Don Herzog, and Michael Rosen as commentators, *Dignity, Rank and Rights*, ed. Meir Dan Cohen (Oxford University Press, 2012).

6. From the 1662 *Book of Common Prayer*, in *The Book of Common Prayer: The Texts of 1549, 1559, and 1662*, ed. Brian Cummings (Oxford University Press, 2011), 267: "O God, the Creator and Preserver of all mankind, we humbly beseech thee for all sorts and conditions of men; that thou wouldest be pleased to make thy ways known unto them, thy saving health unto all nations."

Sortal status, by contrast, categorizes legal subjects on the basis of *the sort of person* they are. Modern distinctions of sortal status are hard to find, and that is a good thing. But historically you can think of villeinage and serfdom. Or you can think of a racist legal system like the system of apartheid in South Africa from 1948 to 1994 or slavery in the United States from 1776 until 1865 — systems which recognized different sorts of human beings and ascribed different statuses to people more or less permanently on the basis of the race they belonged to.[7] You can think of nobility — I mean a status system of nobility amounting to something more than a moniker and a seat in the House of Lords. For a long time, our legal system ascribed separate status to women. These sortal statuses represented people's permanent situations and destiny. They even affected how the conditional statuses operated. For example, a person of low social status would be punished differently than a person of high status; there would be different forms of execution, different kinds of imprisonment.[8]

7. Consider for example the 1856 opinion of Chief Justice Taney in *Dred Scott v. Sandford*, 60 U.S. 393, 407 (1856):

> In the opinion of the court, the legislation and histories of the times, and the language used in the Declaration of Independence, show, that neither the class of persons who had been imported as slaves, nor their descendants, whether they had become free or not, were then acknowledged as a part of the people, nor intended to be included in the general words used in that memorable instrument. . . . They had for more than a century before been regarded as beings of an inferior order . . . and so far inferior, that they had no rights which the white man was bound to respect; and that the negro might justly and lawfully be reduced to slavery for his benefit. He was bought and sold, and treated as an ordinary article of merchandise and traffic, whenever a profit could be made by it. This opinion . . . was regarded as an axiom in morals as well as in politics, which no one thought of disputing, or supposed to be open to dispute.

8. See James Whitman, *Harsh Justice: Criminal Punishment and the Widening Divide between America and Europe* (Oxford University Press, 2005).

One way of thinking about basic human equality is that it denies that there are differences of sortal status correlating to differences of kind among humans. The principle of basic equality repudiates a position that once upon a time almost everyone embraced: that the law has to concern itself with different types of human beings. We now hold that there is just one sortal status: the status of being a human person.[9] To use Gregory Vlastos's term, we are "a single status society."[10] We acknowledge, to be sure, that there are differences of conditional status: statuses like bankruptcy, infancy, felony, and so forth. But we believe there is just one sortal status—one kind of human being—under which these possible conditional statuses are arrayed. The principle of basic equality maintains this as a matter of principle and puts it forward critically as a basis for positive law.

Nowhere is this better reflected than in our doctrines of human rights. We think every society ought to look out for and respect certain basic rights in the case of every human being. These are protections,

9. R. H. Graveson, *Status in the Common Law* (Athlone Press, 1953), 2, maintains that a status is a "special condition of a continuous and institutional nature, *differing from the legal position of the normal person,* which is conferred by law . . . whenever a person occupies a position of which the creation, continuance or relinquishment and the incidents thereof are a matter of sufficient social concern" (my emphasis). On this account, "a single-status society" is an oxymoron. English writers tend to put particular emphasis on status as something exceptional, and accordingly they distinguish their notion of status from Roman law notions, which also comprised the status of the ordinary free man. I have never understood why English writers take this view. Ordinary legal personality seems to me to satisfy every other aspect of the definition of legal status. The law determines the background rights (e.g., human rights, civil liberties), background duties (e.g., duties under tort law and criminal law), and background capacities (e.g., standard freedom of contract, testamentary capacity) of the ordinary person in the first instance without his consent, and it does so as a matter of public policy concern, just as it does for the alien or the orphan. See also the discussion in Waldron, *Dignity, Rank and Rights,* 57–61.

10. Gregory Vlastos, "Justice and Equality" (1962), in *Theories of Rights,* ed. Jeremy Waldron (Oxford University Press, 1984), 41–76.

liberties, powers, and moral benefits that every human is entitled to as part of the concern and respect that his or her human status demands. Maybe some of these rights (or versions of them) are shared with animals, though most of them do not make sense except in relation to distinctively human capacities and potentials. They are bound up with the status and perhaps the dignity of the human person.

3.

There has been intense discussion of social and economic equality in the philosophical literature over the past fifty years: philosophers have discussed the case for and against egalitarianism and, if we are egalitarians, what sort of social or economic equality we should be aiming for.[11] Should we be aiming for equality of well-being, equality of resources, equality of opportunity, equality of primary goods, or equality in the capabilities that are important for people's lives? There

11. Cf. Amartya Sen, "Equality of What?," in *Choice, Welfare and Measurement* (MIT Press, 1982), 353–370. See also Ronald Dworkin, "What Is Equality? Part 1: Equality of Welfare," *Philosophy and Public Affairs* 10 (1981): 185–246, reprinted in Ronald Dworkin, *Sovereign Virtue: The Theory and Practice of Equality* (Harvard University Press, 2000), 11–64; Ronald Dworkin, "What Is Equality? Part 2: Equality of Resources," *Philosophy and Public Affairs* 10 (1981): 283–345, also reprinted in Dworkin, *Sovereign Virtue*, 65–119; David Miller, "Arguments for Equality," in *Midwest Studies in Philosophy*, vol. 7, *Social and Political Philosophy*, ed. Peter French et al. (University of Minnesota Press, 1982), 73; Larry Temkin, "Inequality," *Philosophy and Public Affairs* 15 (1986): 99; Amartya Sen, *Inequality Reexamined* (Harvard University Press, 1992); Derek Parfit, *Equality or Priority?* (University of Kansas, 1995); Harry Frankfurt, "Equality and Respect," *Social Research* 64 (1997): 3; Elizabeth Anderson, "What Is the Point of Equality?," *Ethics* 109 (1999): 287; Richard Arneson, "Equality and Equal Opportunity for Welfare," *Philosophical Studies* 56 (1990): 77; G. A. Cohen, *Rescuing Justice and Equality* (Harvard University Press, 2008); George Sher, *Equality for Inegalitarians* (Cambridge University Press, 2014). There are also two useful anthologies: J. Roland Pennock and John Chapman, eds., *Nomos IX: Equality* (New York University Press, 1967), and Louis Pojman and Robert Westmoreland, eds., *Equality: Selected Readings* (Oxford University Press, 1997).

are all sorts of theories of economic equality: the difference principle, luck egalitarianism, prioritarianism, and so on. (These were terms of art for some members of my audience, though matters of complete mystery to others.) Such topics and theories have been the bread and butter of political philosophy since John Rawls began crafting his conception of justice in the 1960s.[12] What I want to say is that they represent surface-level issues compared with the depth of the questions that these lectures address. They are surface-level; but they are by no means superficial. Among them are some of the most intractable problems of political philosophy, which is why so much has been written about them.

Until very recently, much less was written about basic equality—much less about the idea that I talk about in these lectures: the idea that we humans are fundamentally one another's equals. There was a page or two in an old article by Bernard Williams, another page or two in the piece I mentioned by Gregory Vlastos, and eight important pages toward the end of John Rawls's great book *A Theory of Justice*.[13] I wrote a long research paper on basic equality more than fifteen years ago that has languished unpublished, though it has circulated in samizdat form on SSRN.[14] And that is about it, at least until quite

12. See John Rawls, "Justice as Fairness," *Philosophical Review* 67 (1958): 164–191, reprinted in John Rawls, *Collected Papers*, ed. Samuel Freeman (Harvard University Press, 1999), 47–72; John Rawls, "The Sense of Justice," *Philosophical Review* 72 (1963): 281–305, also reprinted in Rawls, *Collected Papers*, 96–116. See also John Rawls, *A Theory of Justice* (Harvard University Press, 1971) and *Justice as Fairness: A Restatement*, ed. Erin Kelly (Harvard University Press, 2001).

13. Bernard Williams, "The Idea of Equality" (1962), in *Problems of the Self* (Cambridge University Press, 1973), 230–239; Vlastos, "Justice and Equality"; and Rawls, *A Theory of Justice*, 504–512.

14. Jeremy Waldron, "Basic Equality," NYU School of Law, Public Law Research Paper No. 08-61 (December 2008), http://ssrn.com/abstract=1311816. I gave a talk based on this paper in Scotland at the University of St. Andrews as the Sir Malcolm Knox lecture in the

recently.[15] The recent material comprises a couple of edited vol-
umes, one called *Social Equality: Essays on What It Means to Be
Equals* and one asking, in its title, *Do All Persons Have Equal Moral
Worth?*[16]

The first of these includes some important recent work on what it
means for a society (or a family, a business, or a friendship) to be organized so that its members relate to one another as equals.[17] This
involves considering what are called relational (as opposed to distributive) ideas of equality. Relational equality is plainly closer to what
I am calling basic equality than distributive equality is. But the two—
basic equality and relational equality—don't seem to be regarded as
identical. What is sometimes said is that we invoke the proposition

---

year 2000. These Gifford Lectures are a much expanded and reconsidered version of that
piece.

15. Other pieces on basic equality have included Herbert Spiegelberg, "A Defense of
Human Equality," *Philosophical Review* 53 (1944): 101–124; Joseph Margolis, "That All
Men Are Created Equal," *Philosophical Review* 52 (1955): 337–346; John H. Schaar,
"Some Ways of Thinking about Equality," *Journal of Politics* 26 (1964): 867–895; Richard
Wasserstrom, "Rights, Human Rights, and Racial Discrimination," *Journal of Philosophy* 61
(1964): 628–641; John Wilson, *Equality* (Harcourt, Brace and World, 1967), chap. 2;
Stanley Benn, "Egalitarianism and the Equal Consideration of Interests," in Pennock and
Chapman, *Nomos IX*, 61–78; Steven Lukes, "Socialism and Equality" (1974), in *Essays in
Social Theory* (Macmillan, 1977), 98–105; Vinit Haksar, *Equality, Liberty and Perfectionism*
(Clarendon Press, 1979), chaps. 2–3; D. A. Lloyd Thomas, "Equality within the Limits of
Reason Alone," *Mind* 88 (1979): 538–553; Amy Gutmann, *Liberal Equality* (Cambridge
University Press, 1980), chap. 1; Dworkin, "In Defense of Equality"; Louis Pojman, "Are
Human Rights Based on Equal Human Worth?," *Philosophy and Phenomenological Re-
search* 52 (1992): 605–622; John Coons and Patrick Brennan, *By Nature Equal: The Anatomy
of a Western Insight* (Princeton University Press, 1999).

16. Steinhoff, *Do All Persons Have Equal Moral Worth?*; Carina Fourie, Fabian Schuppert, and Ivo Wallimann-Helmer, eds., *Social Equality: Essays on What It Means to Be Equals*
(Oxford University Press, 2015).

17. See Samuel Scheffler, "The Practice of Equality," in Fourie et al., *Social Equality*,
21–44.

that all people have equal moral worth to defend the claim that we should organize our society as a society of equals.[18] Mostly those who write about the relational conception spend their energy talking not about what relational equality is based on but about the structures and practices it requires. There has been interest, too, not only in highlighting the distinction between relational and distributive concerns but also in considering whether relational equality might itself make demands of a distributive kind.[19] And the picture that sometimes seems to emerge is that we proceed from basic equality to relational equality and only thence to distributive equality.[20] I am not sure about that; I believe that basic equality sometimes has distributive implications all by itself. Anyway, relational equality is certainly important. I say a little more about it in Lecture 2, for I believe it comprises some of the most exacting normative consequences of basic equality. In the meantime, let me reiterate that I am not equating basic equality with relational equality. Their exact connection needs to be explored.

The dearth, until recently, of good philosophical work on basic equality is not because the latter was thought unimportant. It is very important: much of the work that has been done on distributive equality as a policy aim presupposes and builds upon the importance of basic equality.

Let me give a couple of examples, inspired by Ronald Dworkin's early work on equality. Dworkin posed questions about what I have called surface-level issues of distribution in the following terms: "Suppose some community must choose between alternative schemes for distributing money and other resources to individuals. Which of the

18. See Samuel Scheffler, "What Is Egalitarianism?," *Philosophy and Public Affairs* 31 (2003): 5–39, at 33.

19. Scheffler, "The Practice of Equality," 44.

20. Scheffler, "What Is Egalitarianism?," 31.

possible schemes treats people as equals?"[21] Someone might say in response that the aim of such schemes should be to equalize the net balance of enjoyment over suffering across persons. After all, "for almost everyone, pain or dissatisfaction is an evil and . . . for almost everyone pleasure or enjoyment . . . is of value, and contributes to the desirability of life."[22] But, says Dworkin, different people in fact give these conscious states different weight in their lives. Athletes may be willing to endure more pain for the possibility of high achievement, while nonathletes would value the enjoyment of achievement lower and the absence of pain higher. Using such conscious states, then, as a metric of equality would not treat people as equals, because it would try to make them equal in aspects of their lives that they value unequally. This argument therefore presupposes that we can appeal to basic equality—the idea of treating people as equals—to criticize some theory about the appropriate measure for distributive equality.

In a later article, Dworkin pursued another argument, this time against the artificial maintenance of equality of resources (equality of wealth, for example) over time. He argued that this ignored the effects of the choices people make, and he said that ignoring people's choices did not treat them as equals.[23] To be respected as an equal is (among other things) to be respected as an agent and a responsible chooser.[24] So, once again, there is a principle of basic equality— Dworkin calls it equality of concern and respect—operating as an underlying major premise. Whether or not equal treatment in some surface dimension is worth achieving is a matter of the relation between such treatment and the idea of deep equality. Dworkin did a tremendous amount over the years along these lines to explore and

---

21. Dworkin, "What Is Equality? Part 1," 185–186.
22. Ibid., 221.
23. Dworkin, "What Is Equality? Part 2."
24. See also Sher, *Equality for Inegalitarians*.

articulate this, providing a seminal account of the relation between basic equality and "choice-sensitive" and "luck-sensitive" aspects of social and economic distribution.[25]

More concretely, it is not hard to see how sometimes treating us as one another's equals may require unequal treatment of various kinds.[26] We recruit strong people, for example, to be firefighters. We recruit young people, not old people, to the fire brigade. We discriminate in these ways, but we think this surface-level discrimination is justified because such a strategy takes all our interests into account. All our interests are taken into account in determining that our firefighters are going to have to be strong and relatively young. So we appeal to a deep notion of equality—equal consideration of interests—to justify unequal treatment of candidates hoping for a job with the fire brigade. We discriminate at the surface level, but we have to be sure not to discriminate in the range of human interests that we cater to when we make this justification. That is, we must be prepared to show that having relatively youthful firefighters benefits the old as well as the young, and that having people as firefighters who are fit and strong benefits those who are in a bad state physically. We treat one another as equals when we appeal to the whole range of human interests to justify these surface-level inequalities. The principle of basic equality operates to patrol and discipline the way we argue in these matters.

As I said, I owe this whole way of looking at things—the distinction between equal treatment and treatment as an equal and the insistence that the latter must underpin and discipline the former—to the work of Ronald Dworkin (though the examples I have given are not his). The distinction between basic equality and surface-level

25. See also the papers collected in Dworkin, *Sovereign Virtue.*

26. This example is taken from Jeremy Waldron, "The Substance of Equality," *Michigan Law Review* 89 (1991): 1350–1370.

equality was fundamental to his work. Yet in his prolific career, Professor Dworkin said next to nothing in detail about the principle of equal concern and respect. He gave us the phrase: he repeated it in almost everything he wrote,[27] but he devoted very little energy to any detailed reflection on basic equality.[28] What does equal concern and respect amount to? What, if anything, in our nature evokes it? What would its denial involve? We know that racists and sexists do not regard all humans as their equals; they divide them up according to race and gender. Often this is done impulsively or inarticulately. But is it worth asking nevertheless what exactly a rational racist, if such can be imagined, would have to believe that we deny? What precisely would have to be refuted if this foundational assumption of equality had to be defended against real-life, articulate opponents?

As I have said, not nearly enough work has been done on this. This has begun to change, however, and in recent years some discussion has started to emerge in political philosophy.[29] This book and the lectures it is based on are a part of that new wave. But my reflections here are a little more wide-ranging than the current philosophical debate. I mean to explore all considerations that are relevant to basic equality, even those that a well-trained philosopher would nowadays eschew.

27. See, for example, Ronald Dworkin, *Taking Rights Seriously* (Harvard University Press, 1977), 180–183, 227, 272–278; Ronald Dworkin, *Law's Empire* (Harvard University Press, 1986), 200–202, 291–295; Dworkin, *Sovereign Virtue*, passim; and Ronald Dworkin, *Justice for Hedgehogs* (Harvard University Press, 2011), 2–4.

28. An exception is Dworkin, "In Defense of Equality," but the discussion there leaves one thirsty for more.

29. See, for example, the papers in Steinhoff, *Do All Persons Have Equal Moral Worth?* See also Nicholas Wolterstorff, *Justice: Rights and Wrongs* (Princeton University Press, 2008), and Nicholas Mark Smith, *Basic Equality and Discrimination: Reconciling Theory and Law* (Ashgate, 2011).

4.

So consider this. In a recent essay called "The Irrelevance of the Concept of Worth," Héctor Wittwer talks about excluding "from scientific and philosophical discourse" propositions like "the religious dogma that all human beings were created in God's image." I have no such privilege (nor would I want to exercise it if I did). Lord Gifford set up these lectures for the stated purpose of

> "Promoting, Advancing, Teaching, and Diffusing the study of Natural Theology," in the widest sense of that term, in other words, "The Knowledge of God, the Infinite, the All, the First and Only Cause, the One and the Sole Substance, the Sole Being, the Sole Reality, and the Sole Existence, the Knowledge of His Nature and Attributes, the Knowledge of the Relations which men and the whole universe bear to Him, the Knowledge of the Nature and Foundation of Ethics or Morals, and of all Obligations and Duties thence arising."[30]

In light of this charge, it would be wrong not to pursue my theme of basic human equality into religious contexts. It would be wrong to say nothing about the idea that we are, all of us, equal in the eyes of God.

Certainly, arguments about basic equality—the self-same idea as the one the philosophers discuss—can be found in that domain, and until the twentieth century such arguments were rarely found anywhere else. When believers say we are created equal or when people of faith say that we are all children of God made in his image, they

---

30. *Trust, Disposition and Settlement of the late Adam Gifford, sometime one of the Senators of the College of Justice, Scotland,* dated 21st August 1885, http://www.giffordlectures.org /lord-gifford/will.

are addressing from their point of view exactly the topic of my lectures. And I discuss their ideas as well. I certainly do not preclude the possibility of a purely secular account of basic equality, and much of what I say in these lectures has a secular character, though occasional religious resonances will be pretty obvious. Lecture 5 in particular is devoted to the idea, common to the Jewish and Christian traditions, that each person's normative equality in her relations with her fellow human beings has something to do with her relation to God. I think it is a complicated something, not anything simple like a divine command or an immortal soul. Religious accounts cite some of the same characteristics that are cited in the secular traditions—human reason, moral agency, personal autonomy, and so on—but they bind these together into a particular narrative structure of creation, redemption, and salvation, which is said to be available to and important, equally important, in the life of each person.

I am not coy or evasive about this in the way the tradition of modern political liberalism sometimes demands we should be, under the fancied constraints of public reason.[31] Basic equality, human dignity, human worth—if these are applicable at all—are supposed to be grounded on what people are really like. If someone thinks that a theologically informed anthropology gives us our deepest and most serious account of what people are really like and what is most important about them, then we have no choice but to consider that point of view in an inquiry like this. It does not overwhelm our discussion, but it is hinted at throughout, and it is the specific topic of that one lecture.

On the other hand, although there is a robust tradition of Jewish and Christian theology supporting the principle of human equality,

31. See John Rawls, *Political Liberalism* (Columbia University Press, 1993), 212ff. I will discuss this further at the end of Lecture 5.

I am conscious that religious doctrine has been cited to the contrary effect as well. Biblical chapter and verse have been invoked to support slavery and racial inequality; people cite Genesis 9:22–26 and Joshua 9:23.[32] I am not saying they interpret those scriptural passages properly, but they do cite them. And gender inequality too—Genesis 3:16 and I Corinthians 11:3.[33] People have sometimes used religious ideas—including some that are gestured at by Lord Gifford in his settlement—to validate their convictions that there are indeed different sorts of human being with differential dignity, rights, worth, and status. It would be wrong to say nothing about that. If we take religious ideas seriously we must follow them where they lead. We cannot rule out the possibility that in the final analysis, appearances to the contrary notwithstanding, great religions like Christianity and Judaism either do not support, rely on, or presuppose human equality or may simply be indifferent to the principle or may even be opposed to it. We have to consider these possibilities, consider what they mean.

32. Genesis 9:22–26: "And Ham, the father of Canaan, saw the nakedness of his father, and told his two brethren without. And Shem and Japheth took a garment, and . . . went backward, and covered the nakedness of their father . . . and they saw not their father's nakedness. And Noah awoke from his wine, and knew what his younger son had done unto him. And he said, Cursed be Canaan; a servant of servants shall he be unto his brethren. And he said, Blessed be the Lord God of Shem; and Canaan shall be his servant." Joshua 9: 22–23: "And Joshua called for them, and he spake unto them, saying, Wherefore have ye beguiled us, saying, We are very far from you; when ye dwell among us? Now therefore ye are cursed, and there shall none of you be freed from being bondmen, and hewers of wood and drawers of water for the house of my God." Note: all biblical citations are to the King James Version.

33. Genesis 3:16: "Unto the woman he said, I will greatly multiply thy sorrow and thy conception; in sorrow thou shalt bring forth children; and thy desire shall be to thy husband, and he shall rule over thee." I Corinthians 11:3: "But I would have you know, that the head of every man is Christ; and the head of the woman is the man; and the head of Christ is God."

5.

Not only do I not ignore these possibilities, but I devote much of the rest of this lecture to a particularly egregious example. We are going to spend time in the unpleasant company of one Reverend Hastings Rashdall, who seems to have been strongly opposed to basic equality. We are going to spend time with his writings, not because his arguments demand an answer from us right now today—he was writing in England around 1907—but because his position is clear in a number of regards that illuminate what it is that we are denying when we say we are one another's equals.

I hope you do not find the example of Rashdall's arguments too offensive. In general philosophy, one sometimes has to pretend to be a weirdo; in a discussion of induction, for example, one has to pretend to believe that one does not know whether the sun will rise tomorrow. Unless one's speculations appear "cold, and strain'd, and ridiculous"[34] by ordinary standards, one is not doing philosophy. Some philosophers can make of this a disarming element of personal charm in their work. In moral philosophy, however, the same method means one sometimes has to pretend to take seriously things which are offensive by ordinary *moral* standards. And that can (and should) make moral philosophy an uncomfortable occupation to pursue. We are going to have to appear to take seriously in this lecture a position that in another context will be dismissed out of hand as unpleasant and wrong.[35] Still, here goes.

---

34. David Hume, *A Treatise of Human Nature*, ed. L. A. Selby-Bigge (Oxford University Press, 1888), 269 (bk. 1, pt. 4, §7).

35. Uwe Steinhoff, "Against Equal Respect and Concern," in Steinhoff, *Do All Persons Have Equal Moral Worth?*, 142–143, thinks I offer this as an excuse for philosophers' failure to reflect at length on the justification (or lack of justification) of basic equality. I assure him I do not. But it is worth mentioning just the same.

Dr. Hastings Rashdall was a philosopher and an ordained Anglican priest. He was a fellow of New College, Oxford,[36] a pupil of Henry Sidgwick and T. H. Green, and a member of the Christian Social Union. Later he was canon of Hereford Cathedral and, later still, dean of Carlisle.[37] In 1922 he was invited to present the Gifford Lectures at St. Andrews, but he had to decline for reasons of ill health.[38] In 1907 he published a two-volume book entitled *The Theory of Good and Evil: A Treatise of Moral Philosophy*, which was a work of ethical rationalism and ideal utilitarianism, in some ways quite similar to the ethics of G. E. Moore.[39] As a theologian and philosopher Rashdall belonged to the liberal wing of Anglican theology.[40] But his biblical learning and his Christian faith and vocation did not seem to inoculate him against a deep philosophical racism.[41]

36. A memorial plaque that one can still see in the cloisters of New College reads, "In memory of Hastings Rashdall DD FBA 1858–1924, Scholar, Fellow and Tutor, and Honorary Fellow of New College and Dean of Carlisle. Historian, Philosopher, Theologian. In thought fearless, in learning various and profound, rich in humour. In his books, in his teaching, in his public duties, he brought to the service of his age a rare passion for virtue, knowledge, and truth."

37. P. E. Matheson, *The Life of Hastings Rashdall DD* (Oxford University Press, 1928).

38. Ibid., 212.

39. Hastings Rashdall, *The Theory of Good and Evil: A Treatise on Moral Philosophy*, 2nd ed. (Oxford University Press, 1924). The comparison is to G. E. Moore, *Principia Ethica* (Cambridge University Press, 1903) and *Ethics* (Williams and Norgate, 1912).

40. See Gary Dorrien, "Idealistic Ordering: Hastings Rashdall, Post-Kantian Idealism, and Anglican Liberal Theology," *Anglican and Episcopal History* 82 (2013): 301: "Rashdall worked hard at exemplifying liberal Christian rationalism. High-minded, earnest, erudite, and deeply pious, he was dedicated to making theology modern."

41. I became aware of this material when it was identified as a target in the opening pages of Vinit Haksar, *Equality, Liberty and Perfectionism* (Oxford University Press, 1979), 2. I had previously been aware of other work by Rashdall, namely, a chapter he wrote on property entitled "The Philosophical Theory of Property," in *Property: Its Duties and Rights: Historically, Philosophically and Religiously Regarded*, ed. Charles Gore (Macmillan, 1913), 37.

In a discussion of justice in chapter 5 of volume 1 of Rashdall's treatise, he considered the question "Whose good is to be pursued and promoted in our social arrangements? And to what extent?" Instead of giving what for us is the obvious answer—"Everybody's good, and equally if possible"—Rashdall began considering the possibility that people differ radically in their capacity to achieve well-being. Like John Stuart Mill, he had a sense of higher and lower forms of happiness; unlike Mill, however, he did not believe that the higher forms were accessible in principle to everybody.[42] Instead Rashdall maintained, "The number of persons capable of highest intellectual cultivation and of enjoying the good incidental to such high cultivation is unquestionably a small minority and it is doubtful that their enjoyment of this well-being is much use to those who are beneath them in the social scale."[43] But Rashdall thought nevertheless that we need to ensure the attainment of this higher good for those who *can*

42. Cf. John Stuart Mill, *Utilitarianism*, ed. George Sher (Hackett, 2002), 13 (chap. 2). Talking of the life envisaged by "the philosophers who have taught that happiness is the end of life," Mill said this:

The happiness which they meant was not a life of rapture; but moments of such, in an existence made up of few and transitory pains, many and various pleasures, with a decided predominance of the active over the passive, and having as the foundation of the whole, not to expect more from life than it is capable of bestowing. A life thus composed, to those who have been fortunate enough to obtain it, has always appeared worthy of the name of happiness. And such an existence is even now the lot of many, during some considerable portion of their lives. The present wretched education, and wretched social arrangements, are the only real hindrance to its being attainable by almost all.

True, Mill made some comments at the beginning of *On Liberty*, ed. Currin Shields (Bobbs-Merrill, 1956), 14 (chap. 1) about his Harm Principle not being applicable to people living in "the infancy of [the] human race," that is, to "barbarians" who need to be governed by people like Mill and his father. But again, he believed that such races of men could be brought eventually into the enjoyment of full liberty as well as full happiness.

43. Rashdall, *The Theory of Good and Evil*, 234.

enjoy it, whatever sacrifices it requires on the part of everyone else.[44]
Otherwise the best we could expect would be "the general diffusion
of dull adult contentment and an education ranging between that of
the Sunday school and that of the Mechanics Institute."[45] (I guess
people talked like that in 1907.) Then he wrote this:

> I will now mention a case in which probably no one will hesi-
> tate. It is becoming tolerably obvious at the present day that all
> improvement in the social conditions of the higher races of man-
> kind postulates the exclusion of competition with the lower
> races. That means that, sooner or later, the lower Well-being—
> it may be ultimately the very existence—of countless Chinamen
> or negroes must be sacrificed that a higher life may be possible
> for a much smaller number of white men.[46]

He added (perhaps unnecessarily) that it was impossible to defend
such a policy on the principle of equal consideration.[47] Rashdall continued: "If we do defend this"—and he seemed to have no doubt that
we would[48]—"we must adopt the principle that higher life is intrinsi-

---

44. Ibid., 238: "It is at least a speculative possibility that the existence of such a life for
the few should only be purchasable by sacrifices on the part of the many which are not
compensated by any appreciable advantage to that many. If under such conditions we pro-
nounce that the higher life ought not to be extinguished, then we do at least depart from the
principle of equal consideration, understood as we have hitherto understood it."

45. Ibid., 238.

46. Ibid., 238–239.

47. Ibid., 239.

48. Cf. Dorrien, "Idealistic Ordering," 303:

> Rashdall took for granted that his audiences shared his assumptions about the inferi-
> ority of black persons and other ethnic communities that the British Empire colo-
> nized. Thus he rarely bothered to defend his prejudice. The inferior humanity of
> blacks was obvious to him, not something to argue about; it was merely a point of

cally, in and for itself, more valuable than lower life, though it may only be attainable by fewer persons, and may not contribute to the greater good of those who do not share it."[49]

As far as I can tell there is nothing ironic in this passage, nothing ironic in its explicit racism or its deprecation of the well-being of "Chinamen and negroes" (to use his terminology). He did say in a footnote that "the exclusion is far more difficult to justify in the case of people like the Japanese, who are equally civilized but have fewer wants than the Western."[50] The outlook that Rashdall was purveying here is as bad it sounds. This is not even the White Man's Burden; this is White Man's Privilege. It is not *mission civilisatrice*; it is a frank insistence that civilization is of very little use to large sections of mankind and that the interests of those sections of mankind should be subordinated to the interests of those who are capable of profiting from civilization. Rashdall's view seems to rest explicitly on the assumption that "our comparative indifference to the welfare of the black races, when it collides with the higher Well-being of a much smaller European population,"[51] is a topic for justification, not condemnation.[52] And he ended this section of his book with the following conclusion: "Individuals, or races, with higher capacities (i.e. capacities for a higher sort of Well-being)

---

reference or example. . . . [I]t was not even necessary to distinguish cultural white supremacism from the more deeply pernicious idea of ontological difference. Race was biological as well as cultural; black persons were truly inferior beings.

49. Rashdall, *The Theory of Good and Evil*, 239.

50. Ibid., 239n.

51. Ibid., 241.

52. Cf. Dorrien, "Idealistic Ordering," 308–309: "Rashdall's prejudices and imperial ambitions were so commonly shared that he was not challenged to defend their dissonance with his rhetoric of liberal enlightenment."

have a right to more than merely equal consideration as compared to those of lower capacities."[53]

I do not think anybody now writing in moral or political philosophy accepts that there is an ethically significant division of the human species into races along the lines presupposed in Rashdall's conception, although outside philosophy there are many who do. Racism remains a curse in modern democracies, and one of the characteristics of the basic human equality principle is its implacable opposition to any such account. True, there is some opposition in philosophical circles to the abstract idea of basic human equality, and we shall consider a version of it—Peter Singer's critique of human speciesism—in detail in Lecture 6.[54] But Singer's concerns about speciesism have nothing whatever to do with Rashdall's philosophical racism, which I am setting out here only in order to make clear the most egregious form of inegalitarian doctrine. Singer's concerns do have to be addressed in a theory of basic equality, but Singer, I am certain, would reject Rashdall's philosophical racism as vehemently as any of us. That said, the easy consensus among us all that a view like Rashdall's is obviously wrong does not excuse us from the task of articulating why it is wrong and what exactly it is that Rashdall is mistaken about. So what in these passages from Rashdall would we want to dispute? Is it just the racism? There is also a question about the tone, the insouciant complacency of the Edwardian Senior Common Room. But which of the assertions and which of the distinctions did Rashdall get wrong here? Our disagreement with him feels fundamental; but is the fundamental dispute about his factual assumptions or the ethical inferences that he draws from them?[55]

53. Rashdall, *The Theory of Good and Evil*, 242.

54. See Peter Singer, "Speciesism and Moral Status," *Metaphilosophy* 40 (2009): 567–581.

55. Dorrien, "Idealistic Ordering," 305, complicates matters by mentioning Rashdall's affirmation of the equality principle as being "essential to the Christian worldview and intrinsic to Christian ethics."

Maybe it is just the utilitarian feel of Rashdall's ideas that bothers us: I mean the idea of sacrificing some people for the sake of the greater good of others. Rashdall might be arguing, on something like traditional utilitarian grounds, that the well-being of "countless Chinamen or negroes" must be sacrificed *for the sake of the general good.* On this approach, the good of those whose welfare is to be sacrificed is counted in the utilitarian assessment of the policy under consideration, and counted on equal terms; it just happens to be outweighed. If this were the best way to understand it, Rashdall's argument would be an instance of a general difficulty in utilitarian theory that is already quite well understood: utilitarianism appears to countenance the sacrifice of some for the greater good of others or the good of a greater number of others to a greater extent than our moral "intuitions" allow. I do not want to underestimate the importance of that difficulty. But it has been very well studied, and it is not my topic here. (Nor do I want to consider the preposterous factual assumptions that would have to be made in order to justify Rashdall's racism on the utilitarian interpretation.)

But Rashdall was not really talking in those terms. He was talking about sacrificing countless people for the good of a much smaller number of people, and no bona fide utilitarian I know would countenance that arithmetic. We have our differences with the utilitarians on all sorts of things, but not on equality. Utilitarians are fundamentally committed to the principle of basic equality: "Everybody to count for one, nobody for more than one."[56] Everybody's pleasure, everybody's good, everybody's happiness, everybody's pain counts the same in the social calculus. But Rashdall seemed to turn his back on that when he said that it was "impossible to defend the morality of such a policy [the racial policy he argued for] upon the principle of equal consideration taken by itself and in the most obvious sense

56. I discuss this dictum in Lecture 2 (Section 7).

of the word."[57] That is why I think the more accurate interpretation
is that he thinks the well-being of "Chinamen or negroes" should not
be given the same weight in utilitarian (or other similar consequentialist or teleological) argument as the well-being of the "white men"
he appeared to favor.

Why not? It is not just a question of color.[58] Rashdall was not like
R. M. Hare's "fanatic," someone who just makes a fetish of white-
ness or puts a thumb on the scale for anyone of the same color as
he is.[59] Rashdall's position seems to involve the correlation of lines
of human descent with fundamental differences in capability, differences significant enough to constitute the humans in the respective lines as different kinds of being for moral purposes. This I think
is what he meant and what we repudiate. But still it is hard to put
one's finger on.

6.

It is not just inconsistency or irrationality, as though Rashdall were
turning a blind eye to properties in one person that are just the same
as, just as good as those in another or to pains and disappointments
for one person that are just as bad as those experienced by another.
Nor is it just partiality, of the sort that people display when they demand advantages for their child, though they know their child is no
more entitled to them than anyone else. Rashdall thought he was responding rationally and consistently to the moral importance of objective and important differences.

57. Rashdall, *The Theory of Good and Evil*, 239. Note, though, that Rashdall goes on to
say that his view can be reconciled with the Benthamite dictum if the latter is rendered as
"*Caeteris paribus*, everyone is to count for one" (240).

58. Smith, *Basic Equality and Discrimination*, 37.

59. R. M. Hare, *Freedom and Reason* (Oxford University Press, 1963), chap. 9.

We see this when we watch him compound the offensiveness of his position by trying to elicit something for human ethics from the way many of us think about our moral obligations to animals. Rashdall noticed that most people—most, not all—have some concern for animals, but their concern for animals is less than or different from their concern for humans and, they think, properly so. We are against animal cruelty, we say, but on the other hand many of us have animals butchered so we can eat them and we turn a blind eye to the torturous cruelty of the way they are raised, bred, fed, and slaughtered. Some of this no doubt is a matter of widespread bad faith. But without condoning cruelty or the mistreatment of animals, we do also think that some sort of human/animal distinction is justified—or many people do. Our moral thinking is already permeated with the idea of there being a big moral discontinuity within the range of mammals. There are all sorts of mammals, and they flourish and suffer in all sorts of ways, but when you are talking about humans, you are talking about something special (some of us say). Significantly, though we deplore the suffering of animals when it is made inescapably visible to us, we do not commit ourselves to anything like a general program of the improvement of animal lives comparable to the programs that even in Rashdall's Edwardian England were being pursued for underprivileged human beings. Partly it is a question of practicability: with enough resources and patience you can teach an impoverished child in London to read and sing, but you cannot do that with a cat, no matter how hard you try. It is not worth attempting, and it just annoys the cat.

So Rashdall asked an embarrassing question, putting those of us who believe all this on the spot: Might there not be divisions within the *human* realm that are also justified in a similar sort of way? Having acknowledged that the pain of animals "ought not to be wholly ignored," Rashdall observed, "But few people would be disposed to spend money in bringing the lives of fairly well-kept London cab-horses up to the standard of comfort represented by a sleek brewer's dray-horse in preference to spending it on the improvement of the higher life in human beings."[60]

We spend money improving the lives of Londoners, human Londoners; we do not spend money improving the lives of the cab horses of London. He continued:

> The lives of animals cannot thus be lightly treated except upon a principle which involves the admission that the life of one sentient being may be more valuable than the life of another on account of its potentialities — apart altogether from the social utilities which may be involved in their realization. However inconsiderable the differences of capacity among human races or individuals may be when compared with the differences between the lowest man and the highest beast, the distinction that we make between them implies the principle that capacity does matter.[61]

Rashdall was not here denying that man is raised above the animals. He was saying that some classes or races of humans are raised above others and that this is like what many of us think when we consider the relation between humans and animals. He was certainly not arguing that humans (or any class of humans) were *like* non-human animals.[62] He was bad, but not that bad. Rashdall used the animal analogy simply to show that we are already familiar with the idea of less-than-equal consideration.

60. Rashdall, *The Theory of Good and Evil*, 239.

61. Ibid.

62. So, once again, Rashdall's position is quite different from the view I discuss in Lecture 6, which I attribute to Peter Singer, arguing for a moral equivalence between certain non-human animals and human persons with profound disabilities.

Now, we are certainly familiar with the idea of differential consideration. A parent does not treat her children as equals if she gives them both equal amounts of scarce aspirin, ignoring the fact that only one of them has a fever. And a state does not treat its citizens as equals if it fails, in its distributive or cultural calculations, to take into account the fact that one person's choices and aspirations are quite different from those of another. Our consideration of others ought to be fine-tuned to variations in their condition, their choices, and so on. We think this is consistent with, even required by the more basic principle of equal concern. But is not the difference between this view and the view that Rashdall seems to hold about sensitivity to different kinds of human just a difference of degree?

Yes and no. If Rashdall is right about the facts (he is not), these are both instances of morally required sensitivity and discrimination (in a good sense of discrimination). But he is postulating something like *a major difference of kind* between the members of different human groups, over and above whatever is required in the way of sensitivity to the details of their individual situations. Many of us believe there is such a major difference of kind between the capacities for good and flourishing as between the lives of humans and the lives of other animals. As a result, there is a whole array of concepts that we can barely deploy in the case of animals, like opportunity, career, personal autonomy, freedom of belief, long-term expectations, and so on. Our moral consideration of humans has to be structured by concepts like these; as a result it is almost completely different in character from our moral consideration of animals. And Rashdall is suggesting that there is a major difference of kind—that sort of major difference of kind—between the lives and capacities for the good and the flourishing of white men and countless Chinamen and negroes.

7.

I said that I introduced Rashdall's philosophical racism into discussion not because he needed or merited refutation[63] but because consideration of his view might help us clarify our own, if only to show us what partisans of basic equality are against. And here we have a preliminary finding. The principle of basic equality is opposed to any claim that there are moral distinctions and differentiations to be made *among humans* like unto or analogous in scale and content to the moral distinctions commonly made between humans and other animals. The principle of basic equality is opposed to this sort of differentiation among humans. We say, with Cicero in *De Legibus*, that there is "no difference of kind between man and man."[64]

I am going to call this principle, which I say is characteristic of basic egalitarianism, "continuous equality" — "continuous" because it denies the existence of major discontinuities in the human realm. I am not saying that when you accept this principle you are therefore committed to a discontinuity between the human and the animal realm. But you know people who do believe in that, and you know the sort of things they have in mind. You want to say that *no such sort of thing applies within the human realm*. The principle of *continuous* equality simply asserts a negative. To repeat: there are no distinctions of the relevant kind between human and human, nothing like the distinctions commonly made between human and animal.

63. Uwe Steinhoff reminds us ("Against Equal Respect and Concern," 143) that there are plenty of good nonracist opponents of basic equality (like himself) to grapple with, without worrying about Hastings Rashdall.

64. Cicero, *De Legibus*, I.10. The passage continues: "In fact, there is no human being of any race who cannot aspire to virtue." My source for this saying is J. A. Rogers, *Nature Knows No Color-Line: Research into the Negro Ancestry in the White Race* (Wesleyan University Press, 2014), 47n.

A separate principle—I shall call it the principle of *distinctive equality*—would add something to this. Distinctive equality says that not only are humans one another's equals in the continuous sense, but also they are one another's equals on a basis that does actually differentiate them from animals. (This, as I said earlier, is often associated with the phrase "human dignity.") So the second position includes the first but takes us much further: it actually asserts the discontinuity with other animals and maintains that all humans therefore exist on a higher plane.

Both of these positions are sometimes associated with what I have called basic equality, and in these lectures I take myself to be exploring both of them—sometimes one, sometimes the two together. (For what it is worth, I personally am a strong believer in distinctive equality.) What our consideration of Rashdall has given us, however, is a confidence that basic equality comprises *at least* continuous equality (and that this is what its racists and sexist opponents deny).

8.

Now, pinning down the meaning of continuous equality is a bit of a problem. This is because it defines itself by reference to a position that it does not necessarily embrace. It says there are no distinctions among humans *of the kind that some people think exist between humans and animals.* Well, what kind of distinctions are those? We may refer to them as "Rashdall-discontinuities." But a label is not an explication.

After all, as I said in Section 6, there certainly *are* distinctions between humans that affect some of the questions of justice that Rashdall is addressing in this part of his book. Humans pursue different goods and styles of living, and some of them think about their lives in ways that are quite different from the way we think about ours. Some give a great deal of thought to the life they are pursuing, and they imbue it with the best of their culture, the best that has been said and thought. Others (I think this is me) just sit down and watch television and say "This is the life!" without thinking too much about it.[65] There are differences too, as Rashdall insisted, in the capacities and inclinations that various humans have for different kinds of enjoyment, for flourishing, for contributing to the lives of others, and for moral agency. These seem to be different ways of engaging with value. In recent years, feminist theorists have paid a great deal of attention to differences in the lives, consciousness, and moral agency of men and women.[66] There are differences in the degree of fatalism and the set of expectations with which people confront the adversities of life and the challenges of subsistence. And so long as there are people of faith, there will be massive differences in the way people relate their choices on earth to exemplars of sanctity whom they have heard about and to their hopes for the life hereafter. These are not just occasional idiosyncratic differences; whole civilizations have organized life for their members on these quite different bases. If we were to sort people and peoples according to such differences, would we not be confronted in effect with Rashdall-discontinuities?

I believe the answer is no. We would be confronted with distinctions, but not with the necessity to deploy a whole different moral apparatus to capture what was important in the life of each person.

65. Cf. Ronald Dworkin, "Liberalism," in *Public and Private Morality*, ed. Stuart Hampshire (Cambridge University Press, 1978), 191: "Each person follows a more-or-less articulate conception of what gives value to life. The scholar who values a life of contemplation has such a conception; so does the television-watching, beer-drinking citizen who is fond of saying 'This is the life,' though of course he has thought less about the issue and is less able to describe or defend his conception."

66. See, for example, Carol Gilligan, *In a Different Voice: Psychological Theory and Women's Development* (Harvard University Press, 1993), and the discussion in Robin West, "Jurisprudence and Gender," *University of Chicago Law Review* 55 (1988): 1–72.

In each of these cases, there would be language, and we would see the need to listen to what the people in question said. In each case, what they said would be related to but not wholly derived from what they shared as a culture with those around them. In each case, we would have a sense of people engaging with value and reflecting on ideals and principles. In each of these cases, there would be familiar modes of engagement with others—family, friends, neighbors, lovers, fellow citizens (not to mention rivals and enemies). In each of these cases, there would be something it is like to be leading a life for the person concerned. In each case, there would be a shared sense—subjectively, on the part of the people concerned, and objectively and normatively for those surrounding them—of improvability.[67] People would understand not only that their own circumstances might be different from what they currently were but that a prospect might be held out for improvement so far as their own knowledge, skills, and experience were concerned.

To deal fairly and properly with beings like that (beings like us) we need an apparatus of understanding and sensitivity that I think does not differ greatly from one individual or social context to another. I don't mean we can arbitrarily impose a common template. I mean that the moral sensibility that we need in order to understand what such beings might have at stake in the various choices and situations that social and political philosophy seeks to evaluate would be

67. One of the remarkable things about humans is the gap within each human life between what that life is like if the person is kept warm and well-fed and what that life is like if the person is educated and cared for and initiated fully into the workings of society and so on. The existence of such a gap means that things like education and opportunity and care play an enormous role in human life over and above just feeding people and keeping them warm. There isn't the same gap in the case of (say) a cat as there is with us humans; I mean there isn't the same gap between the virtue of keeping it warm and fed and the highest that the cat is capable of. I think there is a gap of this kind in the case of every human. And I think Rashdall believes this may be true of some human beings but not others.

fundamentally the same. We would want a sensibility that could listen to people and that could descry love, hope, ambition, and expectation as well as pain, loss, fear, bereavement, defeat, humiliation, and devastation in terms that made sense to those who experienced them. All this we need to deal morally and responsibly with humans—any humans. Some of us believe that we do not need it, or much of it, to deal with non-human animals.

So, what I want to say is that a person who is committed to a Rashdall-discontinuity believes we need the full panoply of such an apparatus to deal responsibly and appropriately with situations and choices involving some kinds of human being but not with situations and choices involving other kinds of human being. They say that situations and choices involving other kinds of humans call for a much cruder apparatus of moral sensitivity. That is the sort of view that the principle of continuous human equality rules out. It holds that basically the same apparatus of moral sensitivity is required for dealing with all kinds of humans. There are not different kinds of humans who have to be dealt with in different ways.[68]

That's all I want to say about the Reverend Hastings Rashdall. Examining his position has helped us to get a grip on this "no discontinuity" thesis, the principle of continuous equality. Despite all the differences you see when you look around you, there are no fundamental discontinuities among us, nothing remotely analogous to what some people believe holds between humans and animals.

You may ask why we devoted all this time to a set of offensively racist views. It is, after all, 2015 (or it was when I delivered these lectures),

---

68. It may seem that we can't rule this out altogether. In Lecture 6, I address issues of children and the profoundly disabled, which may appear to bear out Rashdall's position. I believe these cases need to be dealt with very carefully so we can see why even there we should not accept this idea of a division in the human species. But I leave that part to the end of this series of lectures because I need a few other things to fall into place first.

not 1907, and one of the triumphs of the modern era is that no one these days is prepared to say out loud the sort of things that Hastings Rashdall said about "countless Chinamen and negroes." It is beyond controversy that Rashdall was wrong about race, and it is beyond controversy that similar positions are wrong about gender.

But being beyond controversy is not the same as being fully explicated. Embracing a position is one thing; elaborating, articulating, and understanding it is another. I really do think philosophers have the task of explicating things that everyone else has the luxury of taking for granted. An area of inquiry does not become philosophy until people have seen reason to throw its fundamental presuppositions into doubt, at least for the purposes of deeper understanding. That's why we have philosophers and why we pay them.[69] And that is why we have five more Gifford lectures to go, despite the conviction we share that Hastings Rashdall is wrong.

9.

Let me end this first lecture by considering a more troubling complaint. I distinguished at the beginning between basic equality—supposedly a very deep idea—and what I called "surface-level" issues about the distribution of wealth and income. And I said that basic equality would be the focus of these lectures. Well, someone might complain that this emphasis is misplaced. "We live," as Thomas Nagel has observed, "in a world of spiritually sickening economic and social

---

69. See Jeremy Waldron, "What Plato Would Allow," in *Nomos XXXVII: Theory and Practice*, ed. Judith DeCew Wagner and Ian Shapiro (New York University Press, 1996), 170–171, for an argument that political philosophy requires us to challenge and explicate even the fundamental assumptions that we take for granted in the rest of our normative inquiries.

inequality."[70] Thomas Piketty's book *Capital* has examined the extent and the terrifying significance of explosively increasing inequality in societies like Britain and the United States.[71] Shouldn't we be focusing on this rather than on the allegedly "deeper" abstractions of equality at a fundamental level?

Certainly the trends that Nagel mentions and Piketty analyzes deserve great attention. In view of the nature and effects of modern inequality, the normative principles that apply directly to that phenomenon need to be studied very closely. Perhaps this is the most important task. But there are thousands of political philosophers in the world, and it can't be that they should all devote their lives to the most important topic—every last one of them—and that no one should study the second-most important. So there is that irritating point to be made about the division of academic labor.

There are also other more important points to be made. I have already mentioned that when we evaluate economic inequalities we do so using principles of justice that are predicated upon and answerable to basic equality. Now, everything I know about principles of justice indicates that recent patterns of economic inequality must be condemned as unjust. This may be because the relevant patterns of economic inequality have simply not been held accountable to moral principles of any sort. If they had been held accountable, I think it would be obvious that the principles that would be needed to justify these patterns of inequality could not possibly be made consistent with basic equality. That's my intuition, or hunch. It becomes less of a hunch and more of an argument depending on how well-worked-out our notion of basic equality is. If our notion of basic equality is not well explicated, then we have to live with the possibility that this

70. Thomas Nagel, "Equality and Partiality," in Pojman and Westmoreland, *Equality*, 257.

71. For the "terrifying" implications of modern inequality, see Thomas Piketty, *Capital in the Twenty-first Century* (Harvard University Press, 2014), 571.

argument may not go through because its major premise is misconceived or because our opponents make unrefuted claims about there being different kinds of human being whose economic predicament should excite different levels of concern.

The distance between the two levels may be even shorter than that. Some principles that evaluate surface-level distributions test them directly against standards of human dignity. For example, the familiar formulation of one social and economic right holds that "everyone who works has the right to just and favourable remuneration ensuring for himself and his family an existence worthy of human dignity."[72] Possibly, then, it is part of the function of basic equality to generate principles, criteria, or at any rate a way of determining whether a situation of economic deprivation is in itself compatible with human dignity. In Lecture 2, I argue that basic equality, for all its abstraction, is a normative principle, and in the area of rights, some of its normative work is quite direct. Surface-level inequalities involving absolute deprivation might be denounced on this basis, and perhaps certain levels of relative deprivation come under this scrutiny as well. So we are not necessarily averting our eyes from the sort of inequality that Nagel and Piketty condemn when we reflect on basic equality.

Indeed, we have to consider the possibility that massive economic inequality may leach into our commitment to basic equality, seeping through to undermine our adherence to fundamental principles of equal worth and equal dignity. I have argued elsewhere that how things look in society from the point of view of justice is important (even if it is not as important as how things actually are).[73] I think we need to be concerned about whether our commitment to basic equality, deep and pervasive as it is supposed to be, is actually visible

---

72. Universal Declaration of Human Rights, Article 23 (3).
73. See Jeremy Waldron, *The Harm in Hate Speech* (Harvard University Press, 2012).

on the face of our society. How we look is partly a matter of how we have treated one another, how we have cooperated, and how we have shared the burdens and benefits of social interaction. Do we look as though we have treated one another as equals? Inequalities may be entrenched even when they are not justified; if they become well-established and visible, then we may begin to look like a society which does not accept basic equality because we are evidently not prepared to follow through on its justificatory implications.

Even worse, the fact of economic inequality may come to be written in the visible lives of those who are most deprived. It may look not only as though they are not being treated as equals but as though they are *not* the equals of other prosperous members of society. Let me give an extreme example of this troubling possibility. Ted Honderich, who used to teach philosophy in London, wrote a book many years ago called *Violence for Equality*. (We will leave the "violence" aside and just look at the section of the book he called "The Facts of Inequality.") Honderich said that if you look at the most privileged 10 percent of the population of developed countries and the least privileged 10 percent in developing countries, you will see a sort of disparity between lifetimes—something approaching eighty years' life expectancy on the one hand, and something close to forty years' life expectancy, on the other—that might lead you to conclude, if you knew nothing more, that we were dealing with two different species.[74] Of course we are not. But to the extent that the inequality is remediable and we have not remediated it, then that is what we have made these populations look like.[75]

---

74. Ted Honderich, *Violence for Equality: Inquiries in Political Philosophy* (Penguin, 1977).

75. See also the distressing evidence presented to the Sadler Committee in the United Kingdom in 1831 on the effects of child labor in producing a class of humans that seemed *differently shaped* from others, their bodies bent, crippled, and permanently distorted from

A less extreme version of the same point may be made in terms of what used to be called the "two nations" thesis in Europe and the United States. Holding on to a conviction about equal dignity may be harder for us as the population grows into "two nations"—rich and poor—and as people's ways of life become not just unfamiliar but unintelligible to each other. ("Who knows how *these people* live?") It is possible that the principle of basic equality may become less and less credible to us and our children because we become less and less able to imagine what it would be like to live with *these* others on genuinely equal terms. The living of a human life by the deprived might come to seem so different from the living of a human life by the privileged and the prosperous that the latter might balk at a principle of equality that assigned a common value to the living of a human life as such. We might become so accustomed to economic inequality, so inured to the spectacle of it despite its being unjustified, that we cease to recognize those who are deprived as nevertheless our equals. It may even be morally embarrassing for us to recognize them as such, since we would then have to acknowledge the injustice. Better perhaps to turn away, or to try what it feels like to deny or suppress the proposition that poor people too are entitled to equal concern.

Of course, whether we are one another's equals is one thing; whether we recognize each other as one another's equals is another. In principle, moral reality cannot be affected by the entrenchment in society and in the imagination of its members of forms of life whose disparateness is incompatible with the truth about basic equality. We might say that normatively it is the job of principles like basic equality

---

the conditions of labor that had been inflicted on them in childhood: *Report from the Committee on the Bill to Regulate the Labour of Children*, Cmd. 706, August 8, 1832. I am grateful to Marcia Pally for this source.

just to condemn such circumstances and the failures of moral consciousness they generate. And that is what a philosopher should say. We are certainly entitled to get all normative and objective on these matters.

Still, I worry that such normativity may come to seem to our fellow citizens less and less "realistic," more and more detached from reality. And though it is surely the job of moral principles to detach themselves from objectionable realities for the purpose of criticizing and reforming them, in fact the success among us of the normativity of a given principle might depend on some concrete realization of its demands as an exemplar of practicability. And if that is not forthcoming, if the way things around us look seems to belie the demands of this principle, then we may be in trouble. Then nothing but shrill and sustained insistence on the principle of basic equality and its comrades human worth and human dignity will save us.

That is the nightmare that motivates my sense that it is worth harping on this principle and worth exploring at length, rather than perfunctorily, the role it plays and ought to play in our political morality. I also still believe what I said earlier, that it would be a philosopher's job to understand this stuff anyway even if there wasn't this threat. But enough for now. In Lecture 2, I speak at greater length about the normativity of basic equality and the way it grounds itself in facts about our nature. And I take the opportunity to dispose of a suggestion, made by certain analytic philosophers, that equality of any sort is meaningless—that it does no useful work at any level—and that we would all be better off intellectually if our conversations were turned in a different direction.

2

Prescriptivity and Redundancy

This lecture is perhaps the most difficult of the six. In it, I have to deal with some logical and philosophical matters that may be more familiar to specialists than to the ordinary reader. I want to establish a distinction between equality as prescription and equality as description (Sections 1 through 4). I want to consider whether basic equality is best conceived as a response to certain facts about human nature (Sections 4 through 6). And I want to rebut a criticism that is sometimes made by my philosophical colleagues that equality is a redundant idea and that all we should really worry about is whether other values, like concern and respect, are being applied consistently (Sections 7 through 9). None of this will be easy, but I will try not to let the abstruseness of the discussion get too far out of hand.

1.

When we talk about equality, one of the most important distinctions we have to make is between *prescriptive* and *descriptive* equality. Descriptive statements tell us how things are, and prescriptive statements tell us how things ought to be and/or what things ought to be done. Crudely, we can say descriptively (or deny descriptively) that people *are* equal in some respect; we can say their opportunities are equal or that there used to be less inequality of income than there is now. Or we can say, prescriptively, that people *ought to be* equal. We can say that in general—for example, that they ought to be treated with equal respect—or we can say it in some particular regard, such as their income or opportunities.

Prescriptive statements call for something to be done that might not otherwise be done. Or at least that is their usual employment. Sometimes we may lighten the burden of a prescription by associating it with things that are coming to pass anyway no matter what we do. Alexis de Tocqueville did this with social equality. The growth of equality of status and social condition in the nineteenth century struck him as a "providential" fact: "It is universal, it is durable, it constantly eludes all human interference, and all events as well as all men contribute to its progress."[1] But he still thought there was work for prescription to do, for instance to channel this inevitable development that he described. We, on the other hand, cannot afford to be so optimistic. Though many egalitarians believe that people *are* one another's equals in a moral sense (more in a moment about whether or not this counts as a description)—this, they say, is the "moral reality"—still a tremendous amount of work is called for to actualize this moral reality in the world. Like Rousseau's men who are born free but are everywhere in chains, so people in the modern world are born equal but suffer from great inequality even at birth. Our prescription, then, is that they ought to be accorded the equality of concern and respect that is already theirs by right.

Prescription overlaps with evaluation, and what I am presenting here as a distinction between "is" and "ought"—a descriptive "is" and a prescriptive "ought"—might also be presented in terms of fact versus

1. Alexis de Tocqueville, *Democracy in America* (Knopf, 1994), 6.

value. We can say that equality (in some dimension) is a fact, and leave it at that. Or we can cherish it as a value, something that we think matters in human life. If we cherish something as a value, we are probably also inclined to prescribe its preservation, so there is a loose connection between prescriptive and evaluative equality. How loose it is, is a matter of controversy. In what follows I mainly focus on equality as a prescriptive principle, but much of what I say—and certainly the contrast with descriptions—will apply to evaluative statements about equality as well.

Another term that is sometimes used is "normative." Often "normative" is used as a synonym for "prescriptive," though strictly speaking it ought to be reserved for something like the generation or use of general norms.[2] But that is all right: our discussion of equality will be not only prescriptive but normative even in this strict sense. It will be about principles of equality, particularly the principle that requires us to treat each other as equals. In what follows I mainly use the term "prescriptive," but you can usually infer that normativity is involved as well.

2.

What is the connection between descriptive statements and prescriptive statements in the realm of equality? Consider first nonbasic principles of equality, as I called them in Lecture 1—principles like equality of opportunity or the principle that condemns the present

---

2. Joseph Raz disagrees, dismissing any definitional connection between normativity and general propositions like rules or principles as unhelpful; he uses "normative," I think, as I use "prescriptive." See Joseph Raz, *From Normativity to Responsibility* (Oxford University Press, 2011), 6–7. But his usage is different in *Practical Reason and Norms* (Oxford University Press, 1990), where norms appear to be rule-like considerations and not all prescriptions are norms (which would seem to imply that not all prescriptivity is normative).

inequality of incomes. Clearly these are prescriptive. They represent our convictions as to what ought to happen or not happen. There should be equality of opportunity, we say, or there ought to be less inequality of income. Or, using a prescription in the first-person plural, we say, "Let us arrange things so that economic inequality is diminishing rather than rising." These are all prescriptive statements.

Now, there are definitely descriptive statements associated with these prescriptions. Two kinds. First, a philosopher who puts forward a prescriptive principle has to have an eye on the world as it is, on the descriptive reality that his or her prescription targets or evaluates. If you go around saying that incomes ought to be more equal, then you need to have some idea of how incomes actually are at the moment because that is what you are going to evaluate. That is what you are going to criticize or urge to be changed. So there will be a set of target descriptions that you need to focus on in order to figure out where and how to apply your prescriptive principle.

Sometimes the facts that an equality principle targets include facts about positive law. A moral principle of nondiscrimination of course selects as its target the behavior of potential discriminators and facts about the opportunities or lack of opportunities for the potential victims of discrimination. But it may also target facts about the regime of law that is in place to deal with discrimination. Most jurists insist that the existence and validity of a given law is always in the first instance a matter of fact. As H. L. A. Hart put it, legal positivism involves "the simple contention that it is in no sense a necessary truth that laws reproduce or satisfy certain demands of morality, though in fact they have often done so."[3] Since it is not a necessary truth, we must use our prescriptions and the actions they demand to try to *make* it true. Notice also Hart's use of the phrase "reproduce or satisfy."

3. H. L. A. Hart, *The Concept of Law*, 3rd ed. (Oxford University Press, 2012), 181–182.

Sometimes we subject positive laws to moral tests: positive law is our target, and we evaluate it and the consequences of its application to see whether it satisfies moral principles. Sometimes we go further. We insist (prescriptively) that legal doctrine, legislation, or constitutional provisions should actually *reproduce*—as far as written formulations of law can—the moral principles that ought to be used to evaluate social facts. So, for example, in the United States, the Fourteenth Amendment's commitment to ensuring that no one shall be denied equal protection of the laws reads like a moral principle that is quite close to the heart of basic equality. We can recognize that (and even applaud the law's complicity in our ethic of egalitarianism), but still we take *the law as it is* as a target for our evaluation to see whether it does a good job of embodying the relevant moral principle, and to see how its actual application contributes to the satisfaction of the moral demands that it purports to reproduce.

So, prescriptive equality targets certain facts. Second—and this is something more subtle but very important indeed—a person who puts forward a prescriptive principle will also usually have in mind a *reason* or *grounding* for that principle, something which perhaps comprises a set of facts about the individuals who are within the range of the principle, facts that make the principle (and its prescriptive force) sensible or appropriate. For example, we prescribe equality of opportunity, perhaps because we think that every individual has some talents. We say there ought to be less economic inequality because every human has the same needs. These facts about talents and facts about needs are expressed in descriptions that capture the reasons that underlie our prescriptive principles. They make our principles intelligible, and they help guide our understanding and application of them. I will say much more about the role of this second set of descriptions in the following sections of this lecture and then specifically about their role for basic equality in Lectures 3 and 4.

Here is where we have got to. There are two kinds of descriptions in play: the target description and the descriptive characteristics on which our principle is predicated. We look with a critical (and potentially prescriptive) eye at the facts about economic distribution, for example, and we base our prescriptive scrutiny on something about the individuals whose situation we are scrutinizing. A prescriptive principle of equality is responsive to some set of facts, and it targets some set of facts. There is description as reason and description as target. Some such pair of descriptions is going to be associated with all equality principles; indeed I think this is true of principles in general. It is true also of basic equality in ways I explain in the following sections, though its application there is a little more complicated.

I am not forgetting the point—some philosophers insist on it very stridently[4]—that normative principles are themselves true by virtue of describing certain states of affairs (moral states of affairs, aspects of objective moral reality) that validate their normativity. So we could introduce that as a third set of facts: moral facts, if you like. But I will not do that; I am going to put the meta-ethics of moral facts to one side. I think for the most part you can sing along with what I am saying in this lecture, whatever your ultimate views on moral reality. And I shall use the prescriptive/descriptive distinction in the usual way, without prejudice to the issue of moral objectivity.

3.

Our task now is to apply this analytic apparatus of prescription and description to basic equality as well. Let me begin by insisting that the principle of basic equality is itself *prescriptive*. Indeed, as we shall

4. See, for example, Michael Moore, "Moral Reality," *Wisconsin Law Review* (1982): 1061–1156, and "Moral Reality Revisited," *Michigan Law Review* 90 (1992): 2424–2533.

see in a moment, it comprises a powerful cluster of different forms of prescriptivity, value, and normativity. So the distinction between surface-level principles of equality and foundational or basic principles of equality is not a distinction between prescriptive and descriptive propositions. At both levels we are in the realm of prescription. It is true that we often talk about basic equality in indicative language. We say, "People *are* one another's equals" and "People *do have* equal dignity." But the grammatical mood of the phrase should not mislead us. Evaluations and prescriptions are often expressed indicatively. "This *is* good," we say, or "That *is* the right thing to do." And sometimes we say, "People ought to be respected as the equal beings that they already are." (I wrote like that in the second paragraph of this lecture.) Sometimes philosophers talk this way because they are moral realists: they believe in the objective reality of the values and principles conveyed in their prescriptions. But this way of talking need not depend on any sophisticated thesis in meta-ethics. Sometimes it is just a way of talking, and none the worse for that.

The prescriptions of basic equality are a little more abstract than those conveyed in surface-level principles. This is partly because the principle of basic equality operates prescriptively in a second-level sort of way. Though we can say straightforwardly that the principle addresses the way we deal with one another, it often does so by issuing prescriptions about the way our other moral ideals are to be applied. For example, if we are utilitarians, or to the extent to which we engage in *any* consequentialist calculations, the principle of basic equality prescribes that we should treat the interests and the well-being of all people with equal concern and not count costs and benefits to some as mattering more than similar costs and benefits to others. Or in our use of principles of justice (including social justice), basic equality requires of us that all humans be treated as subjects and beneficiaries of justice, and subjects and beneficiaries on equal terms. It does not

necessarily require that surface-level principles of justice themselves
be principles of equality—though many will be—but it requires that
justice should address us all on equal terms. Nobody is beyond justice. We are all entitled to the full benefit of the principles of justice,
and we are all subject as respondents to the burdens and requirements of justice.

In general, basic equality commands our equal considerability
under moral principles. Everyone is to count for one: that is the prescriptive demand. Any project we pursue in the name of the common
good or in the name of social justice has to be disciplined by that
logic. When a proposal of ours threatens a major setback to somebody's interest, we must take that very seriously. And the principle of
basic equality instructs us to take it equally seriously irrespective of
who the person is. When the stakes of a choice that we face include
the life and fundamental interests of more than one human person,
then the principle of basic equality instructs us to take those stakes
equally seriously for each of those affected. We can sum this up by
saying that basic equality prescribes a broad equality of concern for
the individuals whose interests are at stake in our decisions.

It is sometimes said that equality is a *value* and that it should be
treated just like any other value. There is a grain of truth in this: basic
equality and its prescriptive implications matter to us, so they are
values in that sense. But this formulation is mostly misleading. It is
certainly misleading if it is supposed to suggest that when we consider
the overall value of some public proposal, we should count a gain in
equality as on a par with other benefits, like a gain in well-being or
the advancement of some interest. Equality is not just one interest
among others; its job is to discipline what we do about interests and
values. And a loss to equality, the promotion of inequality, is not be
regarded as just one cost among others, to be offset perhaps by other

benefits. Basic equality does its prescriptive work at a second level, disciplining the way we approach costs and benefits.

Having said that, basic equality is definitely *about* value: it is about the value of each person (and their interests and their standing) in regard to all the decisions we make. I believe basic equality operates in two dimensions here. It operates horizontally by commanding *equal* concern for human beings and their interests, insisting that there is to be no "thumb on the scale" for certain individuals we favor or for the members of some groups (say, groups to which we ourselves belong) as opposed to others. This horizontal range is what is required by the principle we called *continuous equality*: all human beings (at least) are to be accorded equal concern. And it is required too by principles of *distinctive equality*: humans, above all other animals, have a special claim on our concern. But it also operates vertically by insisting on the seriousness and depth of the concern that each person and each person's interests demand. We might call this qualitative dimension the dimension of human worth. Without this second dimension of worth, basic equality might be taken to recommend treating all human lives as equally inconsequential and all human interests as equally matters of little or no concern.

A pedant will want to insist that there are two distinct principles here: a principle commanding the depth of our concern for human beings and a second principle insisting that the first principle be applied consistently. And since consistency is supposed to be a default imperative of all philosophizing, some purists might add that the latter principle is redundant. The only interesting thing that proponents of basic equality are asserting, they will say, is that humans should be treated with great respect. And one can say that without mentioning the word "equality." I shall explain my reasons for rejecting this redundancy claim in Sections 7 through 9. For now it is worth noting that some of those who attribute high worth or great respect to certain people are inclined, consistently or inconsistently, to make this attribution in respect of some humans and not others. These are our opponents, if we are egalitarians. Defenders of basic equality are aware of this inclination, and that is one of the main reasons they insistently associate *equality* with attributions of high worth and great respect. By invoking equality, they are laying down a challenge which they hope people who make this sort of discrimination can be brought to face. I will come back to this point. But let me return first to the issue of basic equality's prescriptivity.

I alluded earlier to a controversy between those who believe that evaluation is one thing and prescription another, and those who maintain that prescription is the more fundamental notion and that all evaluation comes down eventually to prescription of one sort or another.[5] The latter are sometimes called "prescriptivists."[6] I do not want to take sides in the debate about prescriptivism. However, I do want to draw attention to a special class of values which we might describe as "commanding values." Some values have the characteristic that their recognition as values demands certain things of us. They make strident claims on our attention and action, and they are associated with a strong sense that ignoring, sidelining, or failing to respond positively to them would be wrong.

I believe that the worth of the human person is "a commanding value" of this kind. It is not like the value of a painting or a new experience, which we may treasure if we like and which rationality perhaps requires us to estimate correctly in relation to other values with which we may be toying. The worth of a human being is already moral in character, in the sense that it presents the proper response

5. See text accompanying footnote 2.
6. See, for example, R. M. Hare, *The Language of Morals* (Oxford University Press, 1952).

as a moral demand, something exacted from us by morality. This is partly a matter of the value being already interactional. It is not just a something attributed to a thing or state of affairs. It is attached to a person, and the characteristic situation is that the person to whom this worth is attached is aware of it and is ready to speak up for it, to give voice to it on his or her own behalf. The demands of human worth are often demands of the human whose worth is in question. They are, as Stephen Darwall puts it, "second-person" moral claims.[7] This is a special form of prescriptivity. It explains the affinity that basic equality has with the idea of rights, which are (among other things) moral demands which it is appropriate for a person to stand up and make on his or her own behalf in his or her own voice without moral embarrassment.[8]

Concern is not the only thing commanded by the worth of the human person. The legal philosopher Ronald Dworkin made the phrase "equal concern and respect" part of our philosophical vocabulary,[9] and the element of respect is at least as important as the element of concern. Respect is not just a matter of value and solicitude; it is also a matter of deference. We respect someone when we acknowledge and recognize him, when we take seriously his status as a thinking, reasoning moral being and defer to him in various ways and make room for him and his ideas. In this regard, too, human worth is a commanding value. Humans demand our respect; they demand our recognition, acknowledgment, and deference. According to the principle of basic equality, they demand it equally, and according to the *distinctive equality* version of that principle, they demand it

7. See Stephen Darwall, *The Second-Person Standpoint: Morality, Respect, and Accountability* (Harvard University Press, 2006).

8. See also the account of rights given in Joel Feinberg, "The Nature and Value of Rights," *Journal of Value Inquiry* 4 (1970): 243–260.

9. See, for example, Ronald Dworkin, *Taking Rights Seriously* (Harvard University Press, 1977), 180–183, 227, 272–278.

equally in a way that other animals do not; it is a high matter of human dignity. And actually, basic equality's demand for equal respect is much more likely than the demand for equal concern to be associated with a view about the distinctive moral position of human beings. Partly this is a matter of respect being oriented toward capabilities that are themselves distinctively human, such as the capacity for moral or personal autonomy. A very strong version of this is stated by Immanuel Kant in his late work, *The Metaphysics of Morals:*

> In the system of nature, a human being is a being of slight importance and shares with the rest of the animals, as offspring of the earth, an ordinary value. . . . But a human being regarded as a *person,* that is, as the subject of a morally practical reason, is exalted above any price; for as a person he is not to be valued merely as a means to the ends of others or even to his own ends, but as an end in itself, that is, he possesses a *dignity* (an absolute inner worth) by which he exacts *respect* for himself from all other rational beings in the world.[10]

That is the particular sort of prescriptivity we are talking about as associated with basic equality.

This is all, as I said, quite abstract. But basic equality also generates some quite familiar normative positions. For example, it extends its normativity to our rights. Though basic equality does not immediately dictate any particular rights, except perhaps in its very close link to the American constitutional norm of equal protection, it certainly mandates equal rights and human rights, though there is the continuing debate about what those rights ought to be. Some human

---

10. Immanuel Kant, *The Metaphysics of Morals,* in *Practical Philosophy,* ed. Mary Gregor (Cambridge University Press, 1996), 557 (6:434–435). (Note: Numbers in parentheses refer to the Prussian Academy edition of Kant's works.)

rights are specifically connected with the (equal) concern that basic equality mandates: think of the right to life, the right to subsistence, and the antidiscrimination rights that one finds in the Universal Declaration of Human Rights (UDHR).[11] Others flow more from the respect side of things—the right to free expression, for example, or freedom of religion.[12] (I am not citing the UDHR as canonical but as illustrative of what being a right-bearer has been supposed to be.) Also, equal respect for us as thinkers and agents supports principles of personal autonomy for the way we organize our lives. We say, "It is for me to organize my life. Not for you." In political contexts, personal autonomy becomes something like equal authority, or at least it gives rise to the seed of democracy in the idea that no human is to be treated as though he or she were naturally subordinated to others.[13] Any political arrangements among us have to be erected on this foundation of equal initial authority.[14] There are also what Samuel Scheffler and others call principles of relational equality, generated as specific prescriptive consequences of the basic equality principle.[15]

11. Universal Declaration of Human Rights, Articles 2 (nondiscrimination), 3 (right to life), and 25 (right to adequate subsistence).

12. Ibid., Articles 18 (freedom of thought, conscience, and religion) and 19 (freedom of opinion and expression).

13. Cf. John Locke, *Two Treatises of Government*, ed. Peter Laslett (Cambridge University Press, 1970), 287, suggesting that the natural condition of human beings is a condition "of equality, wherein all the power and jurisdiction is reciprocal, no one having more than another, there being nothing more evident than that creatures of the same species and rank, promiscuously born to all the same advantages of Nature, and the use of the same faculties, should also be equal one amongst another, without subordination or subjection" (II, §4).

14. For the claim that equal authority is particularly important in the normative pantheon of basic equality, see Nikolas Kirby, "A Society of Equals" (PhD diss., University of Oxford, 2016).

15. Samuel Scheffler, "The Practice of Equality," in *Social Equality: On What It Means to Be Equals*, ed. Carina Foule, Fabian Schuppert, and Ivo Walliman-Helmer (Oxford University Press, 2015), 21–44.

There is plenty more work to be done in all these cases. Still, one can see how some quite familiar normative positions begin to be built up from and upon the norm of equal concern and respect. All this, by way of reflection on the prescriptivity of our principle of basic equality.

4.

The prescriptions of basic equality are also related to descriptive equality in the two ways I wrote about (for nonbasic equality) in Section 2. There is descriptive equality as a *target* of scrutiny for basic equality, and there is descriptive equality as a *reason* for basic equality.

First, basic equality and the principles associated with it target certain facts. Principles of basic equality are oriented toward certain states of affairs that we are concerned about, states of affairs that we want to scrutinize. We want to make ourselves aware of the concern and respect that is actually being shown for various human beings, both in their depth and in their equality. Are some humans being made the object of more concern than others? Are certain humans not being respected or treated with respect? We will want to look at the way in which people benefit under the auspices of the common good, the way in which they do or do not benefit from human rights, and the way they are or are not treated as subjects and beneficiaries of justice. We are interested in the quality of their social relations. These are the target descriptions of basic equality, the facts about the way we treat each other that prescriptions of basic equality are concerned with.

As I indicated earlier, the basic equality principle is particularly concerned about the way other principles of law and morality are applied. Its subject matter comprises facts about the way these other principles are formulated and put into operation. In a sense, this is morality evaluating morality. But it is morality as prescriptive principle, operating at a second level, targeting and evaluating the descriptive state of affairs constituted, for example, by other principles' being applied consistently or inconsistently across all human beings.

What about the second sort of description? Does the principle of basic equality also *respond* to certain ways we may be described? Is basic equality grounded upon certain facts about human nature? Are there aspects of our nature that provide reasons it is appropriate or morally requisite for us to treat one another in certain ways? Do we need to be aware of certain descriptive equalities in human nature in order to make sense of and guide the application of the prescriptions that basic equality involves? These questions are going to preoccupy us, one way or another, for much of the rest of this series of lectures.

5.

Let me consider first some doubts that people have entertained on this score — doubts about whether basic equality is grounded on or is responsive to any facts about human nature.

I said in Lecture 1 that basic equality is supposed to operate as a major premise for much of our reasoning about surface-level equality and inequality. We say, for example, that it is because we are one another's equals that we must be given fair equality of opportunity. It is because we are one another's equals that we ought to have concern about high levels of economic inequality. Sometimes we even say that it is because we are one another's equals that we must be treated unequally in certain respects (unequal aspirins for unequal fevers, for example). So we assume that the principle of basic equality is way down there in the foundation, supporting what we say about nonbasic equality. But if that is so, how can basic equality have foundations of its own? How can it be grounded or underpinned by anything, if it is itself so deep and fundamental? The point is not about the epistemology of surface-level equality but about the values it honors: what value is honored by basic equality?

Certain theorists have indeed treated basic equality as a sort of rock-bottom principle, incapable of further justification. Some say it is simply because the demand for justification has to stop somewhere. Joel Feinberg offers the opinion that equal respect for human beings is in a sense groundless: it is an ultimate attitude, not itself justifiable in more ultimate terms; you either believe it or you do not; it is, says Feinberg, a "groundless commitment."[16] Others say something similar, not because of any grand metaphysical view about what is ultimate and what is not but just because they believe it is pragmatically a waste of time to trouble ourselves any further about the basis of this principle. They are antifoundationalists. They say, "Let's stop arguing about what equality is based on and start looking instead to its implementation."[17]

A few people say this because they think that predicating basic equality on certain facts about human nature would distort the role of the principle in our practical life. An example is Margaret MacDonald in her 1947 essay, "Natural Rights."[18] MacDonald based her view on a radically decisionist conception of value utterances. Value utterances, she said, are like records of decisions: "To assert that all men are of equal worth is not to state a fact but to choose a side. It

16. Joel Feinberg, *Social Philosophy* (Prentice-Hall, 1973), 93.

17. See, for example, Richard Rorty, *Consequences of Pragmatism* (University of Minnesota Press, 1982); Richard Rorty, "Human Rights, Rationality, and Sentimentality," in *On Human Rights: The Oxford Amnesty Lectures*, ed. Steven Shute and Susan Hurley (Basic Books, 1993), 111–134.

18. Margaret MacDonald, "Natural Rights," in *Theories of Rights*, ed. Jeremy Waldron (Oxford University Press, 1984), 21–40. This paper was originally published in *Proceedings of the Aristotelian Society* 47 (1947): 225–250. It is cited here by page numbers in the 1984 version.

announces: this is where I stand."[19] She acknowledged that somebody might ask, "Yes, but *why* do you choose to stand there? What is it about humans that makes this a sensible place to stand?" But she responded, defiantly, "I affirm that no natural characteristic constitutes a reason for the assertion that all human beings are of equal worth." She went on: "Do we then decide without reason? Are decisions determined arbitrarily, by chance or by whim? No, but the problem is a little bit like asking somebody why do they love their child, or why do they love their spouse or partner? They just do."[20] She even quoted from Montaigne's essay on friendship: "If a man urged me to tell him wherefore I loved him, I feel it cannot be expressed but by telling him: because it is you."[21] The idea is that some of us simply find ourselves committed to a moral outlook organized around basic equality. We may try to attract others to it, but we do not do that by pointing to any other property or fact that is going to compel other people to line up with us in the same way.

I think Margaret MacDonald was absolutely right when she said there is no factual implication that is going to compel a belief in human equality. We are not looking to bridge the gap between description and prescription. We are not looking to abolish the "is / ought gap" or to throw a rope of logical inference between fact and value. But saying we are not compelled by the facts to take any particular position on human equality does not mean that the position we do decide to take has no relation to facts about human beings. It may have a relation to facts about us even though it is not a logically compelling relation. And it may need to supervene upon such facts, just in order to make sense, even as a decision.

19. Ibid., 35.
20. Ibid., 36–37.
21. Ibid., 37.

Now, what I have just said may not be true of particular affections, as in Montaigne's case or MacDonald's asking "Why do I love my child?" But I think it has to be true of general principles like basic equality. The general principle has to have a scope, and it has to have some apparatus associated with it that allows us to apply it consistently to an open-ended array of cases. We have to understand that our principle of basic equality applies to humans (or perhaps all sentient animals) but not to teapots or tadpoles. We have to have some way of managing the principle and some way to make sense of it. I will come back to this in a moment.

A more profound—certainly a more obscure—defense of the claim that equality need not be predicated on any descriptive property of human nature is found in the writings of Hannah Arendt. Arendt is a former Gifford lecturer,[22] and she offered what she called a political concept of equality. She suggested that the members of a society might adopt a principle of treating one another as equals not on account of any natural similarities between them but because such a principle might make possible a form of political community they could not otherwise have.[23] By nature we may be utterly different from one another—in background, talents, and character—but by political convention we *hold* ourselves to be one another's equals. We are not born equal, she says, but we become equals as members of the community on the strength of our decision to guarantee ourselves and each other mutual equal rights. Like everyone else, Arendt of

22. See Hannah Arendt, *The Life of the Mind* (Harcourt, 1974); this book was based on the Gifford Lectures that Arendt delivered in Aberdeen between 1972 and 1974.

23. Hannah Arendt, *The Origins of Totalitarianism*, new ed. (Harcourt, Brace, Jovanovich, 1973), 301. I have explored Arendt's argument about equality in "Arendt on the Foundations of Equality," in *Politics in Dark Times: Encounters with Hannah Arendt*, ed. Seyla Benhabib, with the assistance of Roy T. Tsao and Peter J. Verovšek (Cambridge University Press, 2010), 17–38.

course believes there are differences and similarities among human beings. She said some of the differences arouse dumb hatred, mistrust, and discrimination, while some of the more striking similarities lead us to recoil from our common biology.[24] The important thing is her insistence that there is nothing in our common humanity that compels any moral or practical response. She is famous for saying that in the Holocaust, from which she fled to America in 1940, "the world found nothing sacred in the abstract nakedness of being human."[25]

I have a great respect for the views of Hannah Arendt, but I wonder whether she is not misleading us about the basis of her position. It is true that she found it convenient to pretend that we could just "hold" a group of entities to be one another's political equals, irrespective of what these entities were like. But that proposition—which in itself is slightly mad, as though we could just *decide* to treat trees, tigers, teapots, and teenagers as one another's equals for political purposes—was not what Arendt really thought. Her work made it clear that we can sensibly be held to be one another's equals because of certain facts about what we are like—only these are difficult facts to get at and are certainly not the natural facts about humanity that theorists of equality often cite. Like MacDonald, Arendt acknowledged that we are not compelled logically on the basis of any facts to uphold any particular view about equality. But as in MacDonald's case, that was not the end of the matter.

In Arendt's ethical thought, there *was* something distinctive— indeed something momentous—about human nature. That distinctive something was what she described (in her essay "What Is Freedom?") as "the faculty of freedom itself."[26] She meant the sheer capacity that

24. Arendt, *The Origins of Totalitarianism*, 301–302.

25. Ibid., 295

26. Hannah Arendt, "What Is Freedom?," in *Between Past and Future: Six Exercises in Political Thought* (Viking Press, 1961), 169.

humans have to begin new things. As she put it, the capacity to begin unprecedented things "animates and inspires all human activities, and is the hidden source of the production of greatness and beauty."[27] She said the birth of every human represented the possibility of a new beginning: the occurrence in the world, once again and for the hundred-billionth time, of the possibility of interrupting the life process with something genuinely new.[28] She used the term "natality" to characterize this potential, and she said it was present in all that humans did, political and nonpolitical. It was "a supreme gift, which only man, of all the earthly creatures, seems to have received, of which we can find traces and signs in almost all human activities."[29] It was a potential, and certainly it was not often realized, but you never knew which of these newborns was going to be the one that would begin something new. Arendt's ontology of the human seemed to have this capacity there in each of us as a permanent possibility.

So Arendtian natality, this permanent possibility of new beginnings in the nature and condition of man, is the fact about us on which her commitment to equality supervened. It was not a natural or biological fact; it had a sort of metaphysical force to it. But there is no reason why the facts on which our equality is based have to be natural. There can be descriptions of all sorts. In Lecture 5, we will be looking at a whole host of suggested nonnatural facts on which basic equality may be founded—facts about our relation to God, for example. Arendt's

27. Ibid., 169. See also George Kateb, *Human Dignity* (Harvard University Press, 2011), 174ff.

28. Apparently the total number of humans who have ever lived is 108 billion. Ciara Curtin, "Fact or Fiction? Living People Outnumber the Dead," *Scientific American*, March 1, 2007, http://www.scientificamerican.com/article/fact-or-fiction-living-outnumber-dead/.

29. Arendt, "What Is Freedom?," 169. See also Hannah Arendt, *On Revolution* (Penguin Books, 1973), 211.

natality was not a religious conception, but it was transcendent, and she thought it was of the utmost importance.

6.

I alluded earlier to the idea of *supervenience*, which is a technical concept used in philosophy.[30] "Supervening upon" is a relationship of something like covariance between two types of properties. In the philosophy of mind, it is thought that mental properties like beliefs, ideas, and dreams supervene upon neural or physical properties of the brain, so that there cannot be a change in your mental properties unless there is also a change in your neural properties. Supervenience is not necessarily a reduction of one to the other, but it assumes that there is some underlying basis that the mental properties are either epiphenomena of or at the very least responsive to. We invoke this concept also in moral philosophy when we say that two actions or things cannot be different in their value unless there is some factual difference between them. Two actions, for example, cannot be

---

30. Simon Blackburn, *The Oxford Dictionary of Philosophy* (Oxford University Press, 1996), 368, provides a helpful characterization of supervenience:

> Properties of one kind, F, supervene upon those of another kind, G, when things are F in virtue of being G. Thus a person cannot just be good, but must be good in virtue of possessing other properties, such as courage or kindness. The supervening property relates to the underlying qualities in at least this way: if one thing possesses the underlying properties and is F, then any other thing with the same underlying properties must share the resultant property F.

See also the essays in Jaegwon Kim, ed., *Supervenience and Mind: Selected Philosophical Essays* (Cambridge University Press, 1993). Gideon Rosen, "Metaphysical Dependence: Grounding and Reduction," in *Modality: Metaphysics, Logic, and Epistemology* (Oxford University Press, 2010), 109–136, suggests we talk simply of grounding rather than supervenience. I will use both idioms. But I am not persuaded that we should abandon the term "supervenience."

different in their value unless one of the actions is different from the other. If there is a difference of value, there must be a difference of descriptive characteristics. So moral properties supervene upon the descriptive characteristics.

Actually, putting it that way is not quite right. Jonathan Dancy has pointed out that sometimes one moral difference (or value difference) may supervene on another moral (or value) difference.[31] We say that action X was good, while action Y was not. Why? Because X was generous, and Y wasn't. So we have gone from a general evaluative term ("good") to a more specific evaluative term ("generous"). But then we do also have to ask, "Well, what makes X generous?" And then we come to the level of fact: X was a donation to a worthy cause. So eventually we reach some fact about the action on which its goodness and its generosity supervene.

Supervenience is a highly technical idea. Its application in the moral case is quite different from its application in the philosophy of mind. In the philosophy of mind, it is based on some sort of theory about the relationship between mental events and neural events. In the case of moral philosophy, it is said that we make the evaluations and prescriptions that we do for reasons, and those reasons reference facts in the world; that is what moral supervenience involves. In both areas, supervenience is defended intuitively, but the intuitions are different. I mention supervenience here because it is one way of understanding the second association of a principle with factual statements. The first association is that the principle targets certain facts. The second association is that the principle responds to or is predicated or supervenes upon certain facts.

Let me get even more technical, just for a moment. Does supervenience apply to equality? If I say "These items are of equal value," am

---

31. Jonathan Dancy, "On Moral Properties," *Mind* 90 (1981): 367–385.

I assuming they must share some property? Well, maybe, but not necessarily. A piece of furniture and a bottle of wine may have the same value, but they have it for different reasons: one is worth $500 because of its modern design and exquisite construction; the other is worth $500 because of its taste or its vintage. So when we say all humans are of equal worth, it is possible that the equality may be the upshot of different characteristics in the case of each person. (Even when we call each of two people "priceless," we may not call them priceless for the same reason; one may be priceless on account of her learning, the other priceless on account of her loyalty.) Technically, then, the principle of human equality does not have to presuppose any one property that we all share.

We might reach the same result with the position I described in Lecture 1 as *continuous equality*. Continuous equality is a negative position. It denies that there are important discontinuities in the worth attributable to human beings. Their worth is all about the same. But that does not necessarily involve any affirmative property on which continuous equality is based. Or at least not as a matter of logic: it may be nothing more than the absence of any properties that would generate what I called Rashdall-*dis*continuities. Nevertheless, continuous equality is commonly associated with some affirmative property. This is partly a matter of the difficulty in proving a negative. What makes us so confident that we will not find any major discontinuity in the human range? I think we have to have some affirmative and significant picture of what humans are like that bolsters our confidence that this assertion of a negative makes sense. It may not be logically necessary, but pragmatically maybe even this negative principle is predicated on some feature shared by the individuals who are supposed to be its subject.

And certainly, the more affirmative principle of *distinctive equality*, which says humans are one another's equals on a plane that raises them high above the rest of creation, is going to be grounded on some important distinction between humans and other animals. It will supervene upon their reason or their capacity for autonomy or their relation with God—each of which has been cited in our tradition as a ground for saying of all humans that they have a higher worth or dignity than any non-human animal they might otherwise resemble. The point, then, about distinctive equality is that the property on which the superiority of the human over the non-human supervenes is also the basis on which humans among themselves are designated as equal.

One other point about supervenience. Remember Arendt's insistence that equality was not based on anything? One thing she might have meant is that talk of equality's supervening on some other property misleads us as to the order of argument, as though we *first* notice the other property and *then* are led to assert the prescriptive equality. We first notice that men are rational, and then we say, therefore they must be equal. Or we first notice that all people have a moral sense, and then we proceed to maintaining their equality. Maybe what Arendt intended to say was that things did not necessarily work that way around. We might begin with some conviction about equality or some commitment to it (perhaps a political commitment), and that might inform our search for an underlying property. And then we buy into the whole thing as a package. This sounds like question-begging, but it is connected with an interesting thesis that some philosophers have called "shapelessness."

Consider a predicate like "courage." We know that this predicate seems to face in two directions. On the one hand, it describes a certain characteristic: steadfastness in the face of danger. And on the other hand, it evaluates that characteristic highly. "Courage" is a term that combines evaluation and description. It is what we call a *thick* moral term: it has a strong descriptive element as well as its positive evaluative meaning. But it may not be easy or even possible to separate those two elements from one another—the evaluative and the descriptive—and still be left with something intelligible on both sides. The characteristics that *describe* courage for us may not make much sense apart from the evaluative attitude that unites them. It is as though you were trying to find a description of what makes something "funny" while abstracting from our sense of humor. Sometimes if you peel away the evaluative element, you are left with something that looks amorphous or shapeless—something that, it turns out, makes sense even as a description only in the light of the evaluative commitment.[32]

It is possible that much of our thinking about equality is like this. We come into the discussion with a rough conviction that we are one another's equals, or a determination to behave as though we were; and that informs the way we look for (and what we say about) the properties on which, upon reflection, we say that equality is based. There is no necessary priority of the one over the other, let alone any logical compulsion to move from one to the other. Seeing people in a certain way is perhaps inseparable from resolving to treat them as one another's equals, and somebody who has not resolved to treat them as his equals may complain that he really doesn't "get" the description under which they *are* one another's equals. Something

32. John McDowell makes this argument in "Non-Cognitivism and Rule-Following," in *Wittgenstein: To Follow a Rule*, ed. Steven Holtzman and Christopher Leich (Routledge, 1981), 141–162. Denying that we can always separate a factual from an evaluative component of our value judgments, McDowell says we should "be skeptical about whether the disentangling manouevre . . . can always be effected: specifically, about whether, corresponding to any value concept, one can always isolate a genuine feature of the world . . . that is there anyway, independently of anyone's value-experience being as it is—to be that to which competent users of the concept are to be regarded as responding when they use it; that which is left in the world when one peels off the reflection of the appropriate attitude" (ibid., 144).

like that may be true, or it may be the grain of truth in Arendt's position.

All of this, I hope, will be helpful for Lecture 3, in which our task is not just to identify a set of properties on which equality is based but to make sense of a particular way of looking at those properties. Just to anticipate: Suppose we say that equality is based on human rationality. We all understand that people are rational to different degrees. It looks as though the egalitarian is determined to look past the different degrees of rationality and focus steadfastly on the basic element of rationality itself. Now, that particular way of looking at things has to be motivated; otherwise it will seem pointless and the relevant property may seem shapeless. So that will be on our agenda. We may have to embrace the accusation, often put forward by anti-egalitarians, that we—that is, you and I, dear reader—*see* people as equals, descriptively, only because we are already determined, prescriptively, to treat them as equals. It sounds like we are being accused of cheating. But our embrace of the accusation is supposed to remind our opponents that we are not looking for a descriptive property to *drive us* toward equality or to *prove* that equality is valid. Rather, we are looking for a descriptive property whose conjunction with our prescriptive position will help make sense of the whole egalitarian package.

7.

In all this discussion, I have made the prescriptions associated with equality sound very important—I think they are—and it seems as though anything that important will need a serious grounding. We will be looking for that grounding in Lecture 3. But there is a strain of philosophical analysis which argues that most uses of equality in normative political philosophy are trivial or, worse still, meaningless. These prescriptions, it is said, don't have anything like the importance that egalitarians attribute to them, or, if they do, they are misleading ways of stating the importance of principles other than equality.

Much of this criticism is about nonbasic equality. For example, Peter Westen argues that nondiscrimination claims, typically stated in the language of equality, are really references to the standards that ought to be used in distinguishing justifiable treatment of some from justifiable treatment of others. In an example we considered in Lecture 1, we imagined firefighters being selected for their physical fitness. If a white candidate for the fire brigade is given preference over a black candidate even though they are both quite fit, we say the black candidate is being treated unequally. But actually, what is going on is that he is being treated according to the wrong standard: race has nothing to do with the qualification for firefighting, but physical fitness does. Our claim that candidates should be treated equally means simply that they should be treated according to the standard that ought to be applied to them in this context. So stated, this claim is trivial: what ought to be considered ought to be considered. And it remains trivial until we establish what the standard ought to be. The real debate, Westen says, is not about equality but about which standards are defensible and which are not defensible for recruitment to the fire brigade.[33]

When I reviewed Westen's book many years ago, I wrote that he had a point but that meaningful claims of equality might nevertheless enter into the debate about what the criteria of eligibility for a job on the fire brigade ought to be. In deciding about the social desirability of a physical fitness criterion, we appeal to the interests of everyone

33. See Peter Westen, *Speaking of Equality: An Analysis of the Rhetorical Force of "Equality" in Moral and Legal Discourse* (Princeton University Press, 1990), 110.

in the society that might be served by the fire brigade, and we argue for a fitness standard (if we do) on the grounds that that character-istic is necessary if the interests of all are to be served by this institu-tion. Everyone needs *fit* firefighters to rescue them and their prop-erty when they are endangered by fire. Now, in undertaking this calculation about criteria for the fire brigade, we are required to treat as equals all those who have interests in this matter. We are not to try to justify a race criterion for membership in this glamorous profession on the ground that that will be a better way of affirming the identity of white people (e.g., by presenting whites in this highly laudable role). Such a justification would not treat the interests of black people and white people equally. But arguably a fitness standard does. So equality—equal consideration of interests—does enter meaningfully into the calculation after all.[34] And this is the role of *basic* equality. (You may remember I made a similar argument in Section 3 of Lec-ture 1.)

But there is another response open to Westen. He may concede that all ought to be treated as equals in making the calculation about criteria for recruitment to the fire brigade. But he may observe that this too is a trivial calculation. It does not seem to say much more than that we should consult all the interests that ought to be con-sulted and give them all the weight they ought to have. This is cer-tainly what we should do, and sure, in contexts like this, we should scrupulously do what we ought to do and calculate as we ought to calculate. That much is clear. But does it really tell us anything?

The position I was trying to defend might be phrased in terms of Jeremy Bentham's famous adage, "Everybody to count for one; no-body for more than one," in our calculations of what the interests of

34. Jeremy Waldron, "The Substance of Equality," *Michigan Law Review* 89 (1991): 1357–1359.

all require. As a thoroughgoing and uncompromising utilitarian, Bentham believed that we should evaluate all public policies—including policies about the fire brigade—on the basis of whether they promote the greatest happiness of the greatest number, and he thought that meant we had to keep a kind of ledger of who would benefit and who would suffer under a given rule and adopt only those policies where the total amount of suffering was less than the amount of benefit that would accrue to individuals thereby. Or, if we had no choice but to adopt measures that impose some net suffering, we should choose among the alternatives we face on the basis of the lowest net suffering. We should keep a ledger of anticipated costs and benefits, and in that ledger—in that utilitarian calculus—everybody is to count for one, and nobody for more than one. Of course happiness or suffering might be more or less intense, more or less prolonged, and those dimensions should be taken into account. But they should be taken into account in the same way and on the same scale for each individual. The prolonged happiness of a queen counts for the same, minute by minute, as the prolonged happiness of a commoner. The intense suffering of the most depraved beggar on Edinburgh's South Bridge counts for the same as the equally intense suffering of the professor of New Testament studies. That was Bentham's position, and he, like other utilitarians, was fiercely committed to it.[35] He thought there would be massive changes to law and policy in Britain if we were to stay true to that adage because he thought an awful lot of laws and policies had been justified and enacted in Britain by simply refusing to consider or weigh equally the benefits or suffering of large classes of people.

---

35. Notice, by the way, that it is a principle of *continuous equality*; indeed it is most often invoked these days by those who believe in equal treatment for animals: "Every single animal (human or non-human) is to count for one; none of them for more than one."

I was not arguing that a commitment to equality requires us to be utilitarians in Bentham's image. There are many ways of thinking about interests besides Bentham's hedonic welfarism, and there are many ways of taking all interests into account besides his particular maximizing formula. But his adage "Everybody to count for one; nobody for more than one" can be applied to almost any consequentialist calculation, and, as I said in Section 3, it applies whether such calculations are supposed to be the essence of morality (as the utilitarians think) or simply an important subset of our moral thinking. Now, here's the point. What I am attributing to Westen is the claim that in all these contexts the Bentham adage too is just a tautology: "Everyone to count as they ought to count; no one to count for more or less than they ought to count." Is that what equal concern comes down to?

Or consider this. The Benthamite adage is well known, but it is actually quite difficult to find a source for it in Bentham's writings. David Ritchie observed in his 1903 book, *Natural Rights*, that the phrase is best known from a quotation by John Stuart Mill, for whom Bentham stood as a kind of a secular godfather.[36] "The maxim," said Ritchie, "seems to belong to the unwritten doctrine of the utilitarian master."[37] Bentham did state the adage more concretely when he said, "The happiness of the most helpless pauper constitutes as large a portion of the universal happiness as does that of the most opulent

36. John Stuart Mill, *Utilitarianism*, ed. George Sher (Hackett, 2002), 62 (chap. 5): "The Greatest Happiness Principle . . . is a mere form of words without rational signification, unless one person's happiness, supposed equal in degree (with the proper allowance made for kind), is counted for exactly as much as another's. Those conditions being supplied, Bentham's dictum, 'everybody to count for one, nobody for more than one,' might be written under the principle of utility as an explanatory commentary."

37. David Ritchie, *Natural Rights: A Criticism of Some Political and Ethical Conceptions* (Swan Sonnenshein, 1903), 249.

members of the community."[38] And Henry Sidgwick said something similar: "The good of any one individual is of no more importance, from the point of view . . . of the Universe, than the good of any other."[39] Again, it all sounds very impressive. But Mill offered the following additional gloss on his godfather's saying in a footnote in *Utilitarianism:* "It may be more correctly described as supposing that equal amounts of happiness are equally desirable, whether felt by the same or by different persons. This, however, is not a premise needful to support the principle of utility, but the very principle itself. If there is any anterior principle implied, it can be no other than this: that the truths of arithmetic are applicable to the evaluation of happiness, as of all other measurable quantities."[40] This seems to take the wind out of the Benthamite sails a little bit, and Westen might say, once again, that it reduces the adage to triviality.[41] Or, if not trivial, it seems like nothing more than a discipline of consistency and rationality. Of course double-counting is wrong: it means someone is trying to convince us that there is more at stake for a given person than for someone else, whereas the reality is that there is the same at stake for both.[42] Basic equality tells us only that we ought to apply our principles impartially. Maybe that's a good thing to be reminded of, but it hardly justifies six Gifford Lectures.

---

38. Jeremy Bentham, *Constitutional Code,* bk. 1, chap. 15, quoted in Amy Gutmann, *Liberal Equality* (Cambridge University Press, 1980), 23.

39. Henry Sidgwick, *The Methods of Ethics,* 7th ed. (Hackett, 1981), 382.

40. Mill, *Utilitarianism,* 62n. (chap. 5).

41. For his actual discussion of Bentham's adage, see Westen, *Speaking of Equality,* 252.

42. I am leaving aside the position that says, "People are entitled to put a thumb on the scales for their own loved ones and to count the happiness or suffering of their loved ones more than they count the happiness or suffering of other people's loved ones." See, for example, Samuel Scheffler, "Morality and Reasonable Partiality," in *Equality and Tradition: Questions of Value in Moral and Political Theory* (Oxford University Press, 2010), 41–75. But that is not really a counterexample to the Bentham adage: it operates instead as an account of what valuing involves for humans in certain contexts, and it applies equally to everyone.

8.

The same claim about the triviality or redundancy of equality might apply to the prescription of equal respect as well as equal concern. An Oxford philosopher, J. R. Lucas, says this about the prescription: "We may call it, if we like, the [principle of] Equality of Respect, but in this phrase it is the word "Respect"—respect for each man's humanity, respect for him as a human being—which is doing the logical work, while the word "Equality" adds nothing to the argument and is altogether otiose."[43] We may believe that we ought to respect humans, and what this means is that we ought to respect you and you and you, and each person individually; and we ought to apply that principle of respect impartially, without fear or favor. But equality does not enter into it: I respect one person as she ought to be respected; I respect another as he ought to be respected; and maybe it is the same in each case. Only, the sameness or the equality is not in itself relevant to the calculation.[44]

Hear also what Harry Frankfurt says in his little book, *Inequality*, about the equal rights that everyone is supposed to have.

> Enjoying the rights that it is appropriate for a person to enjoy, and being treated with the appropriate consideration and concern, have nothing essentially to do with the consideration and concern that other people are shown or with the respect or rights that other people happen to enjoy. Every person should be accorded the rights, the respect, the consideration, and the concern to which he is entitled by virtue of what he is and what he

43. J. R. Lucas, "Against Equality," *Philosophy* 40 (1965): 298.
44. See also Westen, *Speaking of Equality*, 102–103; Joseph Raz, "Professor Dworkin's Theory of Rights," *Political Studies* 26 (1978): 130.

has done. The extent of his entitlement to them does not depend on whether or not other people are entitled to them as well.[45]

So much for equality. This critique by Frankfurt and Lucas and others demands an answer.

One thing to say is that it is not true, as Frankfurt claims, that the nature of the rights that X ought to have never depends on the nature of the rights that Y ought to have. In some cases, it is of the essence that the rights be equal. Consider political rights: we might assert that X has a right to a say in who rules him, and so does Y; but we can't determine the extent of X's right without contemplating a system in which X and Y will be political equals and their votes counted the same. We have to say at least that X is entitled to no greater say in who rules him than anyone else (like Y) in the society in which he lives. He is entitled to the greatest say possible consistent with that constraint. But take away the egalitarian constraint on the alleged ground that it is trivial, and we will be all at sea in our calculations. This is an instance of what is called "comparative justice," where we are more sure that X's and Y's share of something should be equal than we are of what cardinal level of that something should be secured to each of them. Another instance of comparative justice is criminal sentencing, where we are sometimes more sure that two felons with similar histories and convicted of similar robberies should be sentenced to equal jail terms than we are about what the length of those terms should be. In general, Frankfurt's argument trades on noncomparative justice, cases where we are confident in the case of each person that *he* should not be tortured and *he* should have freedom of speech and *he* should have enough to live on; and this confidence is matched by a similar confidence for the next person;

45. Harry Frankfurt, *Inequality* (Princeton University Press, 2015), 74–75.

but interpersonal comparisons between them are not really doing any work.[46] But Frankfurt completely fails to consider the topic of *comparative* justice in his little book.

Comparative justice covers a small range of cases. But even for noncomparative cases, we may still say that the principle of basic equality is not redundant. I am in agreement with Vinit Haksar's response to J. R. Lucas: "Lucas is quite wrong in thinking that 'equality' is otiose here. It is a substantial point whether some human beings in virtue of their nature should be given greater respect and consideration than others. To say that they should be given equal respect is to take one side in this substantial controversy."[47] Haksar cites Hastings Rashdall, with his view about "Chinamen or negroes," as someone who takes the other side on this controversy. I think Haksar is saying that you can ditch the word "equality" if you like, but then you may find it more difficult to convey a substantive point that you really do want to make against people and civilizations who have insisted on taking the good of certain individuals and groups more seriously than the good of others. If we want to convey our steadfast opposition to any such perspective, the use of the word "equality" is as good a strategy as any for conveying what it is we are committing ourselves to and what we are committing ourselves against. There is this heritage, for example, of racism and sexism, and the most illuminating way of expressing one's affirmative view in opposition to that heritage is to use the language of equal respect.[48]

46. Cf. Joel Feinberg, "Noncomparative Justice," *Philosophical Review* 83 (1974): 297–338.

47. Vinit Haksar, *Equality, Liberty, and Perfectionism* (Oxford University Press, 1979), 149.

48. See also the discussion by Nicholas Mark Smith, *Basic Equality and Discrimination: Reconciling Theory and Law* (Ashgate, 2011), 22–23, of a similar passage from H. L. A. Hart, "Between Utility and Rights," *Columbia Law Review* 79 (1979): 845. As Smith notes, Hart acknowledges the importance of equality to express objections to (say) cases of "double

Certainly we can formulate our egalitarian convictions using different words if Westen, Lucas, and Frankfurt want us to do so. They are allergic to the term; perhaps we should be sensitive to that. We can say that respect is due to humanity as such, and so are consideration and concern. We do not have to use the eight letter string "e-q-u-a-l-i-t-y." But that word does have the additional and important resonance of indicating the sort of heritage we are struggling against and the heritage of struggling against it. We believe in a profound respect due to humanity, and we maintain that belief in the face of those who claim that there are different kinds of human or that humanity admits of unequal degrees. Words remind us of movements. And "equality" reminds us of that movement in our civilization.

9.

Please bear with me for one final tract of discussion of the redundancy thesis because I think it is important.

I want to focus briefly on a couple of the most famous ethical prescriptions ever issued. When Jesus of Nazareth taught us to feed the hungry, take in the stranger, minister to the sick, and visit those who were in prison—saying that insofar as we did these things "for the least of these my brethren," we did it for him[49]—his commandment might seem to be a prescription about the equal claims of everyone upon us, including those who are apparently the least used to our consideration. But Westen, Lucas, and Frankfurt will say it really just is a prescription about the importance of responding to need. You should respond to need in the case of this person, in the case of that

---

counting, giving the Brahmin or the white man two votes to the Untouchable's or the black man's single vote."

49. Matthew 25:31–40.

person, and in the case of the other person—this prisoner, that sick person, that stranger over there, and so on. You should do so impartially, but you don't need the word "equality" to convey that commitment. So again, we are being told that what are alleged to be principles of equality represent nothing more than a determination to apply moral principles consistently—that is, to treat each human's interest just as it deserves to be treated.

Maybe we don't even need the category of humanity (what Lucas called "Universal Humanity").[50] We might instead tilt toward a certain sort of moral particularism. We might treat each human with the concern due to him or her, each animal with the concern due to it, each plant ditto, each rock, and so on.[51] The last two cases may not detain us for very long, but if we dwell on the humans and animals, it is because each of them has particular needs for us to attend to, not because they are animals or humans or equals. Each of them—the least of them as well as the greatest of them—exhibits needs, and it is just the needs that command our attention.

So: maybe in a world of unlimited time and among people of microscopic moral discernment, we would not have to use principles of equality or inequality, or even principles that use words like "species" and "human." We would just examine each situation very closely and

50. Lucas, "Against Equality," 298.

51. Joseph Raz comes close to this when he says, in *The Morality of Freedom* (Oxford University Press, 1986), 221, that universal principles

> apply to all and thus establish the equality of all with respect to the normative consequences they stipulate. No one is excluded. Who must be the subjects of a principle if it is to be universal? One suggestion may be that "all" should include everything and the content of the principle be allowed to determine whether it is vacuously fulfilled in some cases. "All are entitled to have their interests respected" would apply vacuously to stones because they have no interests.

This, says Raz, is not a good way of determining which principles count as egalitarian principles. But an approach along these lines would help us see that many of what seem to be principles of equality are not really egalitarian principles at all.

figure out what was going on and examine each entity, seeing what its interests and needs were and how to respect them. Whatever we came across or had dealings with, whenever we had to decide about actions that might have an impact on any other entity, we would just pay attention successively to each human, each adult, each man, each woman, each cat, dog, fish, rock, and so on. We would still have principles, but the principles would now express themselves with a very tight connection between the content of the principle and what it was supposed to be an immediate response to. They would say, "If you find something bleeding, try to stop the bleeding," and "If you find something suffering, try to stop the suffering." They would not have to use words like "human." Certainly they would not have to use ideas like "equality." Our principles would simply refer to characteristics directly related to what the principle requires, not characteristics referring to species or types of being. They would be universally quantified, but it would be something like "For all X, if X is thirsty, then give X water," and X would range over everything (people, animals, plants, rocks, etc.).

So: one principle might tell us that if something or someone is hurting, then we should do what we can to alleviate the pain. A principle of first aid might say, "If the thing you're looking at has a limb that is broken, then set and immobilize that limb, if you can." And we would not need to bother ourselves about what the appropriate range of this principle was. "If someone or something would benefit from friendship, or if the person or thing is a stranger in a strange land, then take it in. If it would profit from care or education, then furnish it with that opportunity." The moral particularist might say that *these* are the principles we should follow. We should apply them regularly and consistently, and if we do that, we will no doubt end up applying them to those whom Jesus referred to as "the least of these my brethren." Only we wouldn't need any notion of brethren or the brotherhood of man. We would just be responding to this or that need, this or that interest, as and when it cropped up.

This particularist proposal is not as preposterous as it sounds, especially if it is put forward, as I said, as a limit case for circumstances of infinite time and discernment. I want to respond to it, however, in a different way, and indirectly.

Lord Gifford's endowment talks about natural theology, and I said at the outset that there is some religious resonance in these lectures. My second text is the Parable of the Good Samaritan.

> A certain man went down from Jerusalem to Jericho, and fell among thieves, who stripped him of his raiment and wounded him and departed, leaving him half dead. . . . A certain Samaritan, as he journeyed, came where that man was, and when he saw him, he had compassion on him. He went to him and he bound up his wounds, pouring in oil and wine, and set him on his own beast, and brought him to an inn, and took care of him. And in the morrow, when he parted, he took out two pence and gave them to the host, and said, "Take care of him, and if thou spendest more, when I come again, I will repay you."[52]

You will recall that this story is Jesus's response to a question posed by an irritating lawyer: "Who is my neighbor?" In response to that question, instead of a reiteration of traditional communal divisions, the lawyer is given an answer that cuts straight across ethnic and religious lines. From the standpoint of Jewish law, the Samaritan was definitely not a neighbor of the man he assisted, assuming that that man was Jewish.[53] The story might be compelling enough if it contrasted the

52. Luke 10:27–37.

53. John Bowman, *The Samaritan Problem: Studies in the Relationships of Samaritanism, Judaism, and Early Christianity,* trans. Alfred M. Johnson (Pickwick Press, 1975), 69.

helping behavior of a stranger with the helpful behavior of a priest. But in the words of Herbert Fingarette, Jesus substituted a Samaritan — a geographical neighbor, but one who was despised and hated by the Jews of his time as being uncouth, unclean, immoral, and largely heretical.[54] As Peter Winch has observed, one might as well tell a story about a Palestinian coming to the aid of an Israeli on the road from Jerusalem to Jericho.[55] One other commentator, Philip Esler, has added that there is nothing artificial about imposing a case where the next person to pass by was a non-Israelite; that's what you might expect in life, especially when you are on the road. There is no telling who you will come across when you're on the road.[56]

For our purposes — and, as I said, this is where I have some sympathy for the particularist approach — what is remarkable about the Samaritan is that he simply applies principles of first aid to the individual he confronts in an immediate, no-fuss sort of way. He does not try to answer any of the traditional questions: What sort of person is this? Is this a member of my community, bound to me by communal ties? Is this my responsibility? Is this one of my neighbors, in the strict or traditional sense of neighborhood? He does not ask any of those questions or run his finger down any sort of communitarian checklist. He just applies principles of need and principles of aid. "This individual is bleeding. This is a human who needs care, perhaps for

54. Herbert Fingarette, "Some Moral Aspects of Good Samaritanship," in *The Good Samaritan and the Law*, ed. James Ratcliffe (Anchor Books, 1966), 217–218. I am most grateful to Victor Austin and Andrew Mead for helping me think about the Good Samaritan parable.

55. See Peter Winch, "Who Is My Neighbor?," in *Trying to Make Sense* (Basil Blackwell, 1987), 156.

56. See Philip Esler, "Jesus and the Reduction of Intergroup Conflict: The Parable of the Good Samaritan in the Light of Social Identity Theory," *Biblical Interpretation* 8 (2000): 333–334. See also the discussion in Jeremy Waldron, "Who Is My Neighbor? Humanity and Proximity," *Monist* 86 (2003): 333–354.

days." The glory of the Samaritan's response is that it is uncontaminated by any sense of communitarian divisions in the human ranks. So far, so good.

The moral particularist might invite us to go a step further. He might say the story does not even need to be interpreted in light of any proposition about human equality, which is one way of looking at it: the Samaritan just responded to the predicament of a human on the road, not a Jewish equal but a human equal. Maybe the story does not have to be understood in light of a proposition about human anything—human worth, human dignity, or human status. It is just a story about an immediate and impartial response to bleeding, to wounds, and to things that need to be moved out of danger. Maybe if the Samaritan came across a dog by the side of the road, hit by a car, then the Samaritan would impartially apply the same principles. Stanch the bleeding of the dog; bind up its wounds; carry it to a place of safety. To respond to those imperatives, says the particularist, you do not need any doctrine of equality or the range or human worth or dignity. All you need is the impartial determination to follow your principles wherever they take you.

And perhaps that is right. But it is right only up to a point. The Samaritan is no doubt on *bleeding alert* and *suffering alert* when he is on the road to Jericho. But I think it is important for him to be on *human alert* as well.[57] I said he may come upon a suffering dog. In fact what he came upon was a suffering man, the man who fell among thieves. To deal with this case, the Samaritan had to be prepared to respond to *human* characteristics, which might not apply in the case of the dog. I am not saying we should neglect dogs. But caring for a

57. I do not mean to make it sound like the Samaritan in the parable is a busybody or a professional do-gooder, on the lookout, as it were, for cases to help. It is just part of his (and everyone's) moral equipment, whatever they are doing on the road, that they have the ability to swing into action when they come across these predicaments.

human is different. If the human individual by the side of the road is conscious, then the Samaritan should try to explain what he is doing as he tends to him. The Samaritan should try to allay the man's anxiety for the immediate future because humans have this remarkable capacity to project themselves fearfully or hopefully forward, as well as backward in memory. He might have to tell the man when he takes him to the inn who will take care of the bill at the end. If the man offers his gratitude, then the Samaritan should listen to and respect that. Not only this, but in the case of a human lying injured in the road, there is likely to be somebody to call, some loved one that needs to be got in touch with. And so on. It is part of the principle of human equality that such needs, attributes, concerns, and occasions for respect are always likely to present themselves in the case of humans, *indeed in the case of every single human.* And for this reason we do have to be on *human alert,* even if we are steadfastly not on *community alert,* when we come across these situations on the road.

If there *is* any communitarian element in our response, I guess it may be to find out about particular customs, maybe even particular taboos that affect the person we are trying to help. Is he a Jehovah's Witness with views about blood transfusions? If the man is beyond help, what is the position of his people on burial? But these are exceptions that prove the rule. For *all* humans there are likely to be answers to these questions, and for *all* humans asking such questions is important. The thing about humans is that they have customs and taboos and burial beliefs. And it's important when you're dealing with a human—any human—to find out what these are and respect them.

For these reasons, then, I say—and I think this is the basis of my opposition in the end to the particularist approach—that human beings, as such, are a morally interesting kind of entity. And the idea of special attention to humans just because they are human is at the very least a morally necessary heuristic, which I should take with me when

I go out on the road. For we cannot work in a wholly particularist way, starting at scratch with each entity and each situation that we come across. We always work with some sense of types of beings, even when we are examining some individual like "the least of these my brethren" or "the man who fell among thieves." Human beings are a morally interesting kind, and basic human equality is at the very least a morally necessary heuristic. We need the category human, associated as it is with certain ethical imperatives, and we need it available for equal and indiscriminate use for every case of wounded or vulnerable humanity we come across.

Someone like Hastings Rashdall will say all this is a mistake. He suggests implicitly that one ought to be on *white man alert* when one is on the road because that is a significant kind of being that one has to be on the lookout for when one is dealing with people's interests; that is where the crucial differences will show themselves. Our ethical principles ought to "carve nature at the joints,"[58] and the difference between "white men," on the one hand, and "Chinamen and negroes," on the other, according to Rashdall, indicates one of the major joints that our ethical carving should be responsive to. We believe Rashdall is culpably wrong about that. We think that being on *human alert* is much the better heuristic. And that is partly what we use the language of human equality to convey.

Remember, too, that this is not just about one-on-one interactions like the interaction between the Samaritan and the man who fell among thieves on the road between Jerusalem and Jericho. In moral life and particularly in political life, we are dealing with large populations and we need coarse generalizations that will direct our attention

58. For this metaphor, see Plato, *Phaedrus*, ed. Alexander Nehemas and Paul Woodruff (Hackett, 1995), 64. For extensive discussions in the context of the theory of natural kinds, see Joseph Campbell et al., eds., *Carving Nature at Its Joints: Natural Kinds in Metaphysics and Science* (MIT Press, 2011).

to the effect of the policies we apply to the people who are affected by our administration. Recall that the passage I quoted from Rashdall in Lecture 1 was from the chapter on *justice* in his *Treatise of Moral Philosophy*, not from a chapter on personal ethics. Rashdall was teaching young men at New College how to administer the empire, and that definitely involved the question of how to bring the needs and expectations of countless "Chinamen and negroes" living under imperial authority into relation with the refined interests of a much smaller number of white men living in Holywell Street or Bloomsbury, or—forgive me—in Edinburgh on the Morningside Road.

You may say, "Well, surely Rashdall is right at least to *ask* whether there are discontinuities of this kind, different kinds of capacities for well-being, and whether or not they line up with other broad human characteristics." All right. But when the stakes are so high, that is all the more reason for giving clarity and emphasis to the resounding answer that we have reached: "No. There are no such great differences of capacity for well-being or suffering, no such great differences of moral agency or responsiveness to value or basic rationality among humans. All humans are equal in these fundamental respects." And anyone who goes out on a road where they might come across different kinds of people—whether to administer an empire or to journey down to Jericho—had better go armed with the category of humanity and something like the principle that commands concern and respect for those falling into that category as one another's equals.

3

Looking for a Range Property

The principle of basic equality seems to assume that there must be some factual equality among us. What is this factual equality? That we *are* one another's equals is best regarded as a moral principle: it is prescriptive in spite of its indicative form. The question now is: In virtue of what fact or facts about us is this principle supposed to hold? What's its grounding? That is what I explore in this third lecture.

1.

The question arises for every theory of this kind. John Rawls argued that basic equality entitled each of us to the benefit of principles of justice. But having said that, he acknowledged that "we have yet to consider what sorts of beings are owed the guarantees of justice."[1] Probably it excludes animals, he said.[2] But then what are the features that entitle those who *are* included to equal consideration? Immanuel Kant thought that we had an obligation to treat one another as equals, organizing our actions so that they can "coexist with everyone's freedom

1. John Rawls, *A Theory of Justice*, rev. ed. (Harvard University Press, 1999), 442.
2. Ibid. Rawls added that animals "have some protection certainly, but their status is not that of human beings."

in accordance with a universal law."[3] But who is "everyone" here? How do we distinguish those beings or entities that are entitled to this coexistence under principles of freedom from those that are not? John Locke, writing in the 1680s at the beginning of his *Second Treatise of Government*, thought that there was "nothing more evident than that creatures of the same species and rank, promiscuously born to all the same advantages of Nature, and the use of the same faculties, should also be equal one amongst another, without subordination or subjection."[4] He was calling for the realization in fact of this equality "of jurisdiction or dominion."[5] That was the aim of his egalitarian theory. And he said this demand was based on our equal faculties and our being born to the same advantages of nature. But which faculties? What advantages of nature?

Such questions arise even if we adopt a decisionistic approach to equality, of the sort we discussed in Lecture 2. There we heard some people—Margaret MacDonald and Hannah Arendt—saying, "Look, we can just *decide* to treat a class of beings as our equals. We just *decide* to hold one another to be equal."[6] But, as I said, even if this is so we still have to ask: What features should we understand as delimiting the class of beings in respect of whom this decision is appropriate? What characteristics of the individuals we are talking about make sense of our decision? What properties of candidate entities should we use to apply it? So, decisionistic or nondecisionistic—either way,

3. Immanuel Kant, *The Metaphysics of Morals*, in *Practical Philosophy*, ed. Mary Gregor (Cambridge University Press, 1996), 387 (6:230). (Note: numbers in parentheses refer to the Prussian Academy edition of Kant's works.)

4. John Locke, *Two Treatises of Government*, ed. Peter Laslett (Cambridge University Press, 1988), 287 (II, §4).

5. Ibid., 322 (II, §54).

6. Margaret McDonald, "Natural Rights," in *Theories of Rights*, ed. Jeremy Waldron (Oxford University Press, 1984), 21–40; Hannah Arendt, *On Revolution* (Penguin Books, 1977). See also Lecture 2, Section 5.

we are looking for similarities. We are looking for a "host property," a property that humans share that is key to their equality.[7] The difference may be that on the decisionistic approach, the factual characteristics we are looking for operate simply as indicators of the decision's application, whereas on the deeper, nondecisionistic approach we are looking for grounds, not just for indicators.[8] Still, inasmuch as the decisionist acknowledges an obligation to make sense of her decision, the two ideas come together.

In Lecture 1, I said that principles of basic equality may be of two kinds. There may be a principle of *distinctive equality*, based on our equal possession of some attribute that is supposed to distinguish humans from the animals and that assigns all humans to the same high dignity. A partisan of distinctive equality is going to be looking for some way of understanding the distinctiveness and perhaps the greatness of human nature. Or we may be asserting a more modest position—*continuous equality*—which maintains simply that there are no discontinuities in the range of humanity that would accord some humans a lower status than others. Continuous equality leaves open the question of whether humans are raised above all other living things. Now, strictly speaking, the more modest position does not require us to identify a single property that all humans share. This is because it is a negative position: it says there is no special property that some humans have and others do not. But, as I said in Lecture 2, in light of the difficulty of proving a negative, it is likely that those who believe in continuous equality also base their belief on there being some key property that all humans share (even if they also share it with the higher animals), some key property whose importance justifies their confidence that they will not find any other basis for what I

7. The phrase "host property" is from John Coons and Patrick Brennan, *By Nature Equal: The Anatomy of a Western Insight* (Princeton University Press, 1999), 39.

8. I am most grateful to Jeffrey Stout for this point.

called a Rashdall-discontinuity.[9] They base their confidence that they will not be driven to treat different classes of humans as radically unequal on the fact that humans all possesses some property which, they reckon, is likely to overwhelm any putative basis for discontinuity among them. So really I am assuming that proponents of both these positions are going to be participating in this quest for a property that is the basis of human equality.

One other preliminary—I am talking about finding a *property* on which human equality is based. But at this stage and for the rest of these lectures I use the term "property" very loosely. What we are looking for may be an attribute, a relation, a capability, or a cluster of attributes, relations, and capabilities. As we proceed, the focus will shift quickly to capabilities. And by Lectures 5 and 6, we will be looking not just at capabilities but at a trajectory of the development of an array of capabilities, at the story of their use and the interpersonal relations they give rise to over a whole life. However, we must not get ahead of ourselves. We will begin by considering candidate properties (in the loose sense of "property") one by one.

2.

If we were happy to be blatant speciesists or pure human chauvinists, we might just assert barefacedly that the key property upon which human equality supervenes is human DNA. We might start with that, but it is unsatisfactory even as a starting point. It does little or nothing to make the equality position intelligible, which as I said was an important aspect of supervenience; it does not make sense of basic equality; it does not seem to give us any credible rationale for treating

9. For the idea of a Rashdall-discontinuity, see Lecture 1, Section 8. For the argument about the plausibility of continuous equality depending on recognition of a shared property, see Lecture 2, Section 6.

as equals the beings it credentials. And especially for what I have
called the *distinctive equality* position, it is objectionably question-
begging once the issue of our dealings with non-human animals has
been raised.

Anyway, even if we took human DNA seriously as a host property,
we would have to face up to the point that human DNA is important
not because of what it *is* but because of what it is *for*. The importance
of DNA is infrastructural; it makes other organic properties possible.
And we will want to understand (or we *should* want to understand) the
contribution of DNA to this argument about equality in terms of the
properties that our genome underpins and mobilizes. So by itself
the DNA view is not helpful. It is either question-begging or it leaves
unanswered the crucial questions that we want to get at.

3.

In a 1962 essay called "The Idea of Equality" (one of the few published articles of that era that actually addressed the topic I have taken
for these lectures), the philosopher Bernard Williams dwelt on the
sheer fact of our humanity. He acknowledged that it did not seem to
be a very promising beginning just to remind us that all humans are
human. But then he wrote:

> That all men are human is, if a tautology, a useful one, serving
> as a reminder that those who belong anatomically to the species
> *homo sapiens*, and can speak a language, use tools, live in
> societies, can interbreed despite racial differences, etc., are also
> alike in certain other respects more likely to be forgotten. These
> respects are notably the capacity to feel pain, both from imme-
> diate physical causes and from various situations represented in
> perception and in thought; and the capacity to feel affection

for others, and the consequences of this, connected with the frustration of this affection, loss of its objects, etc.[10]

The capacity to feel pain and the capacity to feel affection for others: like Williams, I think these are worth highlighting. For, as he went on to say, "The assertion that men are alike in the possession of these characteristics is, while indisputable . . . not trivial. For it is certain that there are political and social arrangements that neglect these characteristics in the case of some groups of men, while being fully aware of them in the case of others; that is to say, they . . . neglect moral claims that arise from these characteristics."[11] I think in 1962 Williams had South Africa in mind, particularly with regard to the second of those characteristics: apartheid institutions brutally separated black workers from their families for months, even years, and they did so casually, as though the misery of these separations to those involved was a matter of no concern.

Do the properties cited by Williams establish only a basis for continuous equality, or are they intended to establish the stronger position of distinctive equality? The first characteristic, the capacity to feel pain, seems to be a basis for continuous equality: all humans have it, but then so do many animals have the capacity to feel pain. Jeremy Bentham, the great eighteenth-century utilitarian, is famous for his insistence that this is both the key to moral equality and something we share with the animals. He asked what could be more important than the fact that we and they can feel pain: "What else is it that should trace the insuperable line? Is it the faculty of reason, or, perhaps, the faculty of discourse? But a full-grown horse or dog is beyond comparison a more rational, as well as a more conversable animal,

10. Bernard Williams, "The Idea of Equality," in *Problems of the Self* (Cambridge University Press, 1973), 232.

11. Ibid.

than an infant of a day, or a week, or even a month, old."[12] No, said Bentham, "the question is not, Can they reason? nor, Can they talk? but, Can they suffer?"[13] And since all humans can suffer, then in that sense humans at least are one another's equals, particularly in relation to political arrangements that have the power to cause and distribute such suffering.

Having said this, however, we should note that elsewhere in his writings, Bentham emphasized the fact that "man is not like the animals limited to the present but susceptible to pains and pleasures by anticipation."[14] This seems to take us into the distinctively human range. It was a point Williams alluded to also when he spoke about "the capacity to feel pain, both from immediate physical causes *and from various situations represented in perception and in thought.*"[15] So the Williams criterion seems to straddle the line between continuous and distinctive equality. I think this is what we should expect, as certain properties that we share with animals take on a distinctively human tinge in our experience and we are drawn toward the assignment of moral significance to their distinctively human manifestations.

If we look at Williams's other criterion, the capacity for affection, we see a similar range of possibilities. Animals can have affection for other animals and (as Sue Donaldson and Will Kymlicka have

12. Jeremy Bentham, *An Introduction to the Principles of Morals and Legislation*, ed. J. H. Burns and H. L. A. Hart (Athlone Press, 1970), 282–283 (chap. 17, §i: 1 [note b]). The comparison between infants and animals is something we will come back to in Lecture 6.

13. Ibid.

14. Jeremy Bentham, "Principles of the Civil Code," in *The Theory of Legislation*, ed. C. K. Ogden (Kegan Paul, Trench, and Trubner, 1931), 110. See also the discussion in Stefan Gosepath, "The Morality of Equal Respect," in *Do All Persons Have Equal Moral Worth? On Basic Equality and Equal Respect and Concern*, ed. Uwe Steinhoff (Oxford University Press, 2015), 138.

15. Williams, "The Idea of Equality," 232; my emphasis.

pointed out recently) for humans as well.[16] But the further you take
the capacity for affection in the direction of *love,* maybe the more
distinctively human this becomes. I wouldn't want to press this too
hard. Certainly this is a property that all humans have—a capacity
for love—and it might be significant as a basis for equality. That
humans can love and be moved by love will often be at stake—
fundamentally at stake—in social and political decisions.[17] Now, the
relevant property here includes not just affection and desire but
the capacity to recognize and identify with another person, to involve
oneself existentially in the way things are and how things go for the
other person, and to both lose oneself and find oneself in such a relationship. This feature of our lives, we may think, is part of what makes
sense of the claim that in the more important things we are one another's equals. Certainly we are to attend equally to these capacities
in different people when they are at stake in a decision.

Some Christian thinkers have pursued a theory of this kind, suggesting that humans are equals because they equally have the capacity
to love one another. They suggest that God, having loved us, has
touched us with the ability to love one another. Indeed, if God in a
sense *is* love, then maybe our capacity for love is our bearing of the
image of God.[18] But an emphasis on the human capacity for love and
affection need not be religiously tinged; it is not religiously tinged in
Williams's account. It may be cited simply as an important fact about
us, one that is bound to strike anybody as crucial, whether or not God

16. Sue Donaldson and Will Kymlicka, *Zoopolis: A Political Theory of Animal Rights*
(Oxford University Press, 2011).

17. The apartheid case illustrates this, as do the cases of same-sex and interracial marriage.

18. For some discussion of this possibility, see Roger Ruston, *Human Rights and the
Image of God* (SCM Press, 2004). See also Jeremy Waldron, "The Image of God: Rights,
Reason, and Order," in *Christianity and Human Rights,* ed. John Witte and Frank Alexander
(Cambridge University Press, 2010), 216–235.

created it and taught us to notice it. It is an important fact about us that might be conceived to ground our special worth. Ignoring it, some say, would be an insult to the dignity of the human species.

4.

The capacity most commonly cited in our tradition as the basis of human worth and dignity is *reason*. Listen to Cicero's account of the distinctive character of human beings, from his book *Concerning the Laws (De Legibus)*: "This animal—provident, perceptive, versatile, sharp, capable of memory, and filled with reasons and judgment— which we call a human being, was endowed by the supreme god with a grand status at the time of its creation. It alone of all types and varieties of animate creatures has a share in reason and thought, which all the others lack. What is there, not just in humans, but in all heaven and earth, more divine than reason?"[19] You find the same idea in the Stoics; you find it in the early Christian thinkers, too, in Aquinas and Augustine; and all the way through to the modern era.[20]

The Stoics are particularly interesting in regard to this equation of human reason with a spark of the divine. Cicero's position and the position of philosophers like Epictetus is not only a matter of noticing that God just happens to have favored us by giving us this capacity. Rationality is ours for a reason, they argue. There is a point to our rationality, and the point is that it makes possible a community of sorts

19. Cicero, *De Legibus*, in *On the Commonwealth and On the Laws*, ed. James Zetzel (Cambridge University Press, 1999), 113.

20. For the Stoics, besides Cicero, see Marcus Aurelius, *Meditations*, ed. Martin Hammond (Penguin Books, 2006), 57 (bk. 7); Augustine, *On Free Choice of the Will*, trans. Thomas Williams (Hackett, 1993), 44–46 (bk. 2, chap. 8); Thomas Aquinas, *Summa Contra Gentiles*, bk. 3, chaps. 25 and 37, in *St. Thomas Aquinas on Politics and Ethics*, ed. Paul Sigmund (Norton, 1988), 6–7, 8.

with God or with the gods. "Since there is nothing better than reason," says Cicero, "and [since] this is found both in humans and in gods, reason forms the first bond between the humans and the gods."[21] (I think in Christian teaching too, when reason is identified as part of the image of God, again it is not just seen as a happy endowment; it is an endowment with a point — to make possible fellowship between humans and God, a fellowship that was perhaps ruptured at the time of the Fall.) The Stoics are well known for envisaging a broad polity consisting of all humans, a cosmopolitan vision: "I am not an Athenian or a Corinthian, but a citizen of the world," they would say. That aspect of Stoic teaching is well known;[22] less well known is their insistence that this cosmopolitan community binds together gods and men. As Epictetus put it, "Each human being is primarily a citizen of his own commonwealth, but he is also a member of the great city of gods and men, whereof the city political is only a copy."[23] I find it interesting in this way to push just beyond the claim that humans are rational animals, to the further step of asking why that makes them significant. The worth of human beings is greatly enhanced in this account of the particular purpose for which they are said to be endowed with reason. It is one way in which religious arguments can add extra riches to a secular account of basic equality. We are not just cunning and calculating: our reason is the key to the highest other things of which we are capable, including our highest relations with one another and with the divine. We will consider this more in Lectures 4 and 5.

---

21. Cicero, *De Legibus*, 113 (bk. 1, §23).

22. The quotation is from Diogenes of Sinope. See also the discussion by Martha Nussbaum and others in *For Love of Country: Debating the Limits of Patriotism* (Beacon Press, 1996), 6.

23. Epictetus, *Discourses*, trans. W. A. Oldfather (Loeb Classical Library, 1925), 63–65, 245 (bk. 1, chap. 9 and bk. 2, chap. 5).

I said that this understanding about the significance of human reason runs all the way through to early modern thought. When I wrote *God, Locke and Equality*, I argued that a careful reading of John Locke's work revealed that he too thought reason was the characteristic on which human equality was predicated.[24] Locke actually used the image of God idea—though just once—in the first of his *Two Treatises of Government* (the *First Treatise*, which nobody ever reads). There he said, "God made Adam 'in his own Image after his own Likeness'; makes him an intellectual Creature. . . . For wherein soever else the Image of God consisted, the intellectual Nature was certainly a part of it, and belong'd to the whole Species."[25] In chapter 4 of *God, Locke, and Equality* I argued that Locke presented human rationality as a heritage of every man, not just an intellectual elite. He was wont to contrast the straightforward intellect of the plain man with the "learned gibberish" of scholars, philosophers, and lawyers.[26] That was not a disparagement of rationality; it was an insistence on its wide dissemination.

The account of reason as the host property for equality need not be religious in character. The ability to understand one's surroundings gives a person a distinctive sort of presence in the world, so that the world is no longer something he is just dumbly at the mercy of. Such an understanding in a given individual relates him also to other

24. Of course, Locke is not the only nor even the most prominent or radical of the early modern egalitarians. See Andrew Sharp, ed., *The English Levellers* (Cambridge University Press, 1998). I concentrate on Locke, however, because I know his work best.

25. Locke, *Two Treatises of Government*, 179–180 (I, §30). Also, part of what Locke was doing with this passage was to maintain that this characteristic belonged to Eve as well. See Jeremy Waldron, *God, Locke and Equality: Christian Foundations in Locke's Political Thought* (Cambridge University Press, 2002), 24–28.

26. Waldron, *God, Locke and Equality*, 91, citing John Locke, *An Essay Concerning Human Understanding*, ed. P. H. Nidditch (Oxford University Press, 1971), 453 (bk. 3, chap. 10, §12).

similarly endowed individuals: he not only shares a world with them, but he shares with them knowledge and understanding of that world.

Beyond this, we can say that the creative ability to entertain abstract ideas, to see things in common between experiences and perceptions so that we can grasp and manipulate concepts, to study, reflect, and remember—all this adds up to a capability of breathtaking extent. At its upper extreme, it makes it possible for humans to send spacecraft to the edge of the solar system, to probe the basis of physical reality, to unravel the genome, to eliminate smallpox, to do philosophy, draft codes of laws, write novels, and compose great music. At a lower level it is the ability, if not to share in these scientific and cultural achievements, then at least to enjoy and appreciate their products and to follow some of the lines of thought that their production involved. It is not hard to see why such a capability was identified with the divine. Together with the civilizations it has made possible, human rationality seems to lift us vastly above the other animals—whose reasoning we understand at its most optimistic in terms of the counting and manipulation of bananas. It puts us in a class of our own so far as intellectual achievement is concerned.

5.

Reason is a broad idea: it covers a variety of virtues and no doubt also a variety of sins. Some of the philosophers interested in equality focus on specific rational capacities under this heading. Locke thought the rational attribute that was most important was our ability to engage in abstract reasoning. He believed—something we do not believe—that the capacity for abstract reasoning is both necessary and largely sufficient for figuring out that God exists. And, he argued, a being that could become aware of its maker must have a special significance in the eyes of its maker—a significance that needs to be taken into account in all our dealings with one another.[27] The Lockean idea of the capacity for personhood is in play here also. Someone who can think of herself, abstractly, as a being that endures from moment to moment and as the same being that may commit a sin today and have to account to the Almighty for it tomorrow will regard herself and others like her in these respects as having a special significance in relation to God.

Other, more secular accounts have suggested that human language is the key facet of rationality. George Kateb says that language is the basis of human uniqueness and the crux of rationality: "By making language possible, the human brain makes possible the mind, from which speech and notational systems come. Language not only makes thinking possible, it is the medium of most thinking."[28] This aspect of human nature, Kateb believes, is a basis for distinctive equality: "No other species speaks, much less writes. . . . There is nothing like speech in nature."[29] And it is of momentous importance: "From language comes thinking, a trait that is essential to free agency and moral agency as well as to human stature in general."[30]

For many, it is *practical* reason that is important in its connection with rational agency. Philosophers talk of man's ability to discern and weigh reasons and relate them to one another: "A rational agent can identify available courses of action she might take, discern reasons for and against the options, weigh and assess the reasons she discerns, deliberate and make choices, carry out the action chosen," and so on.[31] What's more, these reasons can be understood abstractly and

---

27. See Waldron, *God, Locke and Equality*, 78–81.

28. George Kateb, *Human Dignity* (Harvard University Press, 2011), 138.

29. Ibid., 139.

30. Ibid., 143.

31. Richard Arneson, "Equality: Neither Acceptable nor Rejectable," in Steinhoff, *Do All Persons Have Equal Moral Worth?*, 34.

universalizably, enabling us to consider and compare their force even apart from the concrete situations in which they are implicated.

One theorist of practical rationality we should spend some time with is Thomas Hobbes, writing in the middle of the seventeenth century. Hobbes had a rather bleak vision of human kind. He was a great believer in human equality, but as its basis he emphasized a chilling characteristic. He thought the rational capacity we shared in common was not our capacity to love or speak or worship or do metaphysics but our equal capacity to *kill*. He said this in *Leviathan* (1651):

> Nature hath made men so equall in the faculties of body and mind as that, though there be found one man sometimes manifestly stronger in body or of quicker mind than another, yet when all is reckoned together the difference between man and man is not so considerable as that one man can thereupon claim to himself any benefit to which another may not pretend as well as he. For as to the strength of body, the weakest has strength enough to kill the strongest.[32]

"The weakest has strength enough to kill the strongest": that is what levels the playing field. In another of his books, *De Cive (Concerning the Citizen)*, Hobbes invited us to consider "how brittle the frame of our humane body is . . . and how easie a matter it is, even for the weakest man to kill the strongest"—how easily killable we are.[33] He thought we should infer from this that there is no reason why any man trusting in his own strength should conceive of himself made by nature above others. "They are equals," said Hobbes, "who can doe

32. Thomas Hobbes, *Leviathan*, ed. Richard Tuck (Cambridge University Press, 1996), 86–87 (chap. 13).

33. Thomas Hobbes, *De Cive: The English Version*, ed. Howard Warrender (Oxford University Press, 1984), 45 (bk. 1, chap. 3).

equall things one against the other, but they who can do the greatest things (namely kill) can doe equall things."[34] Killing, he thought, was the most important thing that one person could do to another, so that people who have equal homicidal capacity are one another's equals by nature.[35]

This is hardly what we would regard as an account of human dignity, but it is emphatically intended to refute any Rashdall-discontinuity within the human range. For example, it has immediate consequences for the alleged inequality between the sexes: "Whereas some have attributed the Dominion to the Man only, as being of the more excellent Sex, they misreckon in it. For there is not always that difference of strength or prudence between the man and the woman as that the right can be determined without War."[36] Any woman can kill any man. So you would be wise not to go around acting as though men and women were not one another's equals.

At first sight, the Hobbesian position seems to involve continuous equality: our ability to kill one another does not distinguish us from many animals. However, a number of features of Hobbesian man that are distinct from the other animals make him also more distinctly dangerous to his fellows than (say) bears or lions—I mean cunning, ambition, reason, mutual fear, and so on. These suggest that Hobbes is mainly interested in distinctive human equality.

All this sounds like a rather brutal account of basic equality. In fact it is supposed to motivate the concern for peace that is the telos of Hobbes's politics. In his theory of natural law, there is a prescriptive aspect to Hobbesian equality, amounting almost to a dignitarian

34. Ibid.

35. There is a good discussion of Hobbes's account and its relevance to basic equality in Jan Narveson, "Equality, Universality, and Impartiality," in Steinhoff, *Do All Persons Have Equal Moral Worth?*, 105–109.

36. Hobbes, *Leviathan*, 139 (chap. 20).

principle of equal respect. Hobbes said, "The question who is the better man has no place in the condition of mere nature where all men are equal. And therefore for the ninth law of nature"—he had about seventeen—"I put this: that every man acknowledge another for his equal by nature."[37] (Or, as he puts it in *De Cive*, people are to be "esteemed" as equal.)[38] No one is to go strutting around saying, "I am born superior to you." It is a condemnation, Hobbes says, of pride.[39]

6.

However, the most important aspects of rationality invoked in discussions of basic equality refer not to homicidal capability but to something almost diametrically opposed to it: our individual powers of moral reasoning. I am still proceeding under the auspices of reason as the key capacity, but looking now not at theoretical reason, not even just practical reason as such, but *moral* reason. Humans can think and calculate not just about what is and about what to do, but also about what they *morally ought* to do. We can figure out what the right thing is, and though we do not always do it, we know we are capable of doing it. This brings us face to face with the enormous influence in these matters of the great eighteenth-century Prussian philosopher Immanuel Kant.

Kant took all human reason seriously. No one can come away from reading *The Critique of Pure Reason* without a sense of his pride in our reasoning powers. True, reason leads us into antinomies; but on the other hand, the intellectual discipline that is required in response to this is itself a product of our rationality, and this gives us confidence

37. Ibid., 107 (chap. 15).
38. Hobbes, *De Cive*, 68.
39. Hobbes, *Leviathan*, 107 (chap. 15). Earlier in *Leviathan*, Hobbes identifies pride with "vaine-Glory" and associates it with the causation of anger (54 [chap. 6]).

in our epistemic powers.[40] However, in Kant's eyes, one of the most important things about human beings—perhaps *the* most important thing—is the capacity, not just to do science and to tame metaphysics, but to grasp and respond to moral law. Humans can come up with and respond to moral reasons even when those reasons are not advantageous for them, that is, even when moral action requires defiance of inclination, interest, and a craving for happiness. Kant thought this was a momentous capacity of counter-causal freedom—an ability to think and act independently of "the determining causes of the world of sense."[41]

There can be no doubt Kant saw this as a basis for what I have called a "distinctive" principle of basic equality. It differentiates us sharply from all other living things; indeed it raises us above our own animality. No mere animal is capable of acting on principle.[42] Here is what Kant said in his late work *The Metaphysics of Morals* (1797):

> In the system of nature, a human being *(homo phaenomenon, animal rationale)* is a being of slight importance and shares with the rest of the animals . . . an ordinary value. . . . But a human being regarded as a *person*, that is, as the subject of a morally practical reason, is exalted above any price; for as a person *(homo noumenon)* he is not to be valued merely as a means to the ends of others or even to his own ends, but as an end in itself, that is,

40. Immanuel Kant, *Critique of Pure Reason*, ed. Paul Guyer and Allen Wood (Cambridge University Press, 1998), 672 (A795 / B824, referring to standard pagination in the two editions of Kant's *Critique of Pure Reason*).

41. Immanuel Kant, *Groundwork of the Metaphysics of Morals*, in Gregor, *Practical Philosophy*, 99, 101 (4:452, 455).

42. Cf. Kant, *The Metaphysics of Morals*, 529 (6:400): "No human being is entirely without moral feeling, for were he completely lacking in it then humanity would dissolve (by chemical laws, as it were) into mere animality and be mixed irretrievably with the mass of other animals."

he possesses a dignity (an absolute inner worth) by which he exacts *respect* for himself from all other rational beings in the world. He can measure himself with every other being of this kind and can value himself on a footing of equality with them.[43]

If we are pursuing distinctive human equality, then this is the sort of account we are looking for. There is something massively important for Kant in our ability to reason morally. The power we have in this regard transforms our sense of what our status is and what is at stake when anyone is dealing with us. There is a wonderful passage in Kant's *Critique of Practical Reason*, which begins, "Two things fill the mind with ever new and increasing admiration and awe . . . : the starry heavens above and the moral law within."[44] The astronomical perspective "annihilates, as it were, my importance as an animal creature." But my moral self-awareness "infinitely raises my worth as an intelligence," as I become aware of a depth in my being not given by my biology. This is what determines the nature and scale of human dignity.

In his best-known book on moral philosophy, *Groundwork of the Metaphysics of Morals*, published in 1785, Kant wrote:

Morality is the condition under which alone a rational being can be an end in itself. . . . [M]orality, and humanity insofar as it is capable of morality, is that which alone has dignity. Skill and diligence in work have a market price; wit, lively imagination, and humor, have a fancy price; on the other hand, fidelity to promises and benevolence from basic principles (not from instinct),

43. Ibid., 557 (6:434–435).
44. Immanuel Kant, *Critique of Practical Reason*, in Gregor, *Practical Philosophy*, 269–270 (5:161–162).

have an inner worth. Nature as well as art contains nothing that, lacking these, it could put in their place.[45]

And he continued, saying that the worth of such a disposition is dignity, which is raised "infinitely above all price, with which it cannot for a moment be brought into comparison or competition at all without, as it were, assaulting its holiness."[46]

Bernard Williams insists we acknowledge that the moral capacity Kant identifies as the basis of human worth is not supposed to be a natural characteristic. It is noumenal; it is transcendent. Williams thinks this makes it difficult for us, here and now, to work with Kant's conception as a basis for mundane equality among ordinary people in ordinary circumstances.[47] Is it possible to eschew Kant's metaphysics while still seeing moral capacity as important? One would presumably say less about the counter-causal character of noumenal will, more perhaps about the simple ability to mobilize abstract moral resources against particular inclinations (even while conceding that these are all made, as it were, of the same stuff). Kantian metaphysics are not required for a grasp of what moral agency involves, nor are they required to underpin the conviction that moral agency is an important capability that all humans have. I do not mean to denigrate the depths of Kant's own account, but we should not exaggerate the extent to which rooting basic equality in moral agency depends on it.

---

45. Kant, *Groundwork*, 84–85 (4:434–435).

46. Ibid., 85 (4:435).

47. Williams, "The Idea of Equality," 235. Martha Nussbaum, in "Disabled Lives: Who Cares?," *New York Review of Books*, January 11, 2001, made much the same point when she said that "for Kant, human dignity and our moral capacity, dignity's source, are radically separate from the natural world. Morality has the task of providing for human needs, but the idea that we are basically split beings, both rational persons and animal dwellers in the world of nature, never ceases to influence Kant's ideas."

7.

Understood in this extended sense, Kantian doctrines about our capability for moral reasoning have been very influential in modern discussions of equality.[48] Unsurprisingly, we find an account along these lines in John Rawls's theory of justice.

That Rawls is an egalitarian is no surprise. We associate surface-level equality with Rawls's difference principle, with his principle of equal opportunity, and with his commitment to equal basic liberties.[49] Ronald Dworkin has argued persuasively that equality is implicated profoundly in Rawls's contractarian thought experiment about "the veil of ignorance" and "the original position."[50] These are all equalizing ideals, and they point us to a commitment to equality deep in the foundations of Rawls's work. For those who persevere to the end of Rawls's long book, there is a section entitled "The Basis of Equality." I suspect it is not widely read, but in it Rawls asks,

What sorts of beings are owed the guarantees of justice[?] [What are] the features of human beings in virtue of which they are to be treated in accordance with the principles of justice[?] Our conduct toward animals is not regulated by these principles, or so it is generally believed. On what grounds then do we distinguish between mankind and other living things and regard the constraints of justice as holding only in our relations to human persons?[51]

48. See, for example, Elizabeth Anderson, "What Is the Point of Equality?," *Ethics* 109 (1999): 312.

49. Rawls, *A Theory of Justice*, 266–267. But for doubts about the extent of Rawls's egalitarianism, see G. A. Cohen, *Rescuing Justice and Equality* (Harvard University Press, 2008).

50. Ronald Dworkin, "Justice and Equality," in *Taking Rights Seriously* (Harvard University Press, 1977), 179–183.

51. Rawls, *A Theory of Justice*, 441.

Rawls responds, "The natural answer seems to be that it is precisely . . . moral persons who are entitled to equal justice."

Now, this answer has been present in Rawls's work since the beginning. In a 1963 article titled "The Sense of Justice,"[52] he maintained that the possession of a sense of justice was sufficient for a person's basic entitlement to justice. In that piece, it seems this position was motivated by a conception of what justice is: "Questions of justice and fairness arise when free persons, who have no authority over one another, are participating in their common institutions and among themselves settling or acknowledging the rules which define them and which determine the resulting shares in their benefits and burdens."[53] They reason about justice together, and it is in virtue of their being able to conduct and their having conducted such reasoning that they owe duties of justice to one another. Of course the idea of such deliberation (the contractarian basis of Rawls's conception) is notional, so the argument just mentioned works at best only inside Rawls's model. Rawls says little in this early piece about why a capacity for justice is necessary and sufficient for the external application, so to speak, of his whole conception. When P, in the real world, has not actually participated in settling or acknowledging the rules which will determine benefits, burdens, and so on, why is P's possession of a sense of justice as such necessary or sufficient for him to be regarded as a subject or beneficiary of justice? What Rawls seems to say is that because P *could have been* a participant in the contractarian conception, he *is* actually owed the benefit of the principles arrived at in that process.[54] He reit-

---

52. John Rawls, "The Sense of Justice," *Philosophical Review* 72 (1963): 281–305, reprinted in John Rawls, *Collected Papers*, ed. Sam Freeman (Harvard University Press, 1999), 96–116.

53. Rawls, "The Sense of Justice," 282.

54. Ibid., p. 301: "The duty of justice is owed to those who could participate in the contractual situation of the original position and act on it."

erates the point in A *Theory of Justice*, though he acknowledges that an argument is not really provided.[55]

Nevertheless, a sense of justice—"a normally effective desire to apply and to act on the principles of justice"—is for Rawls the key to our status and dignity.[56] Notice the reference here to "*the* principles of justice." Coming as it does at the end of the book, this makes it sound as though we already know what the principles are, so that there is no question of the sense of justice having to orient itself to any content other than that of Rawls's own two principles of justice as fairness. But that can't be right. Within Rawls's model, the sense of justice is an admission ticket to the negotiations at the original position, in which it is initially an open question which principles will turn out to be accepted. So the sense of justice must mean something like a desire to apply and act on principles of justice whatever these turn out to be. The orientation is to justice as a concept, not to any particular conception.[57]

8.

Maybe this is all a bit one-sided: all about principle, all about duty, all about morality. What about the times when we are off duty—when we are just living our lives and responding to ordinary reasons, not the starry heavens above or the nagging voice of the categorical imperative? Hobbes made fun of Aristotle for valuing superior wisdom as a basis for inequality; he said this was just what you would expect from

55. Rawls, A *Theory of Justice*, 446.

56. Ibid., 442.

57. For this distinction, see ibid., 5. For some discussion of the difficulties with the idea of the concept of justice (as opposed to conceptions of it), see Ronald Dworkin, *Law's Empire* (Harvard University Press, 1986), 73–76, and Jeremy Waldron, "The Primacy of Justice," *Legal Theory* 9 (2003): 270–271.

a philosopher.[58] And we might say the Kantian conception is just what you would expect from a moral philosopher. To a hammer everything looks like a nail, and to a Kantian it looks as though moral judgment, that part of our lives, is the be-all and end-all of equality.

To answer this point, we may distinguish between *moral* autonomy, which is the capacity Kant is talking about, and *personal* autonomy, by which I mean a person being in control of her life, reflecting on how things are going, working out what to do with her life, and so on. I think it would be a pity to sell short this element of *personal* autonomy, in comparison with the Kantian account of the moral law within. Even considered apart from moral agency, each person has a unique perspective on the course of his or her life over time—thus far, now, and projected into the future. Talk of personal autonomy evokes the image of a person in charge of her life—in Joseph Raz's phrase, authoring or being part-author of her life—not just following inclination as it arises but choosing which of her preferences to follow, and not just for moral reasons but because of the sort of person she wants to be.[59]

Some philosophers elevate this personal autonomy into an exacting ethic in its own right. Like John Stuart Mill, they say that people have a responsibility to identify an authentic path of their own through life, something that answers to their inner destiny. According to Mill, people are responsible for their own individuality, and society ought to organize itself so as to provide an environment conducive to the blossoming of individuality. After all, human nature is not a machine to be

58. Hobbes, *Leviathan*, 107 (chap. 15): "Aristotle in the first booke of his Politiques, for a foundation of his doctrine, maketh men by Nature, some more worthy to Command, meaning the wiser sort (such as he thought himselfe to be for his Philosophy;) others to Serve, (meaning those that had strong bodies, but were not Philosophers as he)."

59. Joseph Raz, *The Morality of Freedom* (Oxford University Press, 1986), 370.

built after a model, but a tree that needs to grow in all its branches, according to the inner forces that determine a person's view of his own life.[60]

I do not want to criticize Mill's doctrine, but it is operating in a different normative mode from the interests we are pursuing. As we track down these properties that are the basis of equality, we are not looking for an all-purpose touchstone of morality. Our interest here is not in laying down any particular ethic for individuals; our interest is in the human capacities on which basic equality, dignity, human worth, and equal concern and respect may be predicated. For us, then, it is enough to say that humans have the ability more or less consciously to lead a life for themselves, to see their lives from the inside out, so to speak, and to make choices in the light of that seeing. That ability, the presence or the potential presence of that perspective, itself commands respect in the case of every human being. It is at stake in most of our dealings with one another. It is an important aspect of morality too, since it conditions our understanding of why others are worth respecting. (Without it—if we had only the Kantian account—we would have no answer to Mill's response to reports of Florence Nightingale's saying that we are put on earth to help others. Mill asked, "And what are the others put on earth for?")[61]

In his 1971 book, John Rawls complemented his own moralistic account of the sense of justice as a basis for equality with an account of our ability to think through and pursue a conception of our own

60. John Stuart Mill, *On Liberty*, ed. Currin Shields (Bobbs-Merrill, 1959), 71 (chap. 3): "He who lets the world choose his life for him, has no other need of any other faculty than the ape like faculty of imitation. He, who chooses his own plan of life for himself, employs all his faculties. He must use observation to see, reasoning and judgment to foresee, activity to gather materials for decision, discrimination to decide, firmness and self-control to hold to his deliberate decision."

61. I have been unable to track down a citation for this bon mot.

good as well. In the formulation to which I have already referred, the two ideas are set out side by side. Rawls asks, "What sort of beings are owed the guarantees of justice?" The answer, as we saw, was "that it is precisely moral persons who are entitled to equal justice."[62] But then he went on: "Moral persons are distinguished by two features. First, they are capable of having a conception of their own good, and second they are capable of having a sense of justice."[63] The combination makes sense. The work that justice does is relative to people's own interests and the pursuit of their own good. We want a society in which those interests are fairly treated. As Rawls put it in *Political Liberalism*, the reasonable must be complemented by the rational: "Merely reasonable agents would have no ends of their own to be advanced by fair cooperation."[64] For this to even arise, people must have interests apart from their moral views on fairness, and the character of their apprehension and pursuit of those interests is an indispensable part of their entitlement to equality.[65]

Immanuel Kant was also interested in this issue of personal as opposed to moral autonomy. In an essay from 1783 with the unwieldy title "On the Common Saying: That may be Correct in Theory, but it is of no Use in Practice," he relaxed the rigor of his moralism enough to say that "nobody can force me to be happy in accordance with his conception of happiness."[66] He went on: "Each may seek his happiness in the way that seems good to him, provided he does not infringe upon that freedom of others to strive for a like end which can coexist with the

62. Rawls, *A Theory of Justice*, 442.

63. Ibid.

64. John Rawls, *Political Liberalism* (Columbia University Press, 1996), 52.

65. Ibid. In the 1963 article, Rawls included only the moralistic element. Somewhere between 1963 and 1971, he added the element of personal autonomy.

66. Immanuel Kant, *On the Common Saying: That May Be Correct in Theory, But It Is of No Use in Practice*, in Gregor, *Practical Philosophy*, 290 (8:290).

freedom of everyone in accordance with a possible universal law."[67] To those brought up in Kantian moral philosophy, this sounds way too generous. On Kant's account as it is usually understood, autonomy and the pursuit of happiness are supposed to operate in utterly different realms. In the *Groundwork*, Kant associated autonomy with the will's ability to determine itself in accordance with the form of universality, unconstrained by nature or inclination.[68] Happiness, by contrast, is supposed to be about needs and inclinations, and as such it must be regarded as "a powerful counterweight to all the commands of duty."[69] Kant says that I become an autonomous being only when I rise above any concern for happiness and follow the moral law for its own sake. Against this background, his privileging of the personal pursuit of happiness is all the more remarkable. On the other hand, he did speak of persons' setting ends for themselves, and these can't just be *moral* ends since part of Kantian morality involves respecting people as ends-setters, as it were. They must be ends that are, in some sense, independent of moral considerations (albeit constrained by them)—ends whose adoption nevertheless commands moral respect.[70]

As with Mill on authenticity, the normative posture of Kant's account of personal autonomy is not quite that of a property grounding equality or dignity. Kant presents his account of personal autonomy in the *Theory and Practice* essay as a principle of political philosophy limiting what states can do. He called the independent pursuit of happiness "the only original right belonging to man by virtue of his

67. Ibid., 290 (8:290–291).

68. See Kant, *Groundwork*, 83 (4:433ff). Autonomy is "the supreme principle of morality," and morality is "the direct opposite of . . . the principle of one's own happiness [being] made the determining ground of the will." See also Kant, *Critique of Practical Reason*, 168 (5:25).

69. See Kant, *Groundwork*, 59 (4:405).

70. See also Andrews Reath, "Setting Ends through Reason," in *Spheres of Reason*, ed. Simon Robertson (Oxford University Press, 2009), 199–220.

humanity,"[71] and he said that a government that abridges it is guilty of "the greatest conceivable despotism."[72] It is unclear whether he also wanted to regard it as an element of human dignity along the lines of his views about humans' moral capabilities. Perhaps it is not so important in the moral theory, which is where Kant's conception of human dignity is located. But it *is* important for Kant's political theory: it is connected with the value of external freedom and independence which is the organizing principle in the *Rechtslehre* (the political part of *The Metaphysics of Morals*), and there it does crucial work in regard to his principle of equal negative freedom.[73] And it may prove difficult after all to drive a wedge decisively between Kant on moral autonomy and Kant on personal autonomy.[74]

One can see why it might be important in our account of the basis of equality. Theories of equality sometimes involve the universalization or outward projection of our own preoccupations. I have an investment in the living of my life according to my plan or conception of the good, and I can infer that others, just like me, will have a similar investment. Much of the time, I may view their actions simply in terms of whether or not they are advantageous to me, but I begin to

71. Kant, *The Metaphysics of Morals*, 393 (6:237). This, Kant said, was the first half of "the principle of freedom" for the constitution of a commonwealth. (The second half added the familiar proviso "provided he does not infringe upon that freedom of others to strive for a like end which can coexist with the freedom of everyone in accordance with a possible universal law.")

72. Kant, *On the Common Saying*, 291 (8:291).

73. Kant, *The Metaphysics of Morals*, 393–394 (6:237–238). In this part of Kant's philosophy, the (negative) freedom that seems to matter is not moral autonomy as such but just people's ability to live their own lives on their own terms. See also Arthur Ripstein, *Force and Freedom: Kant's Legal and Political Philosophy* (Harvard University Press, 2009), 30–56, on the importance of independence for Kant.

74. See also Jeremy Waldron, "Moral Autonomy and Personal Autonomy," in *Autonomy and the Challenges to Liberalism: New Essays*, ed. John Christman and Joel Anderson (Cambridge University Press 2005), 307–329.

treat them as equals when I recognize that they have a point of view on the world and on my actions and on those of other people too that reflects their own preoccupation with the living of their lives. I recognize that, like me, they identify with what they are doing, are seeking to realize purposes of their own to the extent they can, and desire to do all this on their own terms rather than just being the instrument of another's will.[75] The importance of something analogous for me helps me see its importance in their case for them. Williams associates this effort at identification with "our regarding men from the human point of view," recognizing not so much the living of certain particular kinds of life—lives which may or may not be helpful to me or my community—but rather the essentially human purpose of just *living a life on one's own terms.*

9.

So there we have an array of possibilities for the features of human beings on which directly or indirectly their basic equality, their human dignity, their equal worth might supervene. These are the properties of us human beings that are supposed to make sense of our conviction that we should treat one another as equals. They are not the only possibilities; there are others I could mention. Free will is one; I mean our world-making capacity to choose which of several possible worlds will be actuated by our decisions. Hannah Arendt's theme of natality is another.[76] And the aspiration to love and serve

75. This sentence and the next adapt language from Williams, "The Idea of Equality," 234.

76. Hannah Arendt, "What Is Freedom?," in *Between Past and Future: Six Exercises in Political Thought* (Viking Press, 1961), 169. See also the discussion in Jeremy Waldron, "Arendt on the Foundations of Equality," in *Politics in Dark Times: Encounters with Hannah*

God is a third. My main aim in this lecture has been to explore a few such possibilities rather than settle on any one of them.

Let me remind you of what I said at the end of Section 1. The properties I have set out are all, or almost all, capabilities—which, by the way, is one of the reasons the issue of *dis*ability will arise later in these lectures (in Lecture 6). There is obviously some consonance between this emphasis on capabilities as the properties that underlie human equality and the capabilities approach to justice championed in recent writings by Amartya Sen and Martha Nussbaum.[77] Only, I am not invoking capabilities, as Sen and Nussbaum do, as a currency of justice. I am singling out a few capabilities, much fewer than they have to invoke for their purposes, as a basis for our equal worth, a basis for our very entitlement to be regarded equally as the subjects, beneficiaries, and respondents of justice.[78]

Also, many of the capabilities I have cited are complex: there is nothing simple about moral agency, for example, and nothing simple about personal autonomy either. And it is perfectly possible that the capabilities I have described are interrelated. It may not be the case that we have to choose among them. Those themes—complexity and interrelationship—are pursued in Lectures 4 and 5. So there is still lots to talk about.

Arendt, ed. Seyla Benhabib et al. (Cambridge University Press, 2010), 17–38. There is also a discussion in Lecture 2, Section 5.

77. See Amartya Sen, *Inequality Re-examined* (Oxford University Press, 1992), and *The Quality of Life*, ed. Martha Nussbaum and Amartya Sen (Oxford University Press, 1993). See also Martha Nussbaum, *Women and Human Development: The Capabilities Approach* (Cambridge University Press, 2000).

78. There's an excellent account of the relation between these two enterprises in Martha Nussbaum, *Frontiers of Justice: Disability, Nationality, Species Membership* (Harvard University Press, 2006).

10.

But I am sure you are waiting for me to say something about the most important feature of the candidate properties I have set out. You are waiting for me to say something about what is, for egalitarian purposes, their most troubling feature — namely, that these are all capabilities humans appear to possess *in different degrees*.

I mentioned our common capacity to feel affection, but people can feel affection in different ways and to different degrees, and some are hardly capable of love at all. I emphasized reason, but we know that there are great differences here too, unequal degrees of intelligence and insight. As John Coons and Patrick Brennan put it, "Our individual endowments of this crucial good differ radically in degree. Some minds are powerful and thus valued; others are dim and less valued."[79] I mentioned moral qualities, but people are notoriously unequal in their moralizing, in the strength of their moral character, and in their adeptness with values and principles, not to mention the uneven quality of their own moral lives. I mentioned personal autonomy and the lives we all have to lead, but people vary not only in the kinds of life they lead but in the extent to which their actions over time add up to "the leading of a life." Some people stumble from one decision to another, while others lay out the vista of a whole life plan.

These are all differences of degree in various dimensions, and as long as such differences are admitted, we have to ask: how can equality be predicated on such a variable basis? Louis Pojman, who used to teach philosophy at West Point, put it bluntly:

79. Coons and Brennan, *By Nature Equal*, 41.

If reason is really all that makes us valuable, then the more of it the better. . . . If our ability to will the good is what gives us value, then it would seem that some people are more valuable than others. . . . Some people must struggle against great odds to will the good, others find it relatively easy, and still others will not only to do their duty but to do altruistic or supererogatory acts. So we are not of equal worth but of radically differential worth. Shouldn't we be treated in proportion to our ability to will the good?[80]

This is a very common critique, for, in the words of Jack Schaar, "inequalities among men on virtually any trait or characteristic one might mention are obvious and probably ineradicable."[81]

We have to respond to this challenge. Driven by such variability away from capacities that can be tested and measured, should we try to take refuge in the unity and simplicity of something that cannot be measured, like the soul?[82] In a 2008 book called *Created Equal: How the Bible Broke with Ancient Political Thought*, Joshua Berman observed that this problem of differences of degree is bound to crop up whenever we are relying on empirical or natural attributes. So, he said, maybe we should look away from empirical properties and turn our gaze toward some transcendent aspect of our nature to be the basis of human equality.[83] In my view, this will not help. The fact is that many religious properties can be possessed in different degrees

80. Louis Pojman, "A Critique of Contemporary Egalitarianism: A Christian Perspective," *Faith and Philosophy* 8 (1991): 484.

81. John H. Schaar, "Some Ways of Thinking about Equality," *Journal of Politics* 26 (1964): 867.

82. The question is discussed in Coons and Brennan, *By Nature Equal*, 43.

83. Joshua Berman, *Created Equal: How the Bible Broke with Ancient Political Thought* (Oxford University Press, 2008), 168.

as well. If I say we are all created in the image of God, I cannot deny that that image is more blurred in some people than it is in others.[84] I have nothing against religious accounts of equality, as you will see in Lecture 5, but I do not think we should scramble over to them just because we are afraid to face up to this issue of different degrees of what we think of as the empirical capabilities underlying human worth.

So what else can we say about this variability? Perhaps we do not need precise identity. The idea that equality must be based on humans' possession of some characteristic *to an exactly equal degree* stems from an overuse of the Aristotelian proportionality model. Aristotle argued that distributive justice could be construed as equality because justice required an equality of proportion between each person's merit and each person's allocation of some good.[85] From this, one might infer that if people are to be given an equal allocation of anything, then their merit must be exactly equal, otherwise the proportions will be unequal. But even if this makes sense in the case of certain sorts of merit for surface-level principles of distributive justice, there is no reason to think it a sensible basis for approaching our topic of *basic* equality.

Or we might bring in an Aristotelian dictum on the other side: perhaps it is a mistake to demand more precision than the subject matter admits of.[86] Perhaps all we need is broad similarity from one person to another. In this spirit, John Wilson, who was a philosopher of education at Oxford in the 1960s, wrote that "we should not press our criteria of similarity too far."

84. I take up this point again in Lecture 5, in Section 4.

85. See Aristotle, *Nicomachean Ethics*, trans. W. D. Ross (Oxford University Press, 1954), 113 (bk. 5, chap. 3, 1131a): "The just, then, is a species of the proportionate. . . . For proportion is equality of ratios."

86. Ibid., 2–3 (bk. 1, chap. 3, 1094b).

> We can always detect some difference if we try hard enough. . . .
> Two lines can be of equal lengths: yet if we insist on measuring
> them in micromillimetres we could prove one to be a little
> longer. . . . But this leads to the paradoxical view that nothing is
> ever really the same as anything else. . . . The egalitarian might
> say that all he wishes to assert is that there are certain similari-
> ties amongst men, not that there are certain qualities which they
> all possess to the same degree.[87]

Will this do? Unfortunately, we are not just talking about marginal
differences. The differences that worry us are not insignificant or
trivial. There seems all the difference in the world between someone
who has disciplined herself to the clear and fruitful use of reason
and someone who thinks lazily and impulsively without any critical
reflection. There seems all the difference in the world between
someone who struggles as hard as she can to act fairly in her dealings with others and someone who, like many people we know, es-
chews any interest in justice at all. If we believe in the importance
of rationality or in Rawls's shared sense of justice as a basis of
equality, why wouldn't we think that these differences were important? Indeed their importance is undeniable; these are not just trivi-
alities or micromillimeters. So why wouldn't we think that their
undeniable importance was relevant to the determination of human
worth?

    Can we not put all such differences aside and look elsewhere for
some unitary properties, properties that apply (to all humans) in an
all-or-nothing way? I don't know. It is possible to conceive of some
mental attributes like consciousness or the possession of a subjective
point of view as all-or-nothing traits which a being either has or does

87. John Wilson, *Equality* (Harcourt Brace, 1967), 81–82.

not have and which it is fair to say all humans certainly do have and perhaps some non-humans have as well.[88] But as Coons and Brennan point out, equalities that are based upon the mere possession (or lack) of such a unitary property "are generally of little importance, and most, indeed, are trivial."[89] Also, the usual suspects are dangerously close to the properties that do admit of variation, and sometimes there is an air of pedantry or special pleading in the attempt to distinguish the two. Consider this, for example, from John Wilson: "Some people are much more sensitive to pain than others. But the egalitarian may mean merely that men are all, equally,— the commas are important— liable to pain: i.e., one man is liable to pain *just as* another is, not *just as much as* another is."[90]

Wilson's way of putting it alerts us to how delicate this attempt to concentrate on nonscalar characteristics is going to be. I actually think something like this is right, but we have to make sense of the delicacy.

11.

In the passage on "the basis of equality" toward the end of A *Theory of Justice* that I referred to earlier, Rawls proposed a strategy for dealing with these differences of degree. We have seen that Rawls organized basic equality around features of moral personality. But he too faced the problem we are considering. "It may be objected," he wrote, "that equality cannot rest on natural attributes because there is no natural

88. George Sher, "Why We Are Moral Equals," in Steinhoff, *Do All Persons Have Equal Moral Worth?*, 26.

89. See Coons and Brennan, *By Nature Equal*, 11. For an excellent discussion of the difficulties and dilemmas involved in identifying a relevant all-or-nothing property, see Arneson, "Equality," 40–49.

90. Wilson, *Equality*, 83; emphasis and interpolation in original.

feature with respect to which all humans are equal, that is which everyone has . . . to the same degree."[91]

Here is his response: "It is not the case that founding equality on natural capacities is incompatible with an egalitarian view. All we have to do is select a *range property*, as I shall say and to give equal justice to those meeting its conditions."[92] What does he mean by "a range property"? Rawls offers an elaboration which is not helpful (at least not to me): "The property of being in the interior of the unit circle is the range property of points in the plane. All points inside this circle have this property although their coordinates vary within a certain range and they equally have this property, since no point interior to a circle is more or less interior to it than any other interior point."[93] I think there is some fancy mathematics involved in this phrase "the property of being in the interior of a unit circle." But I am not sure. When I tried to figure this out, I did a search on JSTOR. I got twenty references to Rawls's use of this idea, none of which attempted to explain the technicality of being in the interior of a unit circle. I got about seventy references to articles with titles like "Derivations on Algebras of Unbounded Operators" and "Superlogarithmatic Estimates on Pseudoconvex Domains." As far as I could tell, they all assumed that their readers understood the technical idea of a range property and a unit circle and other conceptions like a spanning set. Plus, when I looked up "range property" on *Google* I got a whole lot of stuff about mountain real estate ("Home, home on the range . . .").

But I believe we can simplify. Rawls's idea involves a relationship between two associated properties. There is property R, which operates in a binary way (either you have R or you don't), and property S, which is a scalar property admitting of differences of degree. We say

91. Rawls, A *Theory of Justice*, 444.
92. Ibid.; my emphasis.
93. Ibid.

that R is a range property with respect to S, if R applies to individual items in virtue of their being within a certain range on the scale indicated by S. In the simplest cases, R is like a threshold. If you are over a specified threshold on scale S, you qualify for property R. But the range may have an upper limit as well, or it may be configured in a more complicated way in a two- or n-dimensional model.

Think about the property of *being in Scotland*. Consider the characteristic which a town might have of being in Scotland, as opposed to being in England—I mean as a matter of jurisdiction. Now legal jurisdiction is organized geographically, and geography admits of coordinates and differences. Geographically, I think the city of Stirling is more or less in the center of Scotland, whereas the little village of Gretna Green is just over the line from England. But jurisdictionally Stirling and Gretna Green are both *equally in Scotland*, even though there is this geographical difference between them. Being in Scotland is a range property.

For an American example, think about the state of Ohio. The city of Columbus is more or less right in the center of the state. The city of Cincinnati is on its southern border, just across the Ohio River from Kentucky. But from a jurisdictional point of view, Columbus and Cincinnati are *equally in Ohio*. Though state jurisdiction in the United States is a matter of geography, the scalar geographical difference between these two cities does not matter.

This is the model I think Rawls is suggesting, and the question is whether we can use it to supersede the concern about scalar differences so far as the capabilities underlying basic equality are concerned. If the geographical difference between Stirling and Gretna (or between Columbus and Cincinnati) is superseded by a jurisdictional equality, can we also say that a difference in intelligence or a difference in the quality of people's moral decision making can be superseded by a focus on the range of an underlying rational or moral capability? Rawls seems to think it an obvious model to use,[94] but it has not been discussed as much as one would have thought since 1971.[95] And there is a lot to be discussed. Merely introducing and defining the idea of a range property is not enough. We should not let our familiarity with this technical device (such as it is) blind us to the challenge, indeed the difficulty of applying it in our field of interest.

12.

The idea of a range property definitely works for some of our egalitarians. For instance, Hobbes's conception involves a range property. The scalar property here is "strength of body," and the range property is, for each person P, the property someone else has of being a non-dismissible mortal threat to P.[96] When I look at all the animals around me, I might rank them on a scale of bodily strength. But what should

94. Ibid., 445: "How can it then seem plausible that founding equality on natural attributes undermines equal justice? The notion of a range property is too obvious to be overlooked."

95. There is some discussion of Rawls's own use of the idea of a range property in the following books and articles: D. A. Lloyd Thomas, "Equality within the Limits of Reason Alone," *Mind* 88 (1979): 549; Daniel Wikler, "Paternalism and the Mildly Retarded," *Philosophy and Public Affairs* 8 (1979): 384; Michael Gorr, "Rawls on Natural Inequality," *Philosophical Quarterly* 33 (1983): 11–16; Bailey H. Kuklin, "The Asymmetrical Conditions of Legal Responsibility in the Marketplace," *University of Miami Law Review* 44 (1990): 258n; and Coons and Brennan, *By Nature Equal*, 32–33. More recently, there has been some good discussion in the essays published in Steinhoff, *Do All Persons Have Equal Moral Worth?*, by Sher, Arneson, and Steinhoff himself. There is discussion also in Nicholas Mark Smith, *Basic Equality and Discrimination: Reconciling Theory and Law* (Ashgate, 2011), 30–35.

96. Cf. Coons and Brennan, *By Nature Equal*, 102: "Hobbes has invented the first 'range property' whereby men are simultaneously different and the same depending upon how one wants it."

particularly interest me about that scale (according to Hobbes) is the threshold at which some individual becomes *a non-dismissible threat to my life*. In Hobbes's view all humans are above that threshold,[97] and particular theories of human inequality—such as the suggestion that women are not men's equals—may be refuted by showing that all of the putative unequals are above that threshold too. "When all is reckoned together the difference between man and man is not so considerable. . . . For . . . the weakest has strength enough to kill the strongest."[98] We see here not only a range property underpinning Hobbes's conception of equality but also a motivation for focusing on the range property. That is crucial. One has to explain *why* we are to rivet our attention on the range property rather than the scalar differences. As Ian Carter puts it, "one needs to provide some independent moral reason for focusing on the range property."[99] The focus on mortal threat rather than extent of bodily strength must be *motivated*, and men's fear of sudden death—the *summum malum*, according to *Leviathan*[100]—will do that for Hobbes.

Sometimes the relevant range of a capability is defined by specifying a particular task that has to be performed in a distinctively human life, whatever other tasks a person can or cannot do. In Locke's theory, for example, it is not reason in general that is the basis of our equality, but a very specific rational capacity, namely the ability to know God through engaging in abstract thought. A philosopher may be very sophisticated in the way he does this, but a plain man may do

97. This is even more true in these days of firearms. George Catlin, "Equality and What We Mean by It," in *Nomos IX: Equality*, ed. J. Roland Pennock and John Chapman (New York University Press, 1967), 101, observes, "It was not for nothing that, in pioneer Texas, the Colt revolver was called 'the equalizer.'"

98. Hobbes, *Leviathan*, 86–87 (chap. 13).

99. Ian Carter, "Respect and the Basis of Equality," *Ethics* 121 (2011): 550.

100. Hobbes, *Leviathan*, 70 (chap. 11).

it just as well. Even if humans vary enormously in their intellectual abilities, still for each of them, "it yet secures their great Concernments, that they have Light enough to lead them to the Knowledge of their Maker, and the sight of their own Duties. . . . The Candle that is set up in us, shines bright enough for all our Purposes."[101] Whether or not one can come to know that one has a maker defines a threshold and one that is, in Locke's eyes, incomparably more important than any difference of intellectual ability above that line. As I have argued elsewhere, it is partly on this basis that Locke is committed to a "democratic" conception of the human intellect.[102]

We can see also how the idea of a range property might work for personal autonomy. People organize their lives in different ways and to a different extent, and that may matter for some purposes; but it does not matter for the amount of respect we should show them or for our understanding of what they have at stake in decisions that impact upon them. The members of a Rawlsian elite in Belgravia might each of them set out a formal plan of life and follow it through, year after year, in their investment and educational decisions. And this might seem an order of magnitude different from the mockery that a poor man makes of personal autonomy, distracted as he is by the requirements of subsistence. Still, as Colonel Thomas Rainsborough famously observed in the army debates about manhood suffrage at Putney in 1647, "The poorest he that is in England hath a life to live as the greatest he."[103] Every human, however constrained and inarticulate, has the ability to project a view of herself "into the future as

101. Locke, *An Essay Concerning Human Understanding*, introduction, 45. See also Section 5 above.

102. Waldron, *God, Locke and Equality*, 83–107.

103. "Extract from the Debates at the General Council of the Army, Putney, 29 October 1647," in Sharp, *The English Levellers*, 103.

the continuing subject of a certain kind of life," structured not implausibly by memories, plans, fears, expectations, and hopes.[104]

Let us turn now to moral capacities. In Rawls's model, which, as we saw, combines personal autonomy with a sense of justice, the justification for using a range property is developed by saying, first, that the relevant capacity for moral personality is "not at all stringent." It is, says Rawls, just an "essential minimum."[105] Differences above the minimum may be important for some purposes, Rawls says, but not for the basics of justice and respect: "Certainly some persons have a greater capacity for a sense of justice than others. These persons may properly be placed in positions where the judicial virtues are especially fitting . . . but assuming that a certain minimum is satisfied, these peculiar gifts are not a proper ground for establishing different grades of citizenship. The minimum is sufficient to share in the position of equal citizenship in a constitutional democracy."[106]

I am leaving aside (as Rawls does) — but only for the moment — questions about the massive differences among us that arise in the context of profound disability. The range-property idea is not supposed to meet that challenge. In Rawls's view, "when someone lacks the requisite potentiality either from birth or accident, this is regarded as a defect or deprivation. There is no race or recognized group of human beings that lacks this attribute. Only scattered individuals are without this capacity, or its realization to the minimum degree, and the failure to realize it is the consequence of unjust and impoverished social circumstances, or fortuitous contingencies."[107]

---

104. For this phrasing, I am indebted to Sher, "Why We Are Moral Equals," 23.

105. Rawls, *A Theory of Justice*, 505.

106. Rawls, "The Sense of Justice," 301–302. The suggestion about judges will be taken up in Lecture 4.

107. Rawls, *A Theory of Justice*, 506.

That is all he says (apart from some remarks about children), and we shall have to do better than that in Lecture 6, where I address this issue. For now, we must understand that Rawls's conception is being used to model the "normal" range of human moral abilities.

There is one other point, though, in which his account is incomplete. Rawls says that "nothing beyond the essential minimum is required."[108] But he does not elaborate the term "essential," and so he does not explain this minimalism. That is, he does not provide an argument as to why we should expect the relevant range to extend well into the lower end of normal human moral capabilities. The idea of a range property by itself does not explain this. The closest he comes to an explanation is a suggestion about what is involved in defending one's interests and respecting those of others in the original position.

Kant talks extensively about the "rangishness" of the property that he is counting on (though he does not use that terminology). The relevant trait for Kant is the human capacity to construct, apprehend, and respond to moral reasons even in the face of contrary inclinations. We do not always do this, but we always have the capacity to do it. "To satisfy the categorical command of morality is within everyone's power at all times," says Kant.[109] There is a contrast here with theoretical reason: "In moral matters human reason can easily be brought to a high degree of correctness and accomplishment, even in the most common understanding," whereas theoretical reason is much more demanding.[110] The moral range covers not just Kant's own elite personal moral capacity but also the unsophisticated scruples of the ordinary man[111] and the uneasy conscience of "the

---

108. Ibid., 442.
109. Kant, *Critique of Practical Reason*, 169 (5:36).
110. Kant, *Groundwork*, preface, 47 (4:391).
111. Kant, *Critique of Practical Reason*, 210 (5:88).

boldest evildoer."[112] Even a "child of around eight or nine years old" will undoubtedly answer in the negative if asked whether it is all right to appropriate for one's own use money with which one has been entrusted.[113] The capacity ranges over the good and the bad, the self-aware and the self-deluded, the scrupulous and the unscrupulous, the morally learned and the morally illiterate. Human persons reveal themselves to have these moral capacities even though they cannot necessarily put them into words or articulate them in the language that a Kantian philosopher would articulate them in.

It is not that moral differences between us are unimportant. As Kant puts it, "Before a humble common man in whom I perceive uprightness of character in a higher degree than I am aware of in myself *my spirit bows* whether I want it to or whether I do not."[114] But far from being incompatible with our fundamental equality, the importance to me of my awareness of this difference is precisely that it confirms that the righteous man and I—for all my perversity and foolishness—are basically one another's equals. For as Kant goes on immediately to say, "His example holds before me a law that strikes down my self-conceit when I compare it with my conduct, and I see observance of that law and hence its *practicability* proved before me in fact."[115] I shall talk more about this back-and-forth between capability and exercise in Lecture 4. My point right now is about Kant's motivation for riveting attention on the range property rather than on exercise and achievement. The sheer fact of the existence of the moral capacity, its counter-causal possibilities, present in the will of every man, makes a massive difference to the sorts of beings we are,

112. Ibid., 204 (5:80): "practical reason, whose voice makes even the boldest evildoer tremble and forces him to hide from its sight."

113. Kant, *On the Common Saying*, 288 (8:286).

114. Kant, *Critique of Practical Reason*, 202 (5:76–77); emphasis in original.

115. Ibid., 202 (5:77); emphasis in original.

to our worth and dignity. It is a momentous thing, whose metaphysical significance commands the greatest respect and dwarfs the variations in its all-too-human exercise.

These are just a few examples. But I believe they show that Rawls's idea of a range property is a promising strategy for addressing the challenge posed to the basis of equal worth and equal dignity by the inevitable variations in people's traits and capacities.

13.

There is plenty more to say about range properties, but I am postponing it until Lecture 4. However, there is one issue that needs to be dealt with before we finish this lecture. I have set out an array of possible properties and capabilities that people have, as candidates for the role of "host property" for basic equality.[116] Which one should we choose? Richard Arneson asks, "How do we decide which of these abilities you are going to focus on?"[117] I have talked of reason (practical and theoretical); I have talked of feeling pain; I have talked of love; I have talked of the organization of a life; I have talked of the ability to set ends for oneself, to respond to principles, to differentiate right and wrong and to act on such differentiations. Which of these capacities are we to privilege?

My aim in this lecture has mainly been exploration, but the question is worth considering anyway. Here is the answer: I don't think we are necessarily required to choose. For one thing, almost all the suggested properties are complex in themselves. Most of them are capabilities, and capabilities represent multiple skills, characteristics, and dispositions. And anyway, there is no reason to say that basic

116. Again, the phrase "host property" is from Coons and Brennan, *By Nature Equal*, 39.
117. Arneson, "Equality," 33.

equality must supervene on just one range property. Perhaps we should be looking for a complex account of human equality—a set of range properties, overlapping and complementing each other. Rawls's account in *A Theory of Justice* and, in a much briefer way, Williams's account in "The Idea of Equality" remind us that we may want to focus on several capabilities. People have moral lives of their own to lead, and they have personal lives of their own to lead, and they have rationality to deploy in the leading of their lives. These properties, these capabilities, come together in complexes and narratives; they complement and support one another. And together they help define what is important about a human being. I hope we can bear this in mind in the lectures that follow.

4

Power and Scintillation

The principle of basic equality has a lot of work to do, and whatever we say about the range properties that underlie it, they have to be capable of making sense of that work. In this lecture, I focus once again on the idea of a range property and a little more sharply on what we may think of as the division of labor between range properties as such and the particular scalar differences they are supposed to supersede.

We know that a given range property, R, will be defined in relation to a scalar property, S. For example, human rationality as a basis for equality may be defined in relation to a scale of measurable or ranked intelligence. Or moral agency as a basis for equality may be defined in relation to measurable or ranked competence in moral discernment, deliberation, and action. In each case a certain range within S is specified as a basis for the attribution of R: a range of rationality for the attribution of equal reason or a range of moral competence for the attribution of moral agency. I shall argue that it is a mistake to think of the range property as wholly eclipsing the discernible variations in the scalar property. R has its work to do—quite hard work, as I shall show. But so does S. Understanding a range property is partly a matter of understanding the back-and-forth between recognition of the sheer presence of R and the making of particular judgments within the part of S that is covered by R's range. There is a kind of *scintillation* back and forth between R and S.

Except for the word "scintillation," this is all pretty abstract and algebraic. But if we focus on the moral example—something like Kant's or Rawls's theory of human equality—we can see clearly enough what is going on. Particular moral judgments, responding to the rightness and wrongness of people's actions or their virtues and vices, are very important, and no theory of human equality should be in the business of denigrating or diminishing them. At the same time, it is important to recognize persons—bad persons as well as good—as the bearers of moral agency and to keep faith with the importance of *that* fact, an importance which in many contexts will *not* be sensitive to variations in moral performance. Fundamental rights, basic moral considerability, elementary respect, human worth, human dignity—on Kant's theory and on Rawls's—these constants are underpinned by what people have in common as moral agents.

In this lecture, then, I shall review the specific function of basic equality in our morality, the hard work that has to be done by the underlying range properties to make sense of that function. And I shall argue that while it is important to understand the hard work that the relevant range properties do, it is at the same time important not to overestimate that work or ignore other tasks that morality has to perform besides those mandated by basic equality.

In what follows, please bear in mind what we established in Lecture 3, that the range properties we are looking at are probably capabilities (for thought, choice, feeling, and action of various sorts), not just traits. Bear in mind also that we are likely to be dealing with complex range properties, probably a cluster of related capacities, complementing one another, interacting with one another, and developing over time. For convenience I sometimes use just the bland term "range property" as though it referred to a single trait. Sometimes I will use just the placeholder "R." It is your job to read the more complicated account into my algebraic formulations whenever that is appropriate.

1.

I want to begin with the very idea of a range property and the problem of how we delineate it. How do we determine its dimensions?

We use a range property, R, when we are interested more in *whether* particular cases are located within a given range along a scalar dimension, S, than in *where exactly* they are located within that range. In some conventional cases we do this by stipulation. In the jurisdictional example I used in Lecture 3, we do it simply by drawing a line on a map or responding to some line that has traditionally been there—between England and Scotland, for example, or between Ohio and Kentucky. In the case of human equality, however, the range property is supposed to make sense of our application of concepts like human worth, equal concern and respect, and human dignity. It can hardly do that if it is itself just an arbitrary stipulation.

In some sense, the range property is supposed to be a marker of how things are—carving nature, so to speak, at its joints, by insisting that a line *here* is appropriate and a line *there* is not.[1] We want to insist on certain continuities and reject certain alleged discontinuities— Rashdall-discontinuities, we called them. And some of us want also to identify and endorse certain discontinuities, such as the discontinuity between human and non-human animals. So, how do we do all that? How do we specify the boundaries of a range property that will make sense of all this line drawing? What is involved in that specification? If it is a threshold property, how do we define the threshold

---

1. See the discussion in Lecture 2, Section 9. See also Joseph Campbell et al., eds., *Carving Nature at Its Joints: Natural Kinds in Metaphysics and Science* (MIT Press, 2011).

or calculate where it should be set? What are we supposed to be responding to in making these calculations?

Richard Arneson, who teaches philosophy at the University of California, San Diego, has asked this about Rawls's conception.[2] Focusing on Rawls's idea of moral personality as the relevant range property,[3] Arneson asks how the threshold for the identification of that property is to be set. Is it possible to do this nonarbitrarily? Do we have to have a sort of bright cut-off line and say that everything below misses out and everything above gets into the human range? And what on earth is involved in drawing that bright line? Arneson writes:

> For simplicity, consider just the sense of justice. This is a steady disposition to conform one's conduct to what one takes to be basic norms of fairness along with some ability reasonably to identify these fairness norms. But the disposition to be fair obviously admits of degrees; one can be more or less committed to behaving as one thinks fair. And the ability to deliberate about candidate norms of fairness and select the best of them also varies by degree. Offhand the task of specifying some threshold level of these abilities such that further variations in the abilities above the thresholds should have no bearing on moral status looks hopeless.[4]

One thing here is the familiar issue of the vagueness of whatever boundary we define: perhaps there are gray areas, borderline cases. Now, however we respond to this, we need to bear in mind Rawls's own insistence that we "not confuse the vagueness of a conception of

---

2. Richard Arneson, "What (If Anything) Renders All Human Persons Morally Equal?," in *Singer and His Critics*, ed. Dale Jamieson (Blackwell, 1999), 108–109.

3. John Rawls, *A Theory of Justice*, rev. ed. (Harvard University Press, 1999), 442–443.

4. Arneson, "What (If Anything) Renders All Human Persons Morally Equal?," 108–109.

justice with the thesis that basic rights should vary with natural capacity."[5] And it may be that vagueness as such is not really a problem. Arneson observes generously that the problem about vagueness

> arises from conceiving of the threshold line as very thin, so a tiny difference in possession of a capacity makes a disproportionately huge difference to one's moral status. But one need not conceive the threshold line as very thin. The line separating persons and non-persons might be very thick, such that below the lower boundary of the line it is clear that beings in this range are not persons and above the upper boundary of the line it is clear that beings in this range do qualify as persons. Beings with rational [or moral] capacities that fall in the gray area between the upper boundary and lower boundaries are of indeterminate status.[6]

But still a problem remains. "Even if the line separating persons and non-persons is taken to be thick, it seems arbitrary where exactly the line is placed."[7] Some of those whose theories we considered in Lecture 3 might have an answer to this. John Locke, for example, seemed to have in mind a particular mental operation (abstraction) which, if a being could perform it, would show that that being was a person of distinctive status in the eyes of God. It is arguable too that Kant's theory is of this kind. Arneson acknowledges that Kant appears to solve the difficulty just by specifying a capacity that can be understood in itself, and then looking to see what range of cases it covered,

---

5. Rawls, A Theory of Justice, 445. There are also good discussions of the vagueness problem in Christopher Knapp, "Equality and Proportionality," Canadian Journal of Philosophy 37 (2007): 179–201, and Ian Carter, "Respect and the Basis of Equality," Ethics 121 (2011): 538–571.

6. Arneson, "What (If Anything) Renders All Human Persons Morally Equal?," 108.

7. Ibid.

rather than deciding where on a scale to set a threshold and then addressing the task of defending that threshold.

Tom Christiano thinks the threshold in question "must present some kind of very strong discontinuity" with "a huge difference between the capacities before the threshold is reached and the capacities at the threshold."[8] I wonder if he is right. It may be a mistake to rivet our attention on the threshold in this way. For one thing, a thesis of what I have called continuous human equality may not require this.[9] We may satisfy ourselves that all humans should be treated as one another's equals long before we come to the threshold question of which other beings, of other types or species, should or should not be treated as the equals of human beings.

For the purposes of a principle of equality in ordinary social and political life, I think we will be more concerned with the inside of the range than with its borderlines. It is perhaps a mistake to think that the range must be defined from the outside in, beginning at its boundaries. For example, in the case of moral capacities (Kant's theory, say), what happens is that we notice ourselves and others making and acting on moral judgments from time to time—people of all sorts, moral judgments of all sorts, at all sorts of different levels of quality and competence. They make and act on these moral judgments, and in each case we say to ourselves, "My God, that is interesting!" We do not go around with a moral Geiger counter waiting until the clicking gets to a certain level before we are interested. We just notice that humans do this all the time. Now, sometimes these moral agents seem more morally literate, sometimes less so; but plainly they all

8. Thomas Christiano, "Rationality, Equal Status, and Egalitarianism," in *Do All Persons Have Equal Moral Worth? On "Basic Equality" and Equal Respect and Concern*, ed. Uwe Steinhoff (Oxford University Press, 2015), 57.

9. For the distinction between distinctive and continuous human equality, see Lecture 1, Section 7.

seem to have the capacity to do this thing (even if it is muted by self-ishness or malice in some cases). We notice that humans have the capacity to act on principle, to set ends for themselves, and to respond to value. And what we say is, "This fact about them seems to be very important, more important perhaps than any differences between the ways they exercise these capacities." We are struck by the similarity even in the midst of their differences. And it's our being (justifiably) struck by the similarity, together with our refusal to be distracted by the differences, which constitutes the use of a range property.

Still, a philosopher who wants to defend distinctive equality does have to be preoccupied with the lower boundary. Rawls is in this category: his criterion of *possessing a sense of justice* is supposed to explain why humans are entitled to justice while non-human animals are not.[10] I think Rawls imagines that the relevant threshold can be set at about the lower end of human moral functioning, taking account of our characteristic weaknesses, vices, and irrationalities.[11] Just above the threshold is a human moral reasoner with some sort of sense of justice, but a poor reasoner and one whose sense of justice might have been subordinated selfishly to other desires; below the threshold is (say) a monkey. It seems to me obvious that the threshold marks a massive difference here: a monkey may have some rudimentary sense of fairness—perhaps[12]—but it is orders of magnitude inferior to that of even the morally incompetent human. Even if the human

10. Rawls, *A Theory of Justice*, 441, 448.

11. In Lecture 6, however, I follow Rawls in arguing that the radical absence of moral and cognitive functioning in certain human beings through disability is to be dealt with separately. See Rawls, *A Theory of Justice*, 506.

12. See Sarah Brosnan, "Capuchins Reject Unequal Pay," *YouTube*, December 19, 2012, https://www.youtube.com/watch?v=_Go8tnl21MU. (I am grateful to one of Harvard University Press's readers for this observation.)

doesn't use it, the human has access to a moral capacity which is quite unlike the monkey's. That fact matters more for purposes of elementary human worth than where, exactly, the human is located or has chosen to locate himself on the scale of exercises of this capacity.

2.

In all of this, we must bear in mind the work our range property is supposed to be doing. I have talked about a range property *grounding*, *supporting*, and *underpinning* the principle of basic equality and other principles associated with basic equality. Is it possible to say anything more than this? Is it a relation of entailment or moral argument or what?

In Lecture 2, I said there is not supposed to be any factual implication that will compel a belief in human equality. We are not looking to bridge the "is"/"ought" gap or to throw a logical grappling hook across the chasm between fact and value. But saying we are not compelled by the facts to take any particular position on human equality does not mean that the position we decide to take has no relation to facts about human beings. It may have a relation to facts about ourselves even though it is not a logically compelling relation. Our decision to take up the moral principle of equality may need to supervene upon such facts, just in order to make sense as a decision.

This formulation—of the underlying property "making sense" of the equality principle—is ambiguous. In ordinary usage, to say of something "That makes sense," is to say that it seems right or at least that there is no obvious objection to it. It is a mode of endorsement. But I want the relation between basic equality and the underlying range property to be one that can be apprehended even by opponents of basic equality. An opponent can see a principle as intelligible—see that it makes sense—even while she denies it. So we may want to say that the crucial thing about the relation between the principle of basic equality and the underlying range property is that the latter helps make the former intelligible. (Some opponents might deny that the relevant range property exists or that it applies to the beings to whom the proponents of the principle think it applies, but the opponent may still see that it would *make sense* of the principle if it did obtain or if it did apply.)

This is a vague idea, and philosophers may be frustrated at our inability to make it very much more precise.[13] In using this formulation, I am invoking our intuitive sense of the ways in which moral positions can have a familiar appeal to people. We can see why a moral position, M, might be attractive to people like us; we can see how people might be drawn to a given M; we can understand what people are getting at, what they are moved by, in committing themselves in this way. We use this informal sense when we point to various factual properties in the way we articulate our moral commitments. The idea that a factual property, F, makes sense of a moral position, M, draws partly on the idea of F being a reason for M. And partly it involves the intelligibility of the nexus between fact and moral commitment being expressed as a conditional principle. That F makes sense of M could be captured by saying that "If F, then M" is itself an intelligible candidate for the role of moral principle.

---

13. Some work on this idea of something's *making sense* has been done by Bernard Williams. He deployed the term "MS," I think, to finesse ordinary language issues about "makes sense." See Bernard Williams, "Realism and Moralism in Political Theory," in his (posthumous) collection *In the Beginning Was the Deed: Realism and Moralism in Political Argument*, ed. Geoffrey Hawthorn (Princeton University Press, 2007), 10–11.

Does this mean that the citation of F is supposed to perform a persuasive role in relation to M? Yes and no. No, because the nexus between F and M can make sense even to someone who rejects M. But yes, because its making sense means that even someone who rejects M understands that F explains the attraction of M to those who do embrace it.

In the rigors of moral philosophy, we test arguments for moral positions by asking whether there is a logical connection between F and M or whether F and M are united under the auspices of an overarching moral principle that unites F and M and that might be expected to have some independent appeal. I am not imagining that the alleged connection between F and M—or in our case, between a given range property and the commitment to basic human equality—will survive either of these tests. At best we will have what appears to be the question-begging presentation of a principle "If F, then M" (or, for our case, "If a number of beings each possesses a range property, R, then they are one another's equals"). But there is more to the way moral positions appeal to us than their following from something else to which we are already committed, and not all principles can be presented as the upshot of even higher principles. Justification in morality starts somewhere. And in accounting for the appeal of foundational principles, we are not in a position to invoke anything more rigorous than the idea of such a principle making sense and whatever follows from the fact that many of those to whom it does make sense do actually adopt it.

3.

Apart from all these evasions, there are other things we can say to constrain our choice of range property. It is not enough to just *come up with* some range property that can encompass all human beings for the purposes of basic equality. It must answer to certain specifications.[14]

The most important of these is that there must be something that motivates the use of the range property as such, that is, something to explain why we should be interested in it rather than in the scalar differences of degree. The account we give has to explain our steadfast focus on the range property itself rather than on the associated differences of degree, for purposes of human equality, worth, and dignity. Toward the end of this lecture (Sections 8–12), I am going to argue that the use of a range property is not intended to obliterate the differences that exist among people on the scale that is covered by the range property. The range property is intended to do important work of its own, and that is the work of human equality. But our understanding of the differential merits and the differential abilities that people have—that has work of its own to do as well. We are dealing here with some degree of complementarity rather than competition. So a first constraint on the choice of range property is that it must leave open the possibility that scalar assessments within the range have important moral work to do. It must leave that open, while still being able to explain why, for purposes of equality, the range property is worth focusing on as such.

I said in Lecture 3 that, for some of our candidate capabilities, the motivation for focusing on them as range properties is pretty clear. Thomas Hobbes thought we should be motivated overridingly by fear of violent death, and so we should be more interested in the sheer fact that X can kill Y and vice versa than in any scalar differences be-

14. There is a good discussion in John Coons and Patrick Brennan, *By Nature Equal: The Anatomy of a Western Insight* (Princeton University Press, 1999), 46, who set out what they call "the basic requirements of the host property." Their requirements include moral importance and uniformity, as well as a number of ethical criteria.

tween X's and Y's respective strength or weaponry. That is the basis of equality, said Hobbes; the driving force behind it is the sense of vulnerability, the brittleness of human life, and the power of potential adversaries.[15] But that equality, which unites them all in fear of death at one another's hands, need not be their only interest in physical strength. They may also have an interest in sports which leads them to distinguish various kinds of physical prowess. For the sake of fairness and competitiveness, they may set up women's leagues and distinguish them from men's leagues, even though at the same time they accept—and for certain purposes are transfixed by—Hobbes's point that ultimately every man must fear death at the hands of any woman.

Among more serious candidates for an egalitarian range property, one can see other rationales at work, directing our attention away from scalar variations toward a given capability understood as a range property. Sometimes our focus on the range property is explained by our sense of the specialness that that property, held to whatever degree, confers upon the individual beings who have it. Kant spoke of our awareness of the infinite value of moral personality as competing with the sight of the starry heavens above in the way it brings us to our knees in awe: "Two things fill the mind with ever new and increasing admiration and awe . . . : the starry heavens above and the moral law within."[16] He says we tremble when we detect, whether in ourselves or in somebody else, the presence of what he thinks of as a *counter-causal capacity* to act morally. Of course how we use it matters; how we exercise our moral judgment matters. But our having

15. Thomas Hobbes, *Leviathan*, ed. Richard Tuck (Cambridge University Press, 1996), 139 (chap. 20).

16. Immanuel Kant, *Critique of Practical Reason*, in *Practical Philosophy*, ed. Mary Gregor (Cambridge University Press, 1996), 269–270 (5:161–162). (Note: numbers in parentheses refer to the Prussian Academy edition of Kant's works.)

this power—that momentous fact, in and of itself—makes us creatures of infinite worth and dignity. Kant makes much of the awe that accrues from one's noticing this in oneself, but equally one is awed when one notices it in others.[17]

Sometimes the choice to focus on a certain range property may be explained in relational terms. Interaction of an important or valuable kind between beings may require that they both have properties of a certain sort within a given range. Cicero and the Stoics imagined that we cannot commune with the gods unless in some degree we, like they, are rational beings. There is no question of our rationality being on a par with the gods', but that it is in the same range as the gods' rationality means that we can converse or interact with them, and within that same range converse and interact with one another. Or leave the gods out of it: that a being has a capacity for love means that it can engage in very deep interaction with any other being that has the capacity for love, even though the two capacities may be different in some of their characteristics.

Even Kant's moral capacities—though awesome in each individual—have an important relational dimension. Kant uses a political image *Groundwork of the Mtaphysics of Morals* to characterize our moral capacities; possession of these capacities means that all of us can belong as legislators to a kingdom of ends: an imagined political community in which people reason together to set down the terms, requirements, and constraints that are necessary for a common life together.[18] (The importance of this relational aspect of Kant's kingdom of ends imagery is often neglected because it is imagined

17. As Kant puts it, "Before a humble common man in whom I perceive uprightness of character in a higher degree than I am aware of in myself *my spirit bows* whether I want it to or whether I do not." Ibid., 202 (5:76–77); emphasis in original.

18. Immanuel Kant, *Groundwork of the Metaphysics of Morals*, in Gregor, *Practical Philosophy*, 82–99 (4:432–440).

that he is invoking the image of a lone legislator in the service of a rather solipsistic account of the moral will.)

4.

In all of this, it is not enough just to come up with something that looks like a plausible candidate for a range property (if only one screws up one's eyes and holds one's mouth in a certain way, so as to see a degree of similarity among apparently disparate cases). I said the range property has to be able to do the heavy lifting that human equality requires. It has to make sense of the work that basic equality has to do. Right now I want to say two things about this. One is that this work is a kind of work *across the board*—it is quite comprehensive. Also the relevant range property has to be able to do heavy lifting in the sense that it has to be able to resist a whole bunch of temptations, typical of human life, and it has to be able to trump a number of otherwise plausible moral principles.

Let me begin with the point about comprehensiveness.[19] Whatever range property or combination of range properties we cite, it has got to be credible in light of the array of work that basic equality has to do. If the relation between the range property and the equality principle is that the former makes sense of the latter, then there is a lot to make sense of. In Lecture 2, I said that the normative work of basic equality is at least fourfold: it requires that we are to be counted equally in any calculation of the general good, any utilitarian calculation (if that is what we want to do), or any consequentialist or cost-benefit analysis (where costs to some people must be weighed against

19. This is a different sense of "comprehensive" than the one Rawls uses when he suggests that comprehensive conceptions are out of place in public reason: see John Rawls, *Political Liberalism* (Columbia University Press, 1993), 13. I discuss this latter view at the end of Lecture 5.

the benefits to others). I said that basic equality underpins the entitlement of each of us to justice, to the concern and consideration that
justice requires so far as the fairness of social arrangements is concerned. I said it has to ground the equal basic rights we have (though
there is a further debate to be had about what these equal human
rights are). And it has to ground some sense of our equal authority,
equal respect, leading into democracy as well as the autonomy we are
entitled to in the living of our lives. That is an awful lot of work to be
done. It covers many of the main topics in political philosophy. And
we have to make sure that basic equality is grounded in a way that
enables it to do that much work and work on that considerable scale.

This gives rise, I think, to a problem in discussions of equality. You
will have gathered by now the immense sympathy I have for the position of Immanuel Kant, with his emphasis on human moral capabilities. For Kant this is what underpins our basic equality and our human
dignity. Our rational ability to make and act on moral judgments is
the quintessence of our human worth. Kant thinks it is momentously
important, and we may agree.

Still, I wonder whether the Kantian account really answers to the
comprehensiveness specification. Does it deal, for example, with
equal concern, the equal consideration of our interests? Do we really
want to say that it is because of our capacity as evaluators that attention should be paid to our needs? Or that it is because we are capable
of making moral judgments and acting on them that attention should
be paid to our interests? When Kant says that our humanity is the
"objective end" of morality—"something the existence of which in
itself has an absolute worth, something which as an end in itself could
be a ground of determinate laws"[20]—he means not our human pas-
sions, human susceptibilities, and human affections but our ability

20. Kant, *Groundwork*, 36–37 (4:428).

to rationally evaluate ends or values. Is this really a credible basis for equal concern? I guess one can concoct a theory that connects the two. One can say, "Well nobody can become a moral agent unless he is well fed and well educated, and so the concern about counting people equally for the purposes of interests like subsistence can feed on an account of the importance of moral capabilities." But this may give an inappropriate characterization of the kind and level of concern that is required. People have been known to flourish as moral agents under conditions of adversity and deprivation; should this be taken into account in determining the requisite level of basic concern required for each human person?

The fact is that our interests matter, and, across human beings, interests of the same sort matter equally; our needs matter, and, across human beings, needs of the same sort matter equally. The animal side of our nature matters, and the animal side of our human nature matters equally. And these seem to be points that stand somewhat apart from the Kantian momentousness of our moral agency. Although the moral account gives an account of what is special about us, it does not fully explain why our needs and our interests matter. There is a sort of mismatch between the work equality has to do and this rather narrow account. When you see a human person dying of hunger, you don't say, "Oh, damn! Another opportunity for moral judgment lost to the world." If a human is dying of hunger, we should be concerned with the hunger and the death, not just with the dimming of the moral capacity (which does admittedly depend in some sense on material subsistence).[21] I do not want to deny the many con-

---

21. Some have also balked at Kant's account of human dignity along these lines. They worry that it appears to fetishize our moral capacities rather focus on than the human lives that are led under their auspices and in and around their exercise. See, for example, Michael Rosen, *Dignity: Its History and Meaning* (Harvard University Press, 2012), 80–90, 122–125, for the point that Kant seems to care about moral law and moral capacity, not

nections there are between material need and moral capacities, but I wonder sometimes whether philosophers working in the Kantian tradition have been too careless about this. Too much influenced by Kant's peculiar moralism, they tend to overemphasize range properties that have to do with human moral powers.[22]

Or the attraction may be that we think we need something normative or moral on the factual side of the "is"/"ought" gap. The relevant range property is supposed to make sense of the equality norm. Since the thing we have to make sense of is undoubtedly normative — we talked about all this at the beginning of Lecture 2 — then what better than to begin on the fact side with something about our normative capabilities. But this is a fake advantage. That we all possess Kantian moral capability is a *fact* about us (if it's true) — it is a fact *about* normativity, but it is not normative in itself — and there is just as much of a gap between that fact and the principle of basic equality as there is between the principle of basic equality and any other fact about us (like our needs or our basic interests). We should not feel trapped therefore into offering nothing but an account of moral capabilities on the fact side of the equation. Nothing is lost — and much is gained in the way of the comprehensive work that has to be done — by complementing moral range properties with range properties that concern the basic living of a human life.[23]

---

persons as such. See also the discussion of Kant's notion of respect in Joseph Raz, *Values, Respect, and Attachment* (Cambridge University Press, 2001), 130ff.

22. Cf. Louis Pojman, "Critique of Contemporary Egalitarianism: A Christian Perspective," *Faith and Philosophy* 8 (1991): 485: "Even if we conceded that everyone was equally capable of a good will, we would still question whether this was sufficient for equal human worth. Why should conscientiousness alone constitute our value? On what basis does Kant make one's ability to have a sense of duty the necessary and sufficient condition for value?"

23. I pursued this question, about whether the specification of a given range property is adequate to the scope of the work that basic equality has to do, further in Jeremy Waldron, "Basic Equality," NYU School of Law, Public Law Research Paper No. 08-61 (December 5,

These points are particularly important if we focus on possible beneficiaries of justice who perhaps cannot themselves be regarded as
bearers of the duties that justice gives rise to. Clearly, if our question
is about what underlies the liability to bear the duties that justice generates, it is plausible to invoke a range property connected with
moral agency. But is the same invocation appropriate when our question is about who is entitled to justice as a beneficiary? Those who
believe in some continuous equality between humans and certain
other animals will deny this.[24] They will think that the absence of
moral agency should not lessen our concern for the well-being of an
animal. I don't mean, though, that moral agency can be relevant only
to the question of who bears the duties associated with justice or
equality. We do quite rightly say with Kant that our moral powers
command a powerful degree of respect from others as well as being
the occasion for our assumption of duties. The broader question I am
raising is whether this sort of respect is sufficiently broad to encompass all that basic equality commands. Or must it also be associated
with an equally powerful degree of concern that is not reducible to
such respect?

5.

I said too that the work that basic equality has to do involves *heavy
lifting*. Basic equality has to be able to hold its own in the face of some
very powerful psychological temptations and some equally powerful
moral temptations.

2008), http://ssrn.com/abstract=1311816, 40–44 (§§54–57). There I consider how the point
applies to Locke's account also.

24. See, for example, Laura Valentini, "Canine Justice: An Associative Account," *Political
Studies* 62 (2014): 39–40.

On the psychological front, the insistence that all humans matter and matter equally has to be able to confront and restrain the special favors we think we are entitled to do for ourselves, not to mention our proud and indignant prioritization of family and friends and the strong bonds of nation and community. All of these tend to militate against the application of any principle of equal consideration or equal respect. These are powerful pressures, and the basis of human equality has to have the sort of weight that can explain why the principle stands up against them.

I don't want to dismiss out of hand the claims that special relationships, such as child-parent relationships, have on us, though I think that the principle of basic equality should chasten our enthusiasm for these special claims more than it has done in recent moral philosophy. But focus for a moment on the special tie between parent and child and the priority that it is thought a parent is entitled to accord to a child over strangers on account of this special relationship. The first thing to note about this relationship is that it is characteristic not only of the individual who asserts it but of many if not most adult human beings: they all have children whom they regard as special. Each parent therefore must think sensitively and fairly about other parents' relationships in this regard. There may be circumstances in which parent A is entitled to give priority to A's child, little a, over other children (little b, little c, and so on). But suppose that various parents are attempting to establish together a fair framework within which children will compete (for places at a good school, for example). Parent A is not entitled to support a given framework just because it will advantage little a. She must support a framework that is fair to all—meaning fair to the special concerns of every parent and every child affected and to the special relations between them. What we seek to treat equally, in other words, are humans with their own special concerns. We don't necessarily disparage those special concerns in the name of equality, but we certainly insist on invoking basic equality to underpin a requirement of fairness in the way we approach them. Special relationships do not trump fairness; rather the special relationships that exist are among the things we have to be fair *to*. So, principles of fairness and equality have continuing work to do in determining which special relationships are important for human beings and how the important special relationships that different humans have can be adjusted to one another.

In all this, the principle of basic equality needs to be particularly robust, because morally *we* are not robust. There is a constant temptation toward giving too much weight to our own special relationships. I have in mind particularly one's alleged special relation to one's fellow nationals. In his 1932 classic *Moral Man and Immoral Society*, the theologian Reinhold Niebuhr spoke with great concern about the ability of national feeling and national fellow feeling—my concern for my fellow New Zealanders or, when I live in the United States, for my fellow Americans; your concern for your fellow Scots; and so on. Niebuhr was concerned about the tendency of those feelings to "sluice off" (that was his phrase), to sluice away all that there is of people's altruism.[25] People say, "Of course I am not selfish. I have a huge and massive investment in the well-being of other Scots or a huge concern for other New Zealanders." But if that sort of fellow

25. Reinhold Niebuhr, *Moral Man and Immoral Society: A Study in Ethics and Politics* (Charles Scribner's Sons, 1932), 132:

> Patriotism transmutes individual unselfishness into national egoism. Loyalty to the nation is a high form of altruism when compared to lesser loyalties and more parochial interest. It therefore becomes the vehicle of all the altruistic impulses, and express itself, on occasion, with such fervor that the critical attitude of the individual toward the nation is almost completely destroyed. . . . Thus the unselfishness of individuals makes for the selfishness of nations. That is why the hope of solving the larger social problems of mankind, merely by extending the social sympathies of individuals, is so vain.

feeling begins to monopolize such altruism as I can command, then there is a problem that proper service will not be done to demands of human equality that go well beyond Scotland and well beyond New Zealand. The investment that we have in the nature and character of basic equality has to be able to tip us away from simply focusing on person-referential circles, whether it is the circle of nation or the circle of family.

Do you remember David Hume's observations on the relationship between family feeling and justice? He said that although devotion to family is a "noble . . . affection," yet "instead of fitting men for large societies, [it] is almost as contrary to them as the most narrow selfishness."[26] People may be willing to make sacrifices in the name of morality for themselves, but they're often not willing to make moral sacrifices for their families, even when such sacrifices are commanded by fairness or by a concern for all the members of their society or all the members of the human race. I don't want to discredit family feeling but simply to indicate the discipline that basic equality has to impose on those whose altruism would otherwise be limited by these closed self-referential circles.

6.

Even apart from the work that has to be done in overcoming these psychological obstacles, the principle of basic equality also has to be able to stand up to and if necessary to trump the work of certain other bona fide moral principles. It is a point made familiar in modern political philosophy that sometimes good principles have to prevail over other good principles. Partly this is a matter of moral pluralism; the

26. David Hume, *Treatise of Human Nature*, ed. L. A. Selby-Bigge (Oxford University Press, 1896), 487 (III, ii).

things we value do not fit easily into a tidy set of moral commitments; sometimes hard choices and ragged trade-offs have to be made. But it is not just the untidiness of moral pluralism. Sometimes liberal principles are set up in order to trump moral positions that have a high level of background importance. Rights are developed partly in relation to other elements in the very same political theory in which the rights themselves are included,[27] which means that the considerations that oppose rights cannot be dismissed out of hand. So, for example, individual rights stand up not only against alien justifications like evil tyranny and repression, but they also have to trump the operation of what seem like quite reasonable applications of the principle of utility and other consequentialist considerations. As Ronald Dworkin put it in *Taking Rights Seriously*, "If someone has a right to something, then it is wrong for the government to deny it to him even though it would be in the general interest to do so."[28] Basic equality has to have this sort of trumping power also: it has to have the power to override positions whose moral importance is undeniable. And this trumping power cannot be assumed: it has to be explained.

Also there are respectable moral principles that seem to require us *not* to accord the benefit of basic equality or human dignity to all individuals, but instead to prefer some individuals to others. How can we condemn wrong actions and the moral character of those who produce them without denouncing the moral personalities of their perpetrators? Nothing seems more important, morally, than the distinction between a sadistic mass murderer and an ordinary decent human being. Yet it is a consequence of basic equality as I understand it that Pol Pot, Joseph Stalin, and Adolf Hitler are to be regarded as our equals;

27. This formulation is adapted from Ronald Dworkin, "Rights as Trumps," in *Theories of Rights*, ed. Jeremy Waldron (Oxford University Press, 1984), 165.

28. Ronald Dworkin, *Taking Rights Seriously* (Harvard University Press, 1978), 270.

they have in relation to us equal moral worth and equal human dignity. That seems abhorrent—even, as Uwe Steinhoff puts it, *bizarre*—particularly if one sets up a contrast with some outstandingly virtuous person (the philosophical favorites seem to be Nelson Mandela, Mother Teresa, and, in the following extract, Albert Schweitzer).[29]

> Albert Schweitzer certainly has a higher moral standing and greater moral worth than Adolf Hitler. This is so obvious as not to require argument. (Imagine Hitler and Schweitzer are hurled by some cosmic fluke into your space-time continuum, into the ocean next to your life-boat, and you can save only one of them. Suppose you know for a fact that Hitler will for some reason that has nothing to do with repentance never again hurt anyone. Even then, is there really any question as to which of the two you ought to save? Egalitarians, it would appear, would have you be impartial and throw [toss] a coin. But pretty much everybody apart from egalitarians themselves will find this silly. . . . Genocidal dictators and altruistic doctors are simply not moral equals, and apart from a small number of liberal egalitarians everybody knows that.)[30]

Some of this concern can be allayed by pointing to moral principles that operate outside the realm of basic equality (though under its discipline) and permit all sorts of differentiation, like denunciation of Hitler but not Schweitzer, punishment of Hitler but not Schweitzer,

---

29. The good persons with whom Hitler is contrasted include Schweitzer and Mother Teresa in Stefan Gosepath, "On the (Re)construction and Basic Concepts of the Morality of Equal Respect," in Steinhoff, *Do All Persons Have Equal Moral Worth?*, 125, and Nelson Mandela in Uwe Steinhoff, "Against Equal Respect and Concern, Equal Rights, and Egalitarian Impartiality," in Steinhoff, *Do All Persons Have Equal Moral Worth?*, 157.

30. Steinhoff, "Against Equal Respect and Concern," 168, 170.

maybe even targeted killing of Hitler but not Schweitzer. I will talk about this at length in the last part of this lecture.

But Steinhoff is right. If principles of basic equality, equal worth, and human dignity do any sort of work at all, they have to generate normative conclusions about equal concern and respect for Hitler and Schweitzer that seem immediately offensive. The work that basic equality does for us and among us includes the work that it has to do for terrorists, dictators, mass murderers, and so on. For many people that sounds so massively counterintuitive that they say, "What on earth could be so morally important as to lead us to assert that at bottom Hitler has as much human dignity as a decent law-abiding individual?" Yet that is what basic equality demands, and our conception of it and of the range properties that support it has to be strong enough to do that work and fend off those contrary intuitions. We have to be able to insist unflinchingly that the benefit of basic principles of human worth and human dignity accrues equally to every human being, irrespective of what he or she has done and what he or she is responsible for.

May I give you an example of this unflinching attention? In December 2005, the Supreme Court of Israel, sitting as the High Court of Justice, considered the Israeli government's policy of targeted killing. By that I mean preventative strikes aimed at killing members of terrorist organizations even when they are not actively or immediately engaged in terrorist activities.[31] I mean people who are terrorists on Mondays, Wednesdays, and Fridays but may be found working in their garage in Gaza or the West Bank on Tuesdays, Thursdays, and Saturdays. In a long and very thoughtful opinion, President Emeritus

31. We in the United States have a policy of targeted killing as well: we have death squads and death lists administered by the White House. See Jeremy Waldron, "Death Squads and Death Lists: Targeted Killing and the Character of the State," *Constellations* 23 (2016): 292–307.

Aharon Barak of the Israeli Supreme Court rejected the absolutism of the contention that targeted killing was always wrong.[32] He argued that one couldn't rule out the right of the Israel Defense Forces to use force against people who had engaged and intended to engage in terrorist activities even while they were not actually engaged in combat. There is no alternative, said Justice Barak, to approaching these situations on a case-by-case basis. How regular is the target's participation in terrorist attacks? To what extent is his retreat back into civilian life just an opportunity for rest and preparation? Is the mandated alternative of arrest and trial available in the circumstances? And what is the likely collateral cost in terms of loss of life for civilians who are not unlawful combatants? We may or may not agree with all this; President Barak thought that in certain circumstances, under certain constraints, targeted killing might be permissible, if other forms of apprehension and arrest were not possible, if the number of civilian casualties was limited, and if we were genuinely dealing with somebody who was sallying out to conduct terrorist operations and then coming back for refuge in civilian territory. So he gave a nuanced judgment.

I am not concerned here with the details of the Court's finding; I am concerned with two premises which President Barak said were important before he went on to discuss what the final judgment should be. He said the first premise was that terrorist activity poses a desperate threat to the Israeli people and to Israeli society; this was 2005 and before the recent lull in terrorism. "The State's fight against terrorism is the fight of the state against its enemies"; Israel has paid a terrible cost in the innocent lives of its own people as a result of the

32. *The Public Committee against Torture in Israel and Palestinian Society for the Protection of Human Rights v. Government of Israel and Others* (Israel, HCJ 769/02), December 11, 2005.

thousands of terrorist attacks directed against it.[33] That was the first premise. The second premise I am going to quote exactly as he said it (well, in translation from the Hebrew): "Needless to say, unlawful combatants are not beyond the law. They are not 'outlaws.' God created them as well in his image. Their human dignity as well is to be honored; they as well enjoy and are entitled to protection . . . by customary international law."[34] "Needless to say"—but perhaps it was necessary to say it anyway and to say it in these terms, to pull us up short, to remind us that although we are dealing with a malefactor, a terrorist, an evil person, an enemy of the state of Israel and the Jewish people, a threat to the lives of our loved ones, one who will kill and maim scores of innocent people if he gets the opportunity—*still*, we are talking about a bearer of human dignity. Not a credit to the human race, of course, but a member of it anyway, with all the worth and status that this implies. Again, although we are talking about someone who is justly liable through his actions and intentions to deadly force, we are not just talking about some human beast, which, as Locke put it, "may be destroyed as a Lyon or a Tyger, one of those wild Savage Beasts, with whom Men can have no Society nor Security,"[35] a good animal gone bad, a demon, an outsider to our species, or something that may be manipulated or battered or exploited as a mere tool for our own purposes (the purpose of saving the lives of members of our community). The terrorist may be an evil and dangerous man, but he is also man-created-in-the-image-of-God, and the status associated with that characterization imposes limits on what may be done to him

33. Ibid., §§1, 62.

34. Ibid., §25.

35. John Locke, *Two Treatises of Government*, ed. Peter Laslett (Cambridge University Press, 1988), 292 (II, §11).

and constraints on how lightly we may treat the question of what may be done about him.[36]

I have been talking in these lectures about how nice this principle of basic equality is. But we have to understand the hard and desperately difficult work that it does. The principle limits what we can do to terrorist suspects, even when we are convinced that they are guilty. It limits the punishments we can impose; it limits the peremptoriness with which we can deal with them; and it limits how quickly we can make decisions in the targeted killing case. Barak was mentioning this—under the auspices of a claim that God created the terrorists as well in his image—in order to pull us up short, not in order to settle the matter but in order to say that the greatest consideration and care has to be taken with this judgment, because we are talking about human beings who are, in some sense, precious because of the capacities and abilities we are citing. Kant doesn't flinch from this either; he says that even the greatest human evildoer has dignity and there are limits to what we can do to him. "I cannot deny all respect to even a vicious man as a human being," writes Kant, and he infers that there must be a ban on "disgraceful punishments that dishonor humanity itself (such as quartering a man [or] having him torn with dogs)."[37] The greatest human evildoer is one of us and must be treated as such even if he appears not to deserve it. So we have to have an account of what makes us one another's equals that is deep and serious enough to be capable steadfastly of doing this work. The account has to be able to explain why certain moral differences between people—evident even to the untutored eye—do not count when we are considering

36. See also the discussion in Jeremy Waldron, "The Image of God: Rights, Reason, and Order," in *Christianity and Human Rights: An Introduction*, ed. John Witte and Frank Alexander (Cambridge University Press, 2010), 216.

37. Immanuel Kant, *The Metaphysics of Morals*, in Gregor, *Practical Philosophy*, 580 (6:463).

the benefits of basic equality. That a being possesses the relevant range property in common with all other humans—whatever the startling differences between them—has to be what matters for certain moral purposes.

7.

One may be forgiven for inferring that the use of a range property involves an attempt to reduce the diversity of human beings to one flat ashen trait, like being rational or being an agent, ignoring all the differences between people. The impression is that basic equality requires us to ignore all the interesting facts about people. I would now like to argue that that impression is a mistake. We are not commanded by basic equality to ignore important and interesting differences between people. We are required to do so *for certain purposes,* but for other purposes we are commanded not to do so, and these various purposes are often both in our minds at a given time, requiring us to oscillate (as it were) between our concern for the range property and our concern for the precise location in the relevant scalar range that an individual might have. We oscillate as different moral principles require of us different kinds of response to the human beings in front of us.

So, as we search for a range property that it is plausible to say all people share—one that can plausibly ground their equality and be the basis of the load-bearing work that human equality has to do—it is probably a mistake to look for a bland human uniformity. We don't want a simple similarity, something that will be reductive, reducing us all—all seven billion of us, indeed all humans who have ever lived—to some lowest common denominator. We are certainly looking for a similarity, but the similarity that basic equality seeks to establish must not be incompatible with the idea of the uniqueness of each person, the individuality of each person. That, after all, is part of what we value in the worth of each human person. There may be no point in assigning great weight or importance to the range property or range properties in question unless one is also ready to take the opportunity that such property affords for a unique assessment of each individual. This does not mean we are distracted from the equal significance of the range property. It means rather that our awareness of its egalitarian character is complemented by an interest—a distinct but internally related interest—in its particular manifestation. The property we are looking for must house the distinctiveness of each person, even while it draws attention to facts about us whose similarity is the basis of our equality. So the property we are looking for not only has to equalize its bearers; it has to sparkle so much with their individuality that it is capable of sustaining not just equality but equal respect for the actual persons—the diverse individuals—whom we are calling one another's equals.

There has long been a worry—it emerged in the 1970s and 1980s in criticisms by people like Michael Sandel[38]—that liberal theories of justice imagine us as rather like wraiths that have no real properties, just nothings or next-to-nothings sitting behind a veil of ignorance, not knowing who we are or what matters to us, and trying to work out what justice requires among such vapor-like individuals in the thinnest possible circumstances of justice. I want to avoid that in this discussion if at all possible.

The point of tracking down a range property or set of range properties is not some sort of nominalism in its application to individuals. Michael Gorr worries about something like this in his consideration of the range property of rationality:

---

38. See Michael Sandel, *Liberalism and the Limits of Justice* (Cambridge University Press, 1982).

> While the possession of range rationality (for example) does not entail possessing any given degree of determinate rationality, it most certainly does entail possessing some determinate degree of rationality. For persons are not determinately rational in addition to being range rational—they are range rational in virtue of their being determinately rational (within the specified range). Rationality, that is, cannot exist *in abstracto* (as just indeterminate range rationality) because exemplifying some determinate degree of rationality is just what it means to exemplify range rationality.[39]

Gorr is right: people are rational only inasmuch as they have *a certain degree* of rationality. Still, what that degree is may be important for some purposes and not others.

I am going to use the term "scintillation" to refer to the way our attention moves back and forth between the relevant range property, on the one hand, and the particularity of its manifestation in each individual case on the other hand. Sometimes we are looking at where individuals are on the scale—how they are doing, the quality of their choices, what their life is actually like—and sometimes our attention flits back and rivets itself, for the work that human equality has to do, on the mere presence of the range property in question. We scintillate back and forth. Our understanding of the range property does not efface or obliterate the individual distinctive achievements of each person. It sparkles back and forth between them. Our abstract focus on the range property as such does not preclude a concentration on the concrete uniqueness which is housed by that abstraction; that concentration is needed for other purposes—that is, for work that other values and principles have to do. And equally our attention to the

---

39. Michael Gorr, "Rawls on Natural Inequality," *Philosophical Quarterly* 33 (1983): 15.

concrete achievements of each particular man, woman, and child does not eclipse our foundational interest in the fact that the sort of capacity they are exercising is, for the purposes of equality, momentous and important in itself. As I say, we are looking for some back-and-forth between abstract range-located capacity and scalar individual exercise. And it is not just fortuitous that we are doing that; our flitting back and forth is not due to attention deficit disorder. Because our potential for individuality is a huge element of what is valued fundamentally in each person, it must be part of the point of the range property we are interested in that it makes that individuality possible by accommodating differences of choice and differences of merit.

Let me give a few examples. The first has to do with personal autonomy. When I introduced this as a possible range property in Lecture 3, I mentioned John Stuart Mill's insistence in *On Liberty* that everyone has a capacity for living a life of his or her own. In Lecture 3, we noticed that there was a prescriptive tone in Mill's account: he believed we each had a responsibility to nurture our autonomy. Now, it might seem as though he wanted each of us to become just like him—a million autonomous versions of John Stuart Mill. But of course that wasn't the point at all. The responsibility for personal autonomy was to be discharged by each person opening up the distinctive sparkle of his or her own personality. The whole point of having this capacity for autonomy is that people can allow their particularity to unfold, their particular take on the experience of mankind, their particular talents and circumstances. It is precisely because humans are not all the same and do not all develop in the same way that we value the range property of autonomy which they all share:

> Human nature is not a machine to be built after a model, and
> set to do exactly the work prescribed for it, but a tree, which re-
> quires to grow and develop itself on all sides, according to the

tendency of the inward forces which make it a living thing. . . .
It is not by wearing down into uniformity all that is individual in
themselves, but by cultivating it and calling it forth, within the
limits imposed by the rights and interests of others, that human
beings become a noble and beautiful object of contemplation;
and as the works partake the character of those who do them, by
the same process human life also becomes rich, diversified, and
animating, furnishing more abundant aliment to high thoughts
and elevating feelings, and strengthening the tie which binds
every individual to the race, by making the race infinitely better
worth belonging to. In proportion to the development of his individuality, each person becomes more valuable to himself, and
is therefore capable of being more valuable to others. There is a
greater fulness of life about his own existence, and when there is
more life in the units there is more in the mass which is composed of them.[40]

We can talk in these abstract terms about each individual because the
understanding conveyed in the abstraction is that for each person a
distinctive and particular character will unfold. So there is this scintillation back and forth between insisting on the abstract range property of personal autonomy but at the same time reckoning that the
whole point of that insistence is to allow for an immense variety of
individual life.

Here is another example. In Lecture 2, we spoke about Hannah
Arendt's view that every time a human is born, a possibility of greatness, a possibility of something entirely new comes into the world.[41]

---

40. John Stuart Mill, *On Liberty* (Bobbs-Merrill, 1959), 71 (chap. 3).

41. Lecture 2, Section 5. See Hannah Arendt, "What Is Freedom?," in *Between Past and Future: Six Exercises in Political Thought* (Viking Press, 1961), 169.

And it's that possibility which is the basis of human equality. But again the thing about that possibility is that every so often it will explode into actuality. And we wouldn't be interested in it if it didn't. But we are interested in the possibility for some purposes, and for other purposes we are interested in the particular greatness that actually reveals itself. When we think about the dignity of the human species, we are interested in both. Our interest scintillates, back and forth.

8.

How does this scintillation work for morality and our moral capabilities? The first thing to acknowledge is that it does not always involve charm and sparkle. In the case of moral agency (considered as a range property), we do not delight in the variety of characters it reveals, in the way we do, say, with Mill's account of individuality. Taking proper account of variation of circumstances, morally it might be best if we all made and acted on the same judgments of right and wrong.[42] In fact, though, we will certainly face different options, make different choices, and have to reflect on different past deeds and misdeeds. It is part of the point of being a moral agent—of having and sharing this moral capability—that we can come to terms with this unpredictable and often unmanageable variety. That is one of the remarkable things about moral agency: it won't work as a machine or algorithm. The capability we have is much more subtle than that, nuanced and geared for novelty and capable of coming to terms with what is unusual in human affairs.

42. Novelists (such as Iris Murdoch) will probably disagree, and I am sure there is ample room for a sort of moral aesthetics that can displace the boring monotony of righteousness. Moral aesthetics might even turn us against any version of what is known as the *Anna Karenina* principle. We may say that not only are there myriad ways of acting badly, but each good person is good in his or her distinctive way.

In Section 7, we were asked to consider what range property of moral agency could possibly unite a human monster like Hitler with a human saint like Schweitzer. So imagine: here before us is Hitler, reeking of murder, and familiar moral principles require us to denounce what he has been doing, to stop him, perhaps to kill him—at the very least to do things to him that we wouldn't dream of doing to (say) Schweitzer. Our moral attention is riveted on his murderous misdeeds—his particular crimes—and rightly so. Confronted with his evil, some of us may be tempted to inflict upon him if we can a hideous and torturous death. But exactly at this point principles of basic rights kick in, principles that require us to see Hitler as a human being entitled to elementary protection from cruel or inhuman treatment. Basic equality sees him not as a devil but as a human being with elementary human rights. Then someone dismayed by this constraint asks, "So, do we just let him go free, like everyone else?" The answer is no: we have principles requiring him but not Schweitzer to be apprehended and punished for what he has done.

Now, this is a particular differentiation, but it is required by a broader background principle—a uniform principle—that insists the two of them must be treated as responsible agents. "But surely there doesn't need to be a trial," someone protests. "Can't we just take Hitler out and shoot him?" Well, maybe there is a legitimate debate to be had about that, like the debate between Churchill and his American allies toward the end of the Second World War on what to do about Nazi leaders as and when they fell into Allied captivity. But in conducting that debate, we will for some of the time at least have to consider Hitler simply as a human being, albeit one charged with horrendous crimes. And so we move from principle to principle, perspective to perspective, being sometimes required to see him through the prism of his atrocities and sometimes required to see him through the lens of his humanity. "Scintillation" may not be a good word here because it has connotations of charm, sparkle, and delight. But the structure is the same. We cannot think about this case without moving back and forth between principles that are sensitive to Hitler's evil particularity and principles that are sensitive just to the fact that he is a human being (even if the humanity he shares with the rest of us itself requires that he be held to account). If our morality is well-organized, the relevant principles do not contradict one another. But they do disconcertingly require us to vary our perspective, and so they will seem counterintuitive to those who insist impatiently that any such variation is wrong for the case of Hitler.

Perhaps this thesis of scintillation will be challenged by those who want to describe a wrongdoer like Hitler as a devil.[43] John Kekes believes that liberal egalitarians have forsaken the concept of evil in their willingness to recognize a basically equal humanity in each human being. Certain malefactors, he is convinced, have sunk so low, to such consistently evil depths, that there is nothing left in their case for a thesis of moral equality to stand for.[44] I do not know what to make of this or of the accompanying suggestion that liberal egalitarians are necessarily blind to it. If Kekes means that liberal egalitarians offer Hitler's humanity or his basic equal standing as some sort of mitigation of his crimes, then he is mistaken. Apart from deep—and perhaps troubling[45]—Christian ideas about the possibility in all cases of repentance and redemption (about which I will say a little more in Lecture 5)—the independent operation of a principle of basic

43. See Héctor Wittwer, "The Irrelevance of the Concept of Worth to the Debate between Egalitarianism and Non-egalitarianism," in Steinhoff, *Do All Persons Have Equal Moral Worth?*, 84.

44. John Kekes, "Human Worth and Moral Merit," *Public Affairs Quarterly* 2 (1988): 53–68. See also John Kekes, *The Illusions of Egalitarianism* (Cornell University Press, 2003), chap. 2.

45. My thoughts on this have been troubled by David Daube, "Judas," *California Law Review* 82 (1995): 95–108.

equality and human dignity does not in any respect offset the wrong-doing which other moral principles denounce. Applying the principles of basic equality and human dignity just reminds us of the human status of the wrongdoer, and it demands that we resist every temptation to deploy any sort of concept (in Hitler's case to join *him* in deploying the concept) of the subhuman.

I am reasonably confident in this analysis. But there is a saying that hard cases make bad law. So let us turn away from Hitler and think about how we deal with less drastic differences of moral achievement.

Consider John Rawls's account of basic equality. For Rawls our status as equals depends on our possession of a sense of justice (as well as a sense of our own good). I said in Lecture 3 (at the end of Section 7) that a sense of justice need not be identified with any particular conception or set of principles (like Rawls's own two principles of justice as fairness). The relevant sense of justice must mean something like a desire to apply and act on principles of justice, whatever these turn out to be. Of course, it is important that the sense of justice we all possess be oriented as far as possible toward the truth about justice: it must involve a determination to get at what is *really* just or *really* fair. Notoriously, people disagree about this. Even at the highest level of intellectual contemplation, there is Rawls, there is Nozick, there is Dworkin, there is Sen, there is Nussbaum, there is Walzer, and so on.[46] There have been times when the disagreement seemed like fun, as people declared themselves members of Rawls's

46. Besides Rawls, *A Theory of Justice*, see Robert Nozick, *Anarchy, State and Utopia* (Basic Books, 1974); Martha Nussbaum, *Frontiers of Justice: Disability, Nationality, Species Membership* (Harvard University Press, 2006); Michael Walzer, *Spheres of Justice: A Defense of Pluralism and Equality* (Basic Books, 1983); Amartya Sen, *Inequality Reexamined* (Oxford University Press, 1992); and Ronald Dworkin, *Sovereign Virtue: The Theory and Practice of Equality* (Harvard University Press, 2000).

team or Nozick's team. But disagreement about justice is really a
huge concern for a society. For it is not like religion; we don't lose by
the presence of many different creeds in a multifaith society. But we
do have to administer among us just one conception of justice, or at
the very least, our answers to each particular problem of justice has to
be given in terms of one such conception (even if political competition leads to our answering one problem with Rawls's conception
and another problem with Nozick's). Unfortunately, however, the
need for consensus on justice does not make the disagreement go
away.[47] So the variety of positions that people take up on the question
of justice is a matter of concern, certainly not a matter of delight.

Variation is not just a matter of which conception one subscribes
to. There are also variations in ability, in the way one uses and figures
within a given approach. As well as the principles that respond to the
sheer presence of a sense of justice, there are also principles that respond to these variations. "Certainly some persons have a greater capacity for a sense of justice than others," says Rawls, and this greater
capacity "may qualify a man for certain offices."[48]

> A greater capacity for a sense of justice, as shown say in a greater
> skill and facility in applying the principles of justice and in mar-
> shaling arguments in particular cases, is a natural asset like any
> other ability. The special advantages a person receives for its exer-
> cise are to be governed by the difference principle. Thus if some
> have to a preeminent degree the judicial virtues of impartiality and
> integrity which are needed in certain positions, they may properly
> have whatever benefits should be attached to these offices.[49]

47. Cf. Jeremy Waldron, *Law and Disagreement* (Oxford University Press, 1999).
48. John Rawls, "The Sense of Justice," *Philosophical Review* 72 (1963): 301–302.
49. Rawls, *A Theory of Justice*, 443.

In this respect, then, our attention moves back and forth between the moral and political significance of variations in people's senses of justice and the sheer presence of a sense of justice which determines unitary citizenship and basic rights and liberties.

Consider also what Kant said on the various ways in which our moral capacity and its exercise engage different principles. Kant believed that all humans have the capability for moral agency and action on principle. He knew of course that some people act better than others; he acknowledged that, even with this shared moral capacity, "man is acted on by so many inclinations that, though capable of the idea of a practical pure reason, he is not so easily able to make it effective *in concreto* in his life."[50] He knew that there are hardened malefactors and individuals who have a greater struggle than others to act on principle. And certainly we cannot think that Kant just valued (or thought we should just value) the moral capacity in itself without evaluating how people act on it. So we mustn't deny the importance for Kant of goodwill and moral achievement. Kant could be very severe about this. At times one gets the impression that it is only the well-exercised moral capacity that displays the true sublimity of human worth for Kant. Though he said that dignity attaches to humanity "insofar as it is capable of morality," he also maintained at the very beginning of the *Groundwork* that "it is impossible to think of anything at all in the world . . . that could be considered good without limitation except a good will." A good will—a will that is actually good in the way it is exercised—is the basis of any claim we have to be happy.

Nevertheless there is a point of view in relation to morality where we are simply impressed by the fact that individuals are capable of discerning the moral law, reading, marking, learning, and inwardly

50. Kant, *Groundwork*, preface, 45 (4:389).

digesting it, making it part of their apparatus of action, so that they can then monitor and moderate their behavior accordingly — whether they exercise that capability or not. We are sometimes just blown away by the sheer capacity that people have for the self-application of norms. And that is true in Kant's moral philosophy. As I said in Lecture 3, Kant believed that when I see a humble common man "in whom I perceive uprightness of character in a higher degree than I am aware of in myself *my spirit bows* whether I want it to or whether I do not."[51] Part of my spirit's bowing is my realization that I too have or had that capacity, had I wanted to act on it. We scintillate back and forth between the particular assessment and the realization of the general capacity. A certain respect is due to us as equals because of the capacity within us, and a certain respect under other principles is due to us (or properly withheld from us) by the way we exercise the capacity.

9.

Stephen Darwall, a philosopher at Yale, wrote an article many years ago called "Two Kinds of Respect."[52] He said that sometimes when you say you respect somebody, what you mean to do is to convey a high evaluation of him or her. "I really respect Richie McCaw as an outstanding athlete," someone may say, or "I respect Joe Biden as a good-natured politician." So we sometimes use "respect" as a term of esteem or appraisal. We say, "I respect this person more than that person, when I consider her merits, what she has done, and how she has acted." But, said Darwall, there is a deeper notion of respect, which is somewhat separate, called "recognition-respect." Recognition-respect means

---

51. Kant, *Critique of Practical Reason*, 202 (5:76–77); emphasis in original.
52. Stephen Darwall, "Two Kinds of Respect," *Ethics* 88 (1977): 39.

recognizing that you are dealing with a person here. When you recognize someone as a person, you get out of her way, you don't try to trick her, you don't try to knock her over, you make adjustments in your own conduct so that she has room to live as well. That sense of recognition-respect—owed to persons as such—complements whatever we do by way of appraisal-respect.

Actually the contrast can work even more abstractly, whenever we distinguish between recognizing someone as an X and recognizing him as a good or better X. Recognition-respect doesn't have to be respect for persons. Think about judges as a category. Sometimes a barrister or an advocate will begin a sentence by saying, "With respect, your honor"; this is a phrase that indicates the speaker respects the office of judge and is prepared to make adjustments in her conduct accordingly. But sometimes when the advocates are in the bar—the other bar!—or wherever advocates gather, they say, "Well I respect this judge, but I don't really respect that judge." They say this to convey differential appraisals. One can even make this switch in respecting things like law itself. You may say, "I respect this because it's the law" or "I don't respect this law because I think it's a bad law." We say both things, and they're not incompatible. Both are important: recognition-respect and appraisal-respect. Darwall is absolutely right to make us notice the difference between them and to see how they apply to the fundamental category of person as well as to particular roles or kinds.

Darwall's categories help us see what is going on with this business of scintillation and basic equality. Sometimes we engage in appraisal-respect: we look at what people are responsible for, what they have chosen to do. And sometimes we engage in recognition-respect, responding just to the bare fact of someone's humanity. My point is, and this goes one step beyond Professor Darwall's discussion, is that these are two sides, in many ways, of the same coin because when we respect individuals as persons, we are respecting the very capabilities they have whose exercise will lead inevitably to differences of appraisal-respect.[53] But this is not a contradiction. Sometimes we are doing the work of human equality; sometimes we are doing other work. But the two are tightly related.

10.

In these lectures, I have sometimes talked about human worth; one of the headings under which I am proceeding is the notion of the equal worth that humans have. When people say, "Yes, but what about merit?," I want to reply, "Yes, there is such a thing as merit, and it is definitely not equal. But underlying it there is the notion of human worth, which is a way of thinking about our value when merit is, so to speak, subtracted."

Gregory Vlastos, in his great essay "Justice and Equality," thought it essential for an understanding of our moral practices that we are not just a merit-based society.[54] He said we could imagine living in a purely meritocratic society, where all social decisions and all individual decisions were based on people's merits—on the ability they had to be useful to us and the good things and the bad things they did. But our society is not like that. We recognize an undercurrent of equal human worth that has nothing to do with merit, which greatly affects how we deal with people.

53. See also Stephen Darwall, *The Second-Person Standpoint: Morality, Respect, and Accountability* (Harvard University Press, 2006), 25, for dignity both as the object of recognition-respect and as the basis of the particular claims we make against one another.

54. See Gregory Vlastos, "Justice and Equality," in Waldron, *Theories of Rights*, esp. 49–60.

If I see someone in danger of drowning I will not need to satisfy myself about his moral character before going to his aid. I owe assistance to any man in such circumstances, not merely to good men. Nor is it only in rare and exceptional cases, as this example might suggest, that my obligations to others are independent of their merit. To be sincere, reliable, fair, kind, tolerant, unintrusive, modest in my relations with my fellows is not due them because they have made brilliant or even passing moral grades, but simply because they happen to be fellow members of the moral community.[55]

We are required to respond in these ways to people's worth as well as permitted to respond to their merit when (say) we are punishing them or employing them or admitting them to universities. Vlastos acknowledges that "differences of merit are so conspicuous and pervasive that we might even be tempted to define the moral response to a person in terms of . . . the response to his moral merit."[56] But apart from and behind our meritocratic preoccupations lies a determination to recognize the fundamental worth of each human being. "The human worth of all persons is equal, however unequal may be their merit."[57]

This does not mean that human worth occludes or blocks any consideration of merit. Nor does it mean that we are utterly different from what Vlastos imagines as an M-society, a society that judges, decides, and deals with people on the basis of merit alone. It is not that they use merit and we use worth. Merit has its myriad uses for us also, and the relation is one of scintillation, not contradiction. Indeed, the

55. Ibid., 55.
56. Ibid.
57. Ibid., 51.

two concepts work together. Our insistence, when we make judgments about merit, that everybody has to be judged on the same
scale fairly, is partly rooted in our deep respect for each person, deep
respect for everyone's worth. Our insistence that when we make differentiations of merit, we have to make differentiations that are based
on fair criteria or that are good for the whole society—this too is predicated on a recognition of the human worth of each member of
society, and it bases the meritocratic assessment on that. Do you remember I spoke in Lecture 1 about our preference for strong and
young firefighters?[58] Those are merits for recruitment to the fire de-
partment, and they may seem unfair to old people and to people who
are weak, but the fact is that we look to the interests of everyone in
the community to work out the sort of firefighters we want and what
the meritocratic basis for firefighting ought to be. In that sense, even in
making our differentiations of merit, we are responding to constraints
laid down by our equality of worth. The two things spark off each
other in this way.

The final thing to say about worth and merit is that our understanding of human worth limits our sense of what we can offer by
way of differential rewards and differential penalties to people of high
merit and low merit. I have already suggested that there are certain
things we may not do even to the least meritorious individuals—
terrorists or mass-murderers like Hitler. We may not tear them apart;
on many accounts we may not even kill them. And with regard to the
high merit that certain people have (Schweitzer, for example), we in
a highly meritocratic society say, "Well, we are not allowed to offer a
reward of the entire wealth of the community in a winner-takes-all
sort of arrangement to the most deserving person. For that would

58. Lecture 1, Section 3.

be incompatible with a general concern for the human worth of the other members of the society." We can reward merit, but there are limits imposed by justice as to what the reward may be.

So this is another illustration of how sometimes there is work that has to be done by the scalar property associated with the range property and there is other work that has to be done by the range property itself. The range property helps determine the outer limits of penalty and reward. But the scalar property determines their allocation. In none of this is it the function of the range property to efface, suppress, obliterate, or make us forget about the differences of merit, the differences of capacity, or to denigrate its importance. Merit is important; it is just not all-important.

Some philosophers miss this point. Ian Carter approaches basic equality using the idea of epistemic abstinence. He says we deliberately refrain from looking at any scalar element associated with the range properties that underpin equality. Basic equality, he says, purports to give us

> a particular moral justification for evaluative abstinence—that is, a refusal to evaluate persons' varying capacities. . . . The justification for such a refusal can be said to derive from a particular sense of respect for human dignity. . . . The kind of respect I have in mind involves adopting a perspective that remains external to the person, and in this sense holding back from evaluating any of the variable capacities on which her moral personality supervenes, be they capacities for rational thought or capacities for evaluative judgment or capacities for awareness and understanding of one's place in the world.[59]

59. Carter, "Respect and the Basis of Equality," 550–551.

He says basic equality requires us "to *avoid* looking inside people."[60] I think this involves a mistake. We must not lose sight of individuality and distinction, and it is important to identify range properties that allow these things to sparkle. It is a basis for equality that we are looking for, but it is equality as applied to the individuality, distinction, and uniqueness of each of the billions of persons who are said to be our equals. Are these ideas in destructive tension with one another, papered over by this nice-sounding term "scintillation"? I don't think so, provided we understand that the movement is continual, back and forth (and definitely forth as well as back). The range properties we take as a basis for equality are properties that license rather than preclude our noticing the differences between people. Only, as they do that, they require us for certain purposes to just remind ourselves that each of the different individuals we face is equal to each of the others in being amenable in principle to these evaluations.

11.

What I said earlier about complexity also feeds into this understanding of "scintillation." We do not have just rationality, lives to lead, affections, and a sense of justice as individual capacities, isolated from one another. Each of these is complicated, and many of them are engaged with one another. (We saw this at the end of Section 1.) It is the interplay of all these that generates what I have called "scintillation."

Our emphasis on complexity helps us see another point: that the capabilities we are considering operate not only together but over time. There is a story to be told, or there are stories to be told, in and through and around the possession of these capacities. This is obvious

60. Ibid., 551; emphasis in original.

in the case of personal autonomy, where the key idea is that of having a *life* to lead. But it is also true of moral capacity, which is not just about the instant ability to make moral judgments and decisions at particular points in time but may involve long processes of thought, deliberation, the seeking of advice, the nurturing of a moral sense, the acquisition and use of moral experience, and so on, not to mention growth, education, steadfastness, and uplifting or bitter experience. Even bare rationality is not just this or that calculation or this or that responsiveness to reason. One responds to reason over time; reason and reasonableness can suffuse one's life or extended parts of it. And one can grow in one's ability to notice and respond to reasons.

It is important in all of this to remind ourselves of the truism that the subjects of basic equality are supposed to be human beings, conceived not as momentary time slices but as persons extended over time. Ontologically, the equality we are talking about is equality of whole lives. Our worth, our dignity, and the equality between one person's worth and dignity and another's, are characteristic of human lives—with implications for every moment, sure—but the crucial entity on which we should focus is the trajectory of the whole life, not just something constructed additively out of moments. (These points will be very important in what we say about childhood and disability in Lecture 6.)

All of this connects with what I've been saying about scintillation. What we achieve in the exercise of these capacities is extended in time also, and the back-and-forth of our attention takes place also over time. For we are interested in the scalar aspects of these range properties not just in a scoring or judgmental way but in a way that attends to things like growth, achievement, integrity, and legacy—and mistake, failing, character flaw, repentance, rebuilding, and so on. None of this gets left behind in our selection and focus on a range property. The range property does its work by underlining the elementary requirements of equality, worth, and dignity. But then the range property does its work too by providing an occasion for the exercises and degrees of ability that matter to us in ordinary life as it is lived through time among those who are fundamentally equals.

5

A Religious Basis for Equality?

My theme is equality, the sense in which humans are basically one another's equals, whatever the differences between them and whatever the permissibly and impermissibly different ways in which society treats them. The account of equality I have offered so far in these lectures has been mainly secular in character. There have been hints here and there of religious argumentation—in the Stoic account of our rational capacities, for example, and in several references to the idea of man created in the image of God.[1] But in Lectures 3 and 4, we focused mainly on natural social and moral characteristics, without really considering any transcendent significance they might have. We were trying to find what some authors have called a host property,[2] a property that would help make sense of basic equality, and we talked about the sort of property that would have to be. We focused on rational and moral characteristics, and even when metaphysical elements were introduced, as they arguably

---

1. See Lecture 3, Section 4.
2. John Coons and Patrick Brennan, *By Nature Equal: The Anatomy of a Western Insight* (Princeton University Press, 1999), 39.

were on Kant's account of our noumenal moral powers, those metaphysical elements were not particularly religious.[3] The same is true of
what I said about Hannah Arendt and her account of natality, that is,
of the possibility of human greatness in every life that comes into the
world.[4] Still, all the way through, we have been aware—comfortably
in my case, less comfortably perhaps in the case of some of my
readers—of various religious themes and religious versions of the
themes we explored, lurking around and awaiting our attention. This
lecture is the time when attention must be paid.

Religious arguments about human equality are very common in
our tradition. That the belief in our equality is rooted in a vision of
God's relation to humankind has been a familiar theme for thousands
of years.[5] It is said that we are all equal in the eyes of God, that we
are created in God's image, consecrated by his love, each of us sent
into the world, as John Locke put it, by him and about his business.[6]
We are told that God loves not only the powerful and the mighty but
the poor and the despised. And we are required, according to our religious beliefs—those of us who still have them—to echo the equality
of that love in our own dealings with each other, in our ethics, and
also in our politics.

---

3. Immanuel Kant, *Groundwork of the Metaphysics of Morals*, in *Practical Philosophy*,
ed. Mary Gregor (Cambridge University Press, 1996), 97–108 (4:450–463). (Note: numbers
in parentheses refer to the Prussian Academy edition of Kant's works.)

4. See Hannah Arendt, "What Is Freedom?," in *Between Past and Future: Six Exercises in
Political Thought* (Viking Press, 1961), 169.

5. I elaborated John Locke's version of this in *God, Locke, and Equality: Christian Foundations of Locke's Political Thought* (Cambridge University Press, 2002).

6. John Locke, *Two Treatises of Government*, ed. Peter Laslett (Cambridge University
Press, 1970), 289 (II, §6).

1.

For some of us, as I said, it seems obvious that an adequate conception of human dignity and of the equality that is predicated on that dignity is rooted in an understanding of the relation of the human person to God or in aspects of human nature that matter to God or matter for our relation to God. It seems obvious that human worth and human dignity are going to have to be rooted in something like a theological anthropology, a religiously loaded account of human nature. Human dignity is supposed to be based on what people are really like, and for a person of faith, a theological anthropology purports to provide our deepest and most serious account of what people are like and what is most important about them.

These things seem obvious to me. And much of what follows reflects my own Anglican background and my knowledge of the Jewish-Christian tradition. But in academic writing one hesitates to bring personal faith to the traditional preoccupations of political philosophy. One feels a little shy. This lecture will also explore some reasons for that hesitation. Certainly it will not preclude religious argumentation: the core of an affirmative account can be found in Sections 6 through 9. But those sections are framed on both sides by various misgivings—misgivings as to the intellectual respectability of religious arguments, misgivings as to whether our religious traditions really have anything helpful to offer, and misgivings as to whether it is appropriate to invoke particular religious arguments in political philosophy for a multifaith society. Only an honest exploration of those misgivings can entitle us to attach any significance to the affirmative religious account that I offer in the sections just mentioned.

2.

Many philosophers are inclined to dismiss religious accounts of human equality as superstitious nonsense. They say we should develop our theory of equality, if we want one, in purely secular terms. This is motivated partly by a concern for the integrity and mutual accessibility of public reason: how can one set of believers argue publicly for basic equality when members of their audience do not share any of the presuppositions of their discourse? I will talk about that in Section 10. But the dismissive approach is also motivated by something more substantive, by strong and well-established skepticism about religious arguments set out in the work of thinkers like Richard Dawkins, Daniel Dennett, Sam Harris, and most recently Philip Kitcher.[7] These philosophers and scientists believe that our ethics and political philosophy would be intellectually more respectable if religious conceptions were abandoned.

However, in the context of the Gifford Lectures, particularly in light of the terms of Lord Gifford's endowment,[8] there is no choice but to explore these themes. I don't mean we must assume Dawkins

---

7. See Richard Dawkins, *The God Delusion* (Mariner Books, 2008); Daniel Dennett, *Breaking the Spell: Religion as a Natural Phenomenon* (Penguin Books, 2006); Sam Harris, *The End of Faith: Religion, Terror, and the Future of Reason* (Norton, 2005); Philip Kitcher, *Life after Faith: The Case for Secular Humanism* (Yale University Press, 2014).

8. Lord Gifford set up these lectures in 1886 for the stated purpose of "'Promoting, Advancing, Teaching, and Diffusing the study of Natural Theology,' in the widest sense of that term, in other words, 'The Knowledge of God, the Infinite, the All, the First and Only Cause, the One and the Sole Substance, the Sole Being, the Sole Reality, and the Sole Existence, the Knowledge of His Nature and Attributes, the Knowledge of the Relations which men and the whole universe bear to Him, the Knowledge of the Nature and Foundation of Ethics or Morals, and of all Obligations and Duties thence arising.'" See *Trust, Disposition and Settlement of the late Adam Gifford, sometime one of the Senators of the College of Justice, Scotland, dated 21st August 1885,* http://www.giffordlectures.org/lord-gifford/will.

et al. are wrong. I mean we must face up to all the issues that the possibility of a religious account gives rise to, and that includes facing up to the ethical and intellectual challenges as well.

At the very least, we have to figure out what the implications would be of an abandonment of religious ideas of the sort counseled by Dawkins, Dennett, Harris, and Kitcher. If we were to go ahead with a purge of religious ideas from our account of human worth, human dignity, and basic equality, it is an open question how much that purge would take with it. I know some people believe that equal human dignity can be articulated and defended perfectly well without religion. And, again, perhaps they are right. Many people believe in human dignity without sharing the religious outlook I have mentioned; these are people who, in the words of Hugo Grotius, deny that there is a God or that he has any interest in human affairs, but who still think human beings matter and matter equally.[9] Others deny this. They believe that the idea of human dignity and a purported account of our relation to God constitute an inextricably entangled package—and the whole package is what they want to abandon. They think human dignity itself is an irrational religious idea that is cluttering up clear moral thinking.

We have to take this latter possibility seriously. It cannot be assumed that if we bracket out the religious stuff, we will leave the rest of our ethics intact. It might be like tearing a page out of a paperback novel: when you tear out one page you wreck the binding, and several dozen other pages will eventually litter the floor as well. So we have to ask how much of our account of human dignity, human worth, and basic human equality is bound up with religious ideas, and how much of it would have to be purged as fellow travelers with the creation story, the image of God, the love of Christ, and so on. Some who take the antireligious line—I am thinking of people like

9. Hugo Grotius, *Prolegomena to the Law of War and Peace* (Bobbs-Merrill 1957), 10 (§11).

Steven Pinker (who wrote a book called *The Better Angels of Our Nature*, about the reduction of violence in human affairs)[10]—seem to be willing to acknowledge this implication. They say they would be happy to lose the notion of human dignity as well as arguments about our relation to God. Dignity, said Pinker in a 2008 article in *The New Republic* called "The Stupidity of Dignity," is a "subjective and squishy notion hardly up to the heavy-weight moral demands assigned to it."[11] He thought the idea was hopelessly compromised by its primitive religious associations, and he asked incredulously, "How did the United States, the world's scientific powerhouse, reach a point at which it grapples with the ethical challenges of twenty-first-century biomedicine using Bible stories, Catholic doctrine, and woolly rabbinical allegory?"[12]

Some philosophers argue that it is religious thinking that needs the support of moral thinking, not the other way around. They say that ideas like human dignity come first, and then we choose our religion according to whether its teachings coincide with moral positions to which we are already committed. These days, with cafeteria-style selections of credos, many people choose what they call their faith on this basis. I don't just mean Californian spiritualists. Immanuel Kant in the *Groundwork of the Metaphysics of Morals* said that "even the Holy One of the Gospel must first be compared with our idea of moral perfection before he is cognized as such."[13] Where do we get

10. Stephen Pinker, *The Better Angels of Our Nature: Why Violence Has Declined* (Viking Books, 2011).

11. Steven Pinker, "The Stupidity of Dignity," *New Republic*, May 28, 2008. For some consideration of the consistency of this skepticism with Pinker's optimism in *The Better Angels of Our Nature*, see Jeremy Waldron, "A Cheerful View of Mass Violence," *New York Review of Books*, January 12, 2012.

12. Pinker, "The Stupidity of Dignity."

13. Kant, *Groundwork*, 63 (4:408).

the concept of God or Jesus as embodying the highest good? Kant taught that we begin with the notion of the highest good, which we arrive at by reason, and *then* we bring that to our faith to examine and endorse it as a religion worth believing in. Otherwise we have to reason from what we believe to be the sheer facts of God's power, vengefulness, and desire for dominion, which, as Kant says, are "directly opposed to morality."[14] In 2012 Ronald Dworkin echoed this Kantian argument in *Justice for Hedgehogs*. He wrote that no divine authority can provide a ground for ethical ideals or moral rights because once you are confronted with the notion of a powerful spirit, you need to certify to yourself whether this is a demonic spirit or a good spirit.[15] You cannot do that unless you already have in your armory a set of moral criteria. The possibility that Dworkin is right about this has to be confronted.[16]

3.

Some additional reasons for hesitation arise out of religious discussion itself. We know there are Christian theologians who oppose what I am calling basic equality. I spent time in Lecture 1 exploring the arguments of a distinguished Anglican priest and teacher of ethics at Oxford, Hastings Rashdall, writing at the beginning of the twentieth century, who maintained that we should pay differential attention to the lives and well-being of members of different races.[17] (True,

14. Ibid., 91 (4:443).

15. Ronald Dworkin, *Justice for Hedgehogs* (Harvard University Press, 2011), 339–344.

16. I should also mention the view, held by some Christian thinkers, that the idea of human dignity is a watered-down version of the much more robust religious idea of the sanctity of the human person. See David Gushee, "A Christian Theological Account of Human Worth," in *Understanding Human Dignity*, ed. Christopher McCrudden (Oxford University Press, 2014), 275–288.

17. Hastings Rashdall, *The Theory of Good and Evil: A Treatise on Moral Philosophy*, 2nd ed. (Oxford University Press, 1924), 1:237–238. See Lecture 1, Sections 5–6.

Rashdall did not believe this on religious grounds; my point is that his Christianity did not inoculate him against philosophic racism.) In the United States, all sorts of scriptural citations have been brought forward to support slavery and racial degradation: "hewers of wood and drawers of water" and so on.[18] And we all know about the endemic association of Christian doctrine, Muslim doctrine, and even Jewish doctrine with ideas about the subordination of women.

All of this is out there, and unfortunately, unless our choice of religion is utterly à la carte, it cannot be dismissed out of hand. People of faith are required to believe the ethics laid down in the scriptures. But the ethics may be disconcerting. There may be "hard sayings" in the scriptures,[19] doctrines that we have the greatest difficulty in reconciling with whatever ethical mind-set we bring to our religion. In a book called *By Nature Equal*, John Coons and Patrick Brennan observed that you wouldn't expect John Rawls to begin with the notion that certain kinds of people are privileged over others, but they say there is no telling what religious teachings will begin with.[20] That's the thing about religion: it is inherently strange, and who knows where it will lead a person who takes it seriously?

A religion may be opposed to human equality, or it may be indifferent. We know that, whatever its foundations, the principle of basic equality has mainly secular work to do. It does its work in the world, here on earth among us. Our interest in basic equality is not eschatological—though that doesn't mean it can't have eschatological foundations. Its work is in political morality and law, in the theory of rights and social justice. Hence the thought, I suppose, that we ought to confine ourselves to secular foundations—a line of argument I will come to in Section 10. But even if we do not accept the con-

18. Joshua 9:23.

19. See, for example, Walter Kaiser et al., *Hard Sayings of the Bible* (IVP Academic, 2010).

20. Coons and Brennan, *By Nature Equal*, 152.

straints of public reason, we still must face up to the possibility of a mismatch between secular orientation and religious foundations. Why, for example, would a religion have any interest at all in human equality? The question is only partly rhetorical. Religions have other concerns: they are interested in worship, creed, and the hereafter.[21] Are human dignity and basic equality necessarily on that list? *Our* agendas are not necessarily the agendas of our religions. A religion may teach us to be preoccupied with other things. As I said, that's the thing about religion.

We believers tend to associate our religion with morality, and we assume that our deepest moral convictions are sustained by equally if not more profound convictions about God. Why? Morality is ultimately a worldly entity, of and for this world. Our religious beliefs, by contrast, may have little interest in the virtues and values we have made up for our sojourn here on earth.[22] Augustine, in *The City of God*, made this observation about what we would call theories of self-determination: "As far as this life of mortals is concerned, which is spent and ended in a few days, what does it matter under whose government a dying man lives?"[23] Well, analogously, our lives here are short; what does it matter whether or not these corrupt and decrepit dying organisms are regarded as each other's equals in their brief pilgrimage on earth? Or if Christianity *is* interested in equality, perhaps it is mainly interested in equality in the life of the church.[24] You

21. It is remarkable that the great creeds of the Christian faith—the Apostles' Creed and the Nicean Creed—have no ethical content whatsoever.

22. Joshua Berman, *Created Equal: How the Bible Broke with Ancient Political Thought* (Oxford University Press, 2008), 173, argues that the other-worldly concerns of early Christians meant they were never particularly interested in diminishing hierarchies on earth.

23. Augustine, *The City of God* (Modern Library, 1950), 166 (bk. 5, chap. 17).

24. Cf. Friedrich Engels, extract from *Anti-Dühring* (1877), in *The Idea of Equality: An Anthology*, ed. George Abernethy (John Knox Press, 1959), 197: "Christianity knew only

know the famous passage from Galatians: "There is neither Jew nor Greek, there is neither slave nor free, there is neither man nor woman, for all are one in the body of Christ."[25] If you read what precedes that in Paul's epistle, you will see that it refers to the unity of the congregation of the baptized. It is not, after all, a general thesis about the basic equality of humans as such. So maybe there is nothing here for us to find.

4.

I talk as though we crave a religious account of equality, as though we—I mean we believers—would be disappointed if we didn't find one. Why? In Lecture 3, I mentioned Joshua Berman's suggestion that a transcendent property was needed to ground human equality because all nontranscendent properties, certainly all natural properties, were held in various degrees.[26] I said I did not think this was a good argument for invoking religious authority and that, anyway, there was no reason to suppose that transcendent properties are not also held by humans in various degrees. The idea that humans are created in the image of God might seem to fit the bill, but theologically it is a complicated idea, and in Christian doctrine it does seem to admit of differences of degree, from Jesus Christ alone being the

---

one point in which all men were equal: that all were equally born in original sin—which corresponded perfectly with its character as the religion of the slaves and the oppressed. Apart from this it recognised, at most, the equality of the elect."

25. Galatians 3:28. For diverse perspectives, see also Daniel Boyarin, *A Radical Jew: Paul and the Politics of Identity* (University of California Press, 1994), and Sanford Lakoff, "Christianity and Equality," in *Nomos IX: Equality*, ed. Roland Pennock and John Chapman (Atherton Press, 1967), 115–121.

26. Berman, *Created Equal*, 168.

image of the Father to fallen man being more "like" the devil, in Martin Luther's teaching, than like God.[27]

Still, on other grounds, some of us believe that a religious account is necessary to support the hard work that, as we saw in Lecture 4 (Sections 4–6), basic equality has to do. We face a challenging task: to make sense of and motivate our belief in basic equality. And the work that needs to be done is hard, in a number of respects.

First, there is the fact that we are looking to make sense of an *ultimate* value — that is, a value that has priority in the order in which we make sense of our values. Now, talk of "basic" equality makes it sound as though there shouldn't be anything more fundamental beneath it, but in my experience, whenever you go into a basement, there's always a subbasement holding up the floor. The point is that in looking for a range property, we have to find a way of making sense of human equality as a fundamental idea. This rules out certain candidates. Isaiah Berlin once ventured the suggestion that we should believe in the basic equality of human beings for utilitarian reasons.[28] But that would be question-begging, because utilitarianism itself is partly informed by basic equality: "Everyone to count for one, no one for more than one."[29] So that's a strategy we cannot take. Now, as you go deeper, a number of other familiar moral grounds are ruled out

27. For the point about Christ, see 2 Corinthians 4:4 and Colossians 1:15. For the Lutheran conception, see David Cairns, *The Image of God in Man* (SCM Press, 1953), 131ff. See also Jeremy Waldron, "The Image of God: Rights, Reason, and Order," in *Christianity and Human Rights: An Introduction*, ed. John Witte and Frank Alexander (Cambridge University Press, 2010), 216–235.

28. Isaiah Berlin, "Equality," in *Concepts and Categories* (Princeton University Press, 1960), 81.

29. But see also the discussion in Richard Arneson, "Equality: Neither Acceptable nor Rejectable," in *Do All Persons Have Equal Moral Worth? On "Basic Equality" and Equal Respect and Concern*, ed. Uwe Steinhoff (Oxford University Press, 2015), 31–32.

as ways of making sense of an idea like equality because most turn out to operate, like the principle of utility, at an intermediate level. Having already been explained, they are not available as explanations. Still, it is conceivable that the religious aspect of a person's life and being might fit this bill of priority in the order of explanation. For those who take it seriously, our relation to God is of ultimate significance, and that might be a reason for exploring its application in a foundational case like this.

Second, the property on which we base human equality must be adequate to the breadth of work that has to be done under the auspices of this value. Basic equality has to do work in politics; it has to do work in justice; it has to do work in human rights; it has to do work in human dignity; it has to do work in our calculations of the general good; and it has to do work in our social relations and in our sensitivity to each other's needs and interests. We need a concept that can operate across a broad array of the moral and political problems we face. It may be thought that since God is interested in everything—not only everything we do but how we do it—maybe a religious account can provide a comprehensive grounding for human dignity and human equality.

Third, the basis of human equality has to be robust. The idea has to be sufficiently powerful to displace the psychological variables ranged against it, such as people's preference for themselves or for the members of their family or the members of their particular community. Making sense of human equality—which is what we are doing when we look for a range property on which it might supervene—involves in large part making sense of the motivational power that human equality is supposed to have. Besides its psychological power, the idea needs also to be morally robust enough to trump other moral principles that appear to have bona fides of their own. So, for example, on what appear to be perfectly good consequentialist grounds, one might feel justified in torturing or assassinating a murderous terrorist as though he were "a Lyon or a Tyger, one of those wild Savage Beasts, with whom Men can have no Society nor Security."[30] An ideal like human dignity, applied equally and in an uncompromising way, has to be capable—at least in principle—of stopping such apparently sensible justifications in their tracks. Maybe nothing but a divinely ordained status could have that power.

One additional point I didn't mention in Lecture 4 is the following. The basis of equal dignity has to be not only ultimate, comprehensive, and powerful both psychologically and normatively, but it also has to have a certain resilience in our moral thinking. Philosophers have become accustomed to the methodology of reflective equilibrium, a process by which we bring our abstract and universal commitments into line with our considered judgments about particular matters by making adjustments at both ends—reconstructing our principles and abandoning or modifying a few of our considered judgments. The hope is that we will eventually be left with a set of considered judgments we can cling to, which is in rough equilibrium with a set of principles rigged to generate them.[31] In this process, it seems, we think of the principles we are working on as "ours"—ours to change or modify as the exigencies of reflective equilibrium dictate. Can we still say of the result that it is objectively true? Maybe, but if so, objectivity is a label we paste on to the product of our rethinking, on to the product of our endeavor to find a position we are comfortable with. Now, we know that "objectivity" is a problematic term in many contexts. But one sense of it might convey a sense that some of our deepest principles present themselves to us in an uncompromising

30. The language is from Locke, *Two Treatises*, 292 (II, §11).

31. For reflective equilibrium, see John Rawls, *A Theory of Justice*, 2nd ed. (Harvard University Press, 1999), 18–19, 40–46.

and nonnegotiable way. They are not supposed to be norms that *we* have control over; they are not for us to tamper with.[32] They simply command our deference. Not all of our morality can be like this; there is plenty of constructive work that needs to be done. But perhaps some of the foundations have this nonnegotiable character. That may include the basic equality of all human beings, and I wonder whether a religious grounding might not be a good way of characterizing this particularly strenuous form of objective resilience. Perhaps if we think of a position as commanded by God, we understand ourselves as more passive in the face of the principles put forward for our consideration than moral philosophers generally take themselves to be.

I mention these four requirements—depth, breadth, strength, and nonnegotiability—as possible grounds we might have for thinking that a religious foundation for basic human equality is necessary. It is nowhere near a compelling argument, but it is worth dwelling on nonetheless. It should not lead us to denigrate the attempts that are made by secular thinkers to plumb the depths of these matters. At the same time, it indicates reasons for thinking that religious arguments in this area are something more than mere historical curiosities. They may be exemplars of the seriousness that is undoubtedly necessary for thinking through a momentous issue of this kind.[33]

32. This is adapted from Jeremy Waldron, "What Can Christian Teaching Add to the Debate about Torture?," *Theology Today* 63 (2006): 338, reprinted in Jeremy Waldron, *Torture, Terror, and Trade-Offs: Philosophy for the White House* (Oxford University Press 2010), 269–270.

33. See also Waldron, *God, Locke, and Equality*, 242–243, and the excellent discussion of the possibility of secular theories of rights in Nicholas Wolterstorff, *Justice: Rights and Wrongs* (Princeton University Press, 2008), 323ff.

5.

That said, there are times when religious argument seems to fall short of the intellectual seriousness that is required. In my experience, secular thinkers are often infuriated by the bare citation of scripture, as though that could settle anything. They have to sit and listen to a creation story being told about our common descent and to the citation of the *Mishnah Sanhedrin* to the effect that one man alone was brought forth at the time of creation in order that thereafter no one should have the right to say to another, "My father was greater than your father."[34] They have to sit still while they are taught a doctrine that holds that Adam and Eve were created in the image of God — about fifteen or twenty words in Genesis[35] — and listen patiently while a theory of equality is erected on that. They hear quotations from the Psalms asking, "What is man, that thou art mindful of him?"[36] Or the Prophets, especially Amos and Isaiah, outraged at the oppression of the poor.[37] They are told about Jesus's concern in his ministry for those broken in body and spirit and his apparent privileging of the lowly and the despised,[38] not to mention the great parable of the sheep and the goats and his talk therein about ministering to "the least of these my brethren."[39] And finally there are the

34. "One man alone was brought forth at the time of Creation in order that thereafter none should have the right to say to another, "My father was greater than your father." *Talmud Jerushalmi Sanhedrin*, 4:5, 37a, quoted in Abernethy, *The Idea of Equality*, 65. See also Emanuel Rackman, "Judaism and Equality," in Pennock and Chapman, *Nomos IX*, 155.

35. Genesis 1:26–27.

36. Psalm 8:4–8.

37. Amos 2:6–7, 5:11–12, 8:4–6; Isaiah 3:14–15, 10:1–4, 14:30–32; 41:17–18, 58:6–8.

38. 1 Corinthians 1:26–29. See also Reinhold Niebuhr, *Beyond Tragedy: Essays on the Christian Interpretation of History* (Scribner's, 1979), 196.

39. Matthew 25:31–46.

passages I have already mentioned on equality in Christian community in the Epistles of St. Paul.[40]

We can cite all this and wave it about if we like, coming up with
chapter and verse from Galatians or Genesis or the Psalms that seem
to support our view that humans are all one another's equals. And
certainly people of faith have to take this stuff seriously; *we* cannot
ignore scripture. But from an even slightly detached point of view,
this sort of support can seem contingent, a matter of happenstance.
What if some other form of words had been used? What if some other
doctrine or passage or book had been canonized? Not only that, but
a great variety of things are said and supported in the scriptures:
polygamy, child sacrifice, and so on. If it is just citations we want, we
can justify almost anything. But that can't be what we mean by a religious foundation. We should not be looking for bits of holy paper to
glue to the underside of our convictions. Nor is it just a bit of theology
we want, to spice up an otherwise dull analytic account. Our audience
is entitled to expect something better than that. I don't mean to
eschew scripture altogether, but its use has got to be associated with
argument — argument that addresses systematically, and not just
sporadically or opportunistically, all the challenges and antinomies
that basic equality gives rise to.

At best, the mere citation of scripture might indicate a belief that
basic equality is simply a matter of divine command: "Treat one another as equals!" uttered from on high. Maybe this is what people are
envisaging: simple fiat. The Psalmist asks, "What is man that thou art
mindful of him?"[41] And God's answer might be, "No reason." Often
when people who have no religion imagine what religious arguments
are like, they think about some sort of divine command theory of that

40. Galatians 3:28.
41. Psalm 8:4.

arbitrary and voluntaristic kind. In other cases, however, the determination to cite chapter and verse rather than provide reasons or arguments is explicable as a strategy to solve problems like those we are going to talk about in Lecture 6: concerning profound disability, many people want to say that humans retain their dignity and their status as equals even though they lack some of the properties that equality is supposed to depend on; profoundly disabled people retain their equal human dignity because they have been touched in some unearned way by the grace of God. And the point is supposed to be that one either believes this or one doesn't; there is no argument to be had. That is not the line I take in Lecture 6, but I have heard a number of Roman Catholic thinkers saying something just like that.

6.

When we start looking for more substantial considerations, we might first want to take into account certain negative religious ideas. Rather than making the case for basic equality directly, these ideas warn against various consequences of its denial. So, for example, there has been opposition in Judaism and Christianity to imagined or established forms of inequality if these involve anything like the setting up of idols or human demigods.[42] There have been worries too about the deadly sins of pride and arrogance, and concerns that the celebration of inequality might crowd out the humility and penitence that our

---

42. Tom Wright in his work on St. Paul has been particularly interested in the apostle's concern about the idolatry of emperor worship in Rome; see, for example, N. T. Wright, "Paul and Caesar: A New Reading of Romans," in A *Royal Priesthood: The Use of the Bible Ethically and Politically,* ed. C. Bartholemew (Paternoster Press, 2002), 173–193, and N. T. Wright, *Paul: In Fresh Perspective* (Fortress Press, 2009). See also Niebuhr, *Beyond Tragedy,* 201: "The mighty stand under the judgment of God in a special sense. They are, of all men, most tempted to transgress the bounds of human creatureliness and to imagine themselves God."

religion requires of us. These are warnings about what might follow
from an unhealthy preoccupation with inequality.

Of course these warnings do not mean the inequality claims are
untrue. An analogy may help here. In "The Thirty-Nine Articles" of
the Anglican Church, dating from 1571, the Church's teaching on
the doctrine of predestination is coupled with a suggestion that it has
to be handled very carefully because an unhealthy preoccupation
with it can lead to terrible ethical consequences.[43] Nonetheless predestination is said to be true. The fact that such a warning has to be
issued does not make the underlying doctrine false. Something analogous might be true of inequality, even of the Reverend Hastings
Rashdall variety.

Or — still on the negative side — the religious case for basic equality
may involve disparaging or discrediting the scales on which inequality
is usually measured by those who cherish it. Inequalities involving intellectual excellence may be denounced on the ground that faith
involves forms of belief that do not necessarily draw upon what the
world regards as wisdom. Faith may be "foolishness" from the perspective of the world, and still it is deeply valued.[44] I don't think this

43. In "The Thirty-Nine Articles," the second paragraph of Article 17, "Of Predestination and Election," is: "For curious and carnall personnes, lacking the Spirite of Christ, to
haue continuallie before their yies the sentence of Goddes predestination, is a moste
daungerous dounefeall, whereby the Deuill maie thrust them either into desperation, or
into rechielesnesse of most vncleane living, no lesse perilous than desperation." See Oliver
O'Donovan, *On the Thirty Nine Articles: A Conversation with Tudor Christianity* (Paternoster Press, 1986), 143. For a vivid account of the dangers of a preoccupation with predestination, see James Hogg's 1824 novel *The Private Memoirs and Confessions of a Justified
Sinner* (Wordsworth Editions, 1999).

44. I Corinthians 1:19–27:

For it is written, I will destroy the wisdom of the wise, and will bring to nothing the
understanding of the prudent. . . . [H]ath not God made foolish the wisdom of this
world? . . . For the Jews require a sign, and the Greeks seek after wisdom: But we

point can be taken too far, however, because at the same time there is a strong valuation of human reason in both the Christian and Jewish traditions. On another dimension, inequalities may be proclaimed involving moral virtue or excellence. (We all like to think of ourselves as good people and to contrast ourselves with those who are not.) But claims that contrast the righteous too sharply with sinners may founder on the basis of a doctrine such as original sin. Or, even apart from original sin, moral humility is commanded as a virtue. In this respect, as in others, we say, "Everyone who exalts himself will be humbled, and he who humbles himself will be exalted."[45] Theories of inequality mostly come to us retail, not extolling inequality as such but proclaiming the importance of certain particular bases of inequality, like superior and inferior wisdom or superior and inferior virtue. One contribution that a religion like Judaism or Christianity can make is to cast doubt on the importance of the alleged bases of inequality; that is what I see going on in these suggestions about differential moral virtue versus original sin, and differential intellectual excellence versus the "foolishness" of legitimate faith.

It is not that these differences signify nothing, though their importance in, say, a Christian theory may be different from the way they are valorized in secular ethics. On moral qualities, for example, the religious point of view looks for different differences: the difference

---

preach Christ crucified, unto the Jews a stumbling block, and unto the Greeks foolishness. . . . [T]he foolishness of God is wiser than men. . . . For ye see your calling, brethren, how that not many wise men after the flesh, not many mighty, not many noble, are called: But God hath chosen the foolish things of the world to confound the wise; and God hath chosen the weak things of the world to confound the things which are mighty.

There is a good discussion in Niebuhr, *Beyond Tragedy*, 208–212.

45. Luke 18:9–14.

not just between the good and the bad but also between the penitent and the self-righteous. But neither Jews nor Christians are interested in establishing any ontological distinction between types of human beings on these bases or between types of concern or respect for human beings. What anyone *is* or *achieves* along these dimensions is just a kind of episode in the trajectory of life that is important—and similarly important—in everyone's case. It certainly does not establish that there are different sorts of life, requiring different sorts of response from others.

7.

So far these are all negative arguments, warning against a preoccupation with inequality and difference. What affirmative contribution may we expect? One of the important things about the implication of equality with dignity is that human equality is not just the absence of something or the existence of a rebuttable presumption.[46] Human dignity is not built upon some analytic default position. It is a substantive claim: it purports positively to establish the fundamental equality of all human beings on a substantial basis and at a very high level.

So, what *is* the substantive contribution? In general, we say that the existence of God has the potential to change everything, particularly if God is not just a first mover (in the narrow sense of natural the-

46. For the presumptive approach, see Berlin, "Equality," 84: "If I believe in a hierarchical society, I may try to justify the special powers or wealth or position of persons of a certain origin, or of castes or classes or ranks, but for all this I am expected to give reasons—divine authority, a natural order, or the like. The assumption is that equality needs no reasons, only inequality does so." For a discussion more favorable to the idea of an equality presumption, see Stefan Gosepath, "The Principles and the Presumption of Equality," in *Social Equality: On What It Means to Be Equals*, ed. Carina Fourie, Fabian Schuppert, and Ivo Wallimann-Helmer (Oxford University Press, 2015), 167–185.

ology) but a creator who has an interest in human beings—in who they are, what they are like, and what they do—and is capable of involving them in fellowship with Himself. The relation between God and man (using that term in the gender-inclusive sense) has the potential to consecrate the human person on a basis that goes beyond the terms of value in the world and to confer on humans generally a status and a destiny that transcend what they might make of each other, left to their own devices. Whether he does this and on what terms is, of course, a further question, to be answered through doctrine and scripture; that will affect what the implications are so far as basic equality is concerned. Anything is possible, and, as I acknowledged earlier in this lecture, that includes radical inequality as well.

An account of what I have been calling *distinctive* equality draws on convictions about the momentous character of the human person, and a religious account will try to draw this out in terms of creation and destiny.[47] In the antebellum case of *Dred Scott v. Sandford* (1856), a majority on the U.S. Supreme Court held that African Americans could not become the fellow citizens of white Americans; they were an altogether inferior race fit for nothing but chattel slavery. To this, Justice John McLean responded in his dissent, "A slave is not a mere chattel. He bears the impress of his Maker, and is amenable to the laws of God and man; and he is destined to an endless existence."[48] I have spoken at various times in these lectures about the doctrine of humans' being created in the image of God.[49] The idea is that we

47. For the difference between distinctive equality and continuous equality, see Lecture 1, Section 7.

48. *Dred Scott v. Sandford*, 60 U.S. 393, 550 (1856), Justice McLean dissenting.

49. This doctrine has been explored most thoroughly at the level of Christian and Jewish theological argument: see, for example, Cairns, *The Image of God in Man*; John Kilner, *Dignity and Destiny: Humanity in the Image of God* (Eerdmans, 2015); Yair Lorberbaum, *In God's Image: Myth, Theology, and Law in Classical Judaism* (Cambridge University Press, 2015).

have been created with attributes that enable us to echo God in certain ways and to be capable of fellowship with God, or perhaps to be like icons revealing and maintaining, as it were, the sacred presence of God on earth. These ideas convey a profound sense of the sanctity of the human person—each of us unimaginably and incomparably sacred because of this relation to the Most Holy. That's a sort of "wholesale" sanctification.

More modestly and at a retail level: in Lecture 3, we considered a number of possible properties or capabilities that might ground basic equality or contribute to human worth or dignity. The most important of these were personal autonomy, reason, the capacity for moral thought and action, and the capacity for love. Each of these can be understood in religious as well as in secular terms, only the religious account in each case transforms our understanding of the relevant capacity and gives it a significance that goes beyond mere worldly concerns.

(I also want to show that, in a religious account, these capabilities or their exercise can combine in a narrative for each person, which itself confers a momentous significance on that person's life and on every person's life. One of the main contributions of a religious account— given what our religious traditions involve—will be to complicate the logic of the underpinning of basic equality in this way.)

Let us begin with rationality. I referred in Lecture 3 (Section 4) to the Stoic idea of reason and of the bond it can form between humans and the gods: we not only resemble the divine, but our similitude makes possible fellowship with the divine. That's a pretty extreme religious gloss on the significance of our possession of reason. More modest accounts—if "modesty" even has an application in these transcendent arguments—see human reason as fitting beings like us for certain important ethical and juridical tasks in the world. For example, our reason means we are capable of being stewards of God's creation and viceroys of the order he has created.[50]

We may want to refer, too, to the Lockean suggestion that we need at least a modicum of rationality to know our Creator and to be able to apprehend what he requires of us. In *God, Locke, and Equality*, I identified and attributed to Locke the thesis that the significance of this capacity to know God was key to the basic equality that he built his system around. No great intellectual power is required for this, said Locke. Humans might vary enormously in their intellectual abilities, but "it yet secures their great Concernments, that they have Light enough to lead them to the Knowledge of their Maker, and the sight of their own Duties. . . . The Candle that is set up in us, shines bright enough for all our Purposes."[51] Locke believed that anyone with the capacity for abstraction could reason to the existence of God, and such a person could relate the idea of God to there being a law that applied to him (the human person) both in his conduct in this world and as to his prospects for the next. The idea is that God has conferred on those whom he intends to serve him the rational power that is required for easy recognition of his existence. Thus we can identify the class of those whom God intends to serve him by discerning which beings have and which beings do not have these powers. The fact that a person can get this far, intellectually, shows that he is a creature with a special moral relation to God. As a creature who knows about the existence of God and who is therefore in a position to answer responsibly to his commandments, this is someone whose existence has a special significance.[52]

50. See the discussion in Waldron, "The Image of God," 229–231.

51. John Locke, *An Essay Concerning Human Understanding*, ed. P. H. Nidditch (Oxford University Press, 1975), introduction, 45.

52. This is adapted from Waldron, *God, Locke, and Equality*, 78–80.

In the Islamic, Jewish, and Christian traditions, knowing God is
not easily separated from loving God: "Thou shalt love the Lord thy
God with all thy *mind*" as well as "with all thy heart." Nor is it easy to
separate the love of God from loving and respecting other humans:
our capacity to love is in part our capacity to echo God's love in our
love for each other. These religions encourage us to see beyond ourselves and our own selfish interests, to see something like ourselves
in the other, in any human other—and they tell us too that it is important to see God in our seeing ourselves in the other. Notice also that
what are stressed here are capacities which are relational in character.
They are not just features of the individual who has them; they relate him or her to others: knowledge to God, love in our relation to
God and to our neighbor, and so on. Dignity lies in our relational
capacities.

In Lecture 3, we talked also about personal autonomy—the capability that each person has of making a life for himself or herself and
of seeing the life that is being led from the inside, as it were, as something with meaning and purpose. That this can be understood in
purely secular terms is undeniable.[53] But in the light of a relation to
God, the narrative of each person's life takes on an additional and
special significance.[54] No one approaches autonomy simply in the
spirit of whim or taste. The best secular accounts pay attention to the
ethical significance of the way one shapes one's life and to the way
one's choices answer to one's character and potential.[55] I don't want
to pretend there is anything shallow about secular accounts of personal

53. For a particularly rich account, see Joseph Raz, *The Morality of Freedom* (Oxford
University Press, 1986).

54. For a fine discussion, see Robin Lovin, *An Introduction to Christian Ethics: Goals,
Duties, and Virtues* (Abingdon Press, 2011), chap. 2.

55. See John Stuart Mill, *On Liberty* (Bobbs Merrill, 1959), 71 (chap. 3); Raz, *The Morality of Freedom*, 378–390.

autonomy. But religious accounts add to that an awareness of the significance that one's choices have under the watchful eye of God. They are informed by the prospect of having to give an account of oneself to God. Also, the obligation that one has to one's own character and talents takes on a firmer foundation. The horizon of the life one is leading stretches beyond death to the prospect of glory.[56] And though the lives that are led and the stories that are told vary from individual to individual, the significance of what is happening is similar—operates within a similar range—for each individual and is structured by the same inflections of choice, vocation, sin, penitence, redemption, salvation, and so on.

This brings us to the religious view of moral capacities. In Lecture 3, we outlined an account of the momentous power of moral reason and moral agency in the work of Kant. Our ability to think through to moral principles and apply those principles practically in our choices and actions seems to be one of the most important facts about us, and the sheer importance of its existence in a person's repertoire of human capabilities—quite apart from how it is exercised—seems to establish it as a range property in our thinking about equality. As we saw in Lecture 3, Kant insisted that satisfying "the categorical

56. I have in mind the great peroration at the end of C. S. Lewis, *The Weight of Glory* (Harper Collins, 2001), 45–46:

> It is a serious thing . . . to remember that the dullest and most uninteresting person you talk to may one day be a creature which, if you saw it now, you would be strongly tempted to worship, or else a horror and a corruption such as you now meet, if at all, only in a nightmare. All day long we are, in some degree, helping each other to one or other of these destinations. . . . There are no *ordinary* people. You have never talked to a mere mortal. Nations, cultures, arts, civilization—these are mortal, and their life is to ours as the life of a gnat. But it is immortals whom we joke with, work with, marry, snub, and exploit—immortal horrors or everlasting splendours.

I am more grateful than I can say to Tómas Kennedy-Grant for bringing this passage to my attention.

command of morality is within everyone's power at all times."[57] He did not think it mattered much whether this capacity presented itself as highly sophisticated ethical reasoning or as the barely articulate intuitions of a young child or as the late-night lonely thoughts of the most hardened criminal.[58] The striking thing about his account was that even while he sought the lowest common denominator of human moral capacity, so to speak, Kant still maintained the momentousness of the capacity in question. I am referring to the great passage in the *Critique of Practical Reason* that begins: "Two things fill the mind with ever new and increasing admiration and awe . . . the starry heavens above and the moral law within."[59] It was a transcendent capacity that Kant was pointing to. It involved among other things the idea of moral autonomy, which is not just the authorship of a life but free will, that is, the choice of worlds implicated in the free counter-causal decision of each or any human agent where moral issues are involved.

Bernard Williams said that Kant's account was "a kind of secular analog of the Christian conception of the respect owed to all men as equally children of God."[60] The point is not quite right, because both Kant's moral philosophy and the Christian understanding of morality emphasize agency, not just the passive status of being a child of God. But Williams is right to notice the connection. The momentous power of autonomous agency, which Kant places at the center of moral life, is matched in a religious conception by our receptivity to

57. Immanuel Kant, *Critique of Practical Reason*, in Gregor, *Practical Philosophy*, 169 (5:36).

58. Ibid., 169 (5:36), 204 (5:80), 210 (5:88). See also Immanuel Kant, *On the Common Saying: That may be Correct in Theory, but it is of no Use in Practice*, in Gregor, *Practical Philosophy*, 288 (8:286).

59. Kant, *Critique of Practical Reason*, 269–270 (5:161–162).

60. Bernard Williams, "The Idea of Equality," in *Problems of the Self* (Cambridge University Press, 1973), 235.

grace as something empowering and dignifying the choices we make.

There is also of course religion's role in the incentives of moral life. Kant believed that morality needed to postulate the ideas of God and immortality in order to assure people that moral agency made sense from a practical point of view.[61] For the believer, however, this role of religion is real, not assumed; it is not just a necessary postulate for morality's sake. Moreover, it is not posited as just an external sanction. As we saw a moment ago, it furnishes a notion of accountability, under which we have the dignity of providing something like an explanation of ourselves and of participating through penitence and the hope of glory in the judgment that is brought to that account.

In all of this we are not only noticing things about our capabilities, as though the religious person just *sees* different features than are seen by his secular counterpart. The person of faith sees these capabilities in a different light, in light of various doctrines that are taught in his religion. He believes in things like judgment, forgiveness, and so on, and part of this belief is creedal and propositional. This affects the way we present them. I have phrased it all mostly in a sort of third-person voice, saying, for example, "This is the significance moral choice has in the eyes of the believer." But of course the believer holds this also in a detached and objective spirit, and we can say if we like, "This is what *is the case* if he is right." And—again if the person of faith is right—this is what the case is for everyone, as an objective matter, whether it is believed by a given person or not. (Like other moral philosophies, religious ethics helps itself to the apparatus of realism. That invocation is not self-justifying, of course, but the same applies to secular invocations of moral realism as well.)

61. See Kant, *Critique of Practical Reason*, 139–141 (5:4–6).

One last self-conscious thought: I have made little effort to trans-
late the religious side of all this into a sanitized "philosophese."[62]
Terms like "sin," "redemption," "glory," and "a personal relation with
God" seem indispensable features of the account I have given. They
stem from my own familiarity with Christian faith. Should I be embarrassed by the detail and particularity of this account? I don't
know. What I have written will put off and annoy those who are already ill-disposed to religious argumentation. On the other hand, I
don't want to pretend, through vagueness or equivocation, that this
is any less challenging than it is. If one of these lectures is going to
be devoted to religious accounts of equality, one might as well call it
as one sees it. Whether there is something offensive about giving
voice to all this will be explored in Section 10. In the meantime,
readers will no doubt have decided how much attention they want
to pay.

8.

I have mentioned a number of ideas: the sacralization of man; his or
her knowledge of God; the love of God and its reiteration in love between and among humans; the living of a life under the auspices of
faith and the prospect of eternity; free will; moral knowledge; the possibility of sin; moral orientation toward one's own sin—in repentance and the quest for forgiveness; and salvation generally. Faced
with this array of possibilities, the question will occur as to whether
we have to choose just one religious basis for equality, or whether
there are religious analogues to the points made in Lecture 4 about

---

62. I take the term from Jaco Gericke, *The Hebrew Bible and Philosophy of Religion*
(Society of Biblical Literature, 2012), 215.

complexity. Is it important for us to locate a religious basis for human dignity in just one of these ideas: the capacity to know God, moral capacity, personal autonomy, or the capacity for love? There is no reason, I think, to suppose so and several reasons to suppose the contrary.

For one thing, the narrower the focus on just one human capacity as the basis of equal dignity, the less adequate that conception may be to the comprehensive work that equal dignity has to do. What we are looking for is not just something upon which human equality can supervene but a basis for human dignity as a broad *status* with application across the moral board.

Second, each of the relevant capabilities is in itself internally complex; its exercise involves not a simple doing but complex forms of sensitivity to the world and to the presence and actions of others as well as the characterization of choice that is revealed in action. Third, each of the capabilities we have mentioned looks odd and naked considered in isolation from the others. In a theological account, our moral capacities are not separate from our ability to know God, nor are they separate from our capacity for love. Our capacity for love is intimately tied up with our knowledge of God, and our ability to repent is understood as a turning toward God, reviving or bringing to life our capacity to know and love him. Our understanding of wrongdoing is associated with our reason, and when it is oriented toward others, or the way we have treated others, it often involves love and an awareness of love's demands.

So maybe the possible bases of equality that have been mentioned should not be regarded as separate from one another. Instead we might think of them as *adding up to* a religious account of human dignity. It may be a gestalt—in the way, for example, that our bearing the image of God must be understood as some sort of gestalt, for an image does not bear to its subject just a single point of resemblance.[63] It seems to me that one important point on which a religious thinker might want to insist is that many of these capabilities—whether they are mental, moral, intellectual, affective, or voluntaristic—complement each other and feed in as parts of a single account that may be given for each of us within this tradition, not as a static description but as something that has movement to it. Both the relationality and the array of capabilities and relations that are involved add up to something like a kind of story that might be told about the significance of the life of every human being.[64]

So, for example, the image of God is treasured and consecrated not for its own sake but for the fellowship with God that it will eventually make possible if things go as they should.[65] The capacity to love others involves the possibility of a process in real time as well as the consummation of that process in the life to come. Knowledge of God moves from childish familiarity to creedal faith to something that takes us beyond faith to the immediate vision of God, no longer in a glass darkly but face to face.[66] Judaism, Christianity, and Islam posit

63. I owe this point to George Fletcher, "In God's Image: The Religious Roots of Equality under Law," *Human Rights Review* 3 (2002): 94–95. For a secular equivalent, see Francis Fukuyama, *Our Posthuman Future: Consequences of the Biotechnology Revolution* (Farrar, Straus and Giroux, 2002), 171, identifying human dignity with "a sort of Factor X which cannot be reduced to the possession of moral choice, or reason, or language, or sociability, or sentience, or emotions, or consciousness, or any other quality that has been put forth as a ground for human dignity. It is all of these qualities coming together in a human whole that make up Factor X." I owe this last citation to Neomi Rao, "Three Concepts of Dignity in Constitutional Law," *Notre Dame Law Review* 86 (2011): 199.

64. See also the discussion in Berman, *Created Equal*, 142, of the importance of the dozens or hundreds of stories told in the Hebrew scriptures about the lives led in the light of God's special concern for the destiny of his people Israel.

65. For the idea of the image of God as a sort of trajectory, see John Kilner, *Dignity and Destiny: Humanity in the Image of God* (Eerdmans, 2015), 276.

66. I Corinthians 13:12.

the *specialness* of the human person, but not simply in terms of the human person's having a certain static feature or badge of worth. Nor do they posit one special momentous property that all humans share, but they intimate a special story or trajectory or range of narrative possibilities that apply to each person. Each human is seen as the recipient of a high calling, a possible subject of faith, a subject and object of love, and a subject of penitence and object of redemption. These are processes, not just properties, and they point us toward a dynamic account of human dignity.[67]

So, to return to our theme of equality and the range properties that underlie it: instead of just looking for a property or a set (or gestalt) of properties whose static possession is supposed to confer sanctity equally upon every human person, we should think instead of the importance that attaches to the commonality of human nature inasmuch as the same story of creation, life, faith, sin, penitence, and redemption is to be told about us all, each and every one of us. That there is a story *of this kind* to be told about each individual; that processes of this kind are available for characterizing the life of each individual; that these processes are set in motion by our Creator even if the pathways that are taken are the subject of our own free will—this, it might be said, is the sort of thing that grounds human dignity on a religious account. We are each of us subjects of such a narrative, and though the narrative goes differently for each person, the range of possibilities—the possible trajectories—applies without differentiation to us all.

This seems to be an account of the right heft and shape. It is a story that rises up from the depths of our being, indeed from Being as such.

67. Cf. James Hanvey, "Dignity, Person, and *Imago Trinitatis*," in McCrudden, *Understanding Human Dignity*, 221: "The dignity of the human person has a teleology. . . . When seen within this teleological horizon, [a] person grounded in the *imago Dei* is not a static reality but one that possesses dynamism."

It is a story where the array of possibilities define stakes that are un-imaginably high. It is a characterization with the right scope, for the story I am referring to bears an intense relation to almost everything we do. The way we live our lives, what we think, say, do, hope for, and the way we interact with others are all moments in this story with various kinds of significance for it.[68]

I said earlier that this emphasis on narrative is one of the ways in which I believe the religious account can illuminate possibilities for a secular account as well. There is no reason why someone who is a secular believer in human equality shouldn't find the relevant range property in a narrative too rather than a static description. Our thinking about basic equality is often too static, as if we were hunting down a single isolable feature of human life on which equality could be based rather than contemplating the possibility of a variegated cluster of properties, operating together over time in the life of each person. It is surely of the utmost importance that the entities that are said to be one another's equals live their lives over time; they grow and decay in reason, love, and moral agency and in the complemen-tarity and interlocking of these; they make false starts and recover from them; and each makes what he or she can of the contingent trajectory of his or her particular life. What we accord equality to, where we find dignity, are human lifetimes, not just privileged mo-ments or fragments of those lifetimes.

9.

In Lecture 4, I spoke of the way our understanding of the capabilities underlying basic equality scintillates back and forth between seeing

---

68. See Charles Taylor, *Sources of the Self: The Making of Modern Identity* (Cambridge University Press, 1989), chap. 13: "God Loveth Adverbs."

them as range properties and seeing them as particular achievements with differences of degree in the scale on which the capabilities are exercised. I wanted to emphasize in that lecture that we do not lose interest in the latter just because for the purposes of basic equality we have to focus on the former.

The point is relevant in the present context as well, I mean the movement back and forth between concern for certain capabilities that humans have and for the way those capabilities are exercised over a lifetime. When we are doing the work that human equality has to do—sustaining human dignity, respecting rights, maintaining an equality of concern, and in our relations as equals—we are mainly interested in the potential, in the capabilities, and in the common structure of the story that is going to unfold. For other purposes, however, like comparing or judging merit, we are interested in the particular way the capacities have been exercised. And our interest in individuality never goes away. The Swiss theologian Emil Brunner insisted that our being created, all of us, in the image of God did not detract from the fact that each person was created different from the rest: "The differences between human beings are . . . just as much God's will and creation as the equality of personal dignity."[69] Brunner went on:

> In Christian thought . . . the two elements of equality and un-likeness are not in competition with each other and do not limit each other, because they are on a different plane. Men are equal in their relation to God, and therefore in their dignity. They are unlike in their individuality. . . . There is but one and the same dignity for all, just as theirs is only one and the same destiny

---

69. Emil Brunner, "Christianity and Civilization" (1948), excerpted in Abernethy, *The Idea of Equality*, 299.

whether they are men or women, children or adults, black or
white, whether they are strong or weak, intelligent or dull. Their
final destiny being the same, their personal dignity cannot but
be the same. All the same, the individual differences are not
negligible.[70]

I believe this notion of scintillation (as I called it in Lecture 4) works
particularly well in the context of the narrative account I have been
pointing to. It works because we have our attention drawn back and
forth for various moral tasks that have to be performed in our assessment of how life is going for any particular individual. What I have
been trying to avoid is any doctrine that we should be looking for
some small polished unitary soul-like substance to cite as the basis of
human equality. We are not; we are looking for something messy, dynamic, and complicated, something that can be attributed to everyone
while maintaining a sense of the importance of how in particular the
story goes for each person.

10.

I said at the beginning that there are many people who believe in
human dignity and basic equality who will not acknowledge a scin-
tilla of religious belief. They have little interest in the quest I am pursuing in this lecture; they see nothing important or even intelligible
in the considerations that have been mentioned. So once again a self-
conscious question: Should that have given me pause in my articula-
tion of these ideas?

Is it offensive to air a religious conception of basic equality in
public, in the company of such people? They are fellow citizens, after

70. Ibid.

all, members of the public to whom these things are important. For those who believe in them equality and dignity are matters of public concern; they are certainly matters to be discussed in the public forum. We need to talk about human dignity and the rights it is supposed to support; we need to talk about human equality and the view of justice that it is supposed to shoulder as well as the view of the general good and political democracy that it is supposed to underpin. These are issues of public concern, shared in a community that comprises religious believers and nonbelievers as well.

So, for example, human dignity with its egalitarian implications is put forward as a cardinal value of social and political life—for example, in Article 1 of the Basic Law of Germany—and it is widely regarded as the basis of human rights.[71] In some countries respect for human dignity is treated as an element of public order.[72] In the United States, dignity is a constitutional value, though not one you will find in the constitutional text.[73] Basic equality is certainly a constitutional value in the Fourteenth Amendment. So some will say that

71. Basic Law for the Federal Republic of Germany (1949), Article 1: "(1) Human dignity shall be inviolable. To respect and protect it shall be the duty of all state authority. (2) The German people therefore acknowledge inviolable and inalienable human rights as the basis of every community, of peace and of justice in the world." See also Universal Declaration of Human Rights (1948): "Whereas recognition of the inherent dignity and of the equal and inalienable rights of all members of the human family is the foundation of freedom, justice and peace in the world, Now, Therefore the General Assembly proclaims this Universal Declaration of Human Rights as a common standard of achievement for all peoples and all nations. . . . Article 1: All human beings are born free and equal in dignity and rights."

72. Cf. the decision of France's Conseil d'État in "the Dwarf-Tossing Case" (Commune of Morsange-sur-Orge, 1995).

73. See, for example, *Trop v. Dulles*, 356 U.S. 86 (1958) and *Furman v. Georgia*, 408 U.S. 238 (1972). See Gerald Neuman, "Human Dignity in United States Constitutional Law," in *Zur Autonomie des Individuums: Liber Amicorum Spiros Simitis*, ed. Dieter Simon and Manfred Weiss (Nomos, 2000), 249–271.

since the endpoint of this discussion is public property for public discussion in a well-disciplined set of forums accessible to all, the introduction of religious ideas into that forum represents an attempt to hijack it by people whose arguments cannot possibly make contact with the beliefs and reason of their fellow citizens. They say therefore that any published analysis of human dignity must take place under the discipline of public reason. If the discipline of public reason forbids or frowns upon the introduction of comprehensive religious or metaphysical views into public discourse, as John Rawls has argued in *Political Liberalism*,[74] then it follows that an account of the type I have been presenting in this lecture should be withdrawn or at best offered only on condition that it does not convey anything that could not also be expressed in secular terms. On a view like this, it is disrespectful to talk in public debate about the image of God or God's forgiveness or our destiny in glory to people to whom those phrases mean nothing—certainly if one does not propose to offer a secular "translation." Moreover if I intend to vote on that basis (where justice or rights are sat stake), then I cannot really justify my vote to my fellow citizens since I do not speak about these matters in terms they can comprehend. Given this deep concern about the introduction of religious or metaphysical thinking of any sort into the choices and deliberations of public life, maybe it is inappropriate to present this material in a series of public lectures at the state-supported University of Edinburgh.[75]

I don't buy any of this, for several reasons. First, even if one accepts the strictures of Rawlsian public reason, surely it cannot follow that we must hold our tongues altogether on the question of religious

74. John Rawls, *Political Liberalism* (Columbia University Press, 1996), lecture 6.

75. For some excellent discussion, see Nicholas Wolterstorff and Robert Audi, *Religion in the Public Square: The Place of Religious Convictions in Political Debate* (Rowman and Littlefield, 1996).

foundations or that it is always and in every context wrong to look into that topic. The issue of what is appropriately cited in liberal argument is one thing; the issue of the implications of our own religious faith is another. We have to be able to bear witness to the latter. Moreover, to the extent that Rawls's account of public reason makes use of the idea of an overlapping consensus[76]—overlapping upon certain principles of justice and the common good from a variety of points of view—surely each of those points of view has to be allowed the opportunity of articulating its way to that consensus, the route that it follows to that overlapping position.

I have indicated elsewhere my reasons for rejecting the Rawlsian account.[77] I believe that the idea of public reason threatens to distort as well as truncate public discussion and that it is better and in the end more respectful for people just to call things as they see them, giving the fullest possible account and bearing the fullest possible witness to the grounds on which they adhere to publicly important positions, among which the foundations of basic equality are likely to be prominent. The Rawlsians say this is disrespectful to our fellow citizens, for it involves our proposing as grounds for public principles (that we expect to impact their lives, perhaps coercively) considerations that they cannot make sense of. But the extent to which the story I have given in this lecture literally *cannot be made sense of* by a secular audience is often exaggerated, and the significance of that audience's incomprehension, such as it is, is often distorted.

The fact is that the public world we inhabit, as theologian Robin Lovin has pointed out, is a world in which "those who know and love

---

76. Rawls, Political Liberalism, 133ff.

77. Jeremy Waldron, "Public Reason and 'Justification' in the Courtroom," *Journal of Law, Philosophy and Culture* 1 (2007): 107–134; and Jeremy Waldron, "Two-Way Translation: The Ethics of Engaging with Religious Contributions in Public Deliberation," *Mercer Law Review* 63 (2012): 845–868.

God are mixed up with those who love only themselves" (or each other)—mixed up in complicated ways that do not allow us to separate them out into different and well-defined audiences.[78] Those who know and love God are themselves a mixed bunch with varying degrees of faith and understanding, and those who pursue secular reason are a mixed bunch as well, more or less distant from, more or less able to understand religious conceptions, which in some cases they have left behind in their own lives, having once been familiar with them. The whole thing is a mélange. In public life, we talk not with an undifferentiated public, but back and forth with various people in various settings. It may not always be realistic to expect conviction or even comprehension when one offers an account along the lines I have offered in this lecture. But bits and pieces of it may be understood or resonate here and there, and one can at any rate bear witness to the depth and character of one's conceptions.[79] Moreover even secular thinkers should be curious as to what if anything can be made of the religious grounds that have been adduced for human equality—for whether we like it or not, such grounds *have* been adduced; there *is* this heritage, there *are* these traditions, and

78. Robin Lovin, *Christian Realism and the New Realities* (Cambridge University Press, 2008), 190.

79. See Jürgen Habermas, "Religion in the Public Sphere," *European Journal of Philosophy* 14 (2006): 11. See also Waldron, "Two-Way Translation," suggesting that someone who produces a theological account of dignity or the wrongness (say) of torture *may* be trying to convince his fellow citizens to support a political position. But he may also think of himself as simply bearing witness to a particular view of what torture involves, a speech act that is communicative only to the extent that it tries to convey even to nonbelievers the seriousness and the high stakes that the speaker sees as bound up with the issue. He may just be trying to warn people about how seriously this is regarded; consider, for instance, the abolitionists' characterization of the U.S. Constitution in 1845 as "a covenant with death" and an "agreement with hell."

they *are* worth exploring (maybe with a skeptical eye, but worth exploring nonetheless).

The key to the matter, I think, is that some of those who *have* inquired into this business of theological anthropology claim to have found there the deepest and most troubling or the deepest and most inspiring account of what humans are really like. Others who have inquired found nothing. But the members of the first group have at least an obligation to speak out about what they think they have found. For consider this: Suppose we are moved by the scalar differences of degree that we see among human beings (in moral agency or rationality or whatever), and we are inclined to think that these differences should always be the basis of the way we respect and the concern that we show for the people around us. Before we act on that, we should want to be sure that we have heard everything there is to be said in favor of the opposite position, that is, in favor of basic human equality. To the believer, we will say, "Now is the time to mention any aspects of your theological account that might have a bearing on this." No doubt the atheist will deride the possibility and stand pat on what he is convinced is the full account. But it cannot be considered impertinent for the person of faith at this stage to play whatever cards he has. And conversely: suppose we are transfixed by the importance of the range properties and range narratives that I have spoken about in these lectures and that as a result we are counseling people to ignore for the time being the massive differences of virtue, the massive differences of cognitive and affective powers that exist among people. Then, again, we will want to be sure that we have heard everything, not just some of the things that can be said on the other side.

So it seems to me that the general strategy of everybody calling it as they see it and giving the fullest and most honest account they can is superior to a strategy of embarrassed self-censorship about a matter this important. These issues of human dignity, human equality, and basic worth are supposed to go to the heart of what is most important about human beings, and people must be allowed to say out loud and to each other in public gatherings what they think of as the best way to get at the most important truths there are on these matters. For all these reasons, then, I make no apology for giving a religious account this evening.

6

The Profoundly Disabled
as Our Human Equals

In the first five lectures we strove to see in the light of difference and inequality some basis for human worth and human dignity that constitutes us all as one another's equals. I think I have shown that this task is by no means straightforward, and in this lecture I am going to add even more layers of complexity.

1.

There is one challenge we still have to face, and that is the one referred to in the title of this sixth lecture. We have to come to terms not only with variation of mental, moral, and spiritual characteristics that human persons exhibit every day in the ordinary course of their lives but also with certain extreme differences that qualify some people as tragically and profoundly disabled. I mean disabled perhaps in the very capacities on which our account so far has made everything turn. This lecture addresses the predicament and the status of human beings who are severely cognitively impaired, suffering profound intellectual disability with a very limited ability to think and reason, individuals who can barely respond to those who care for them. Some of these cases are congenital, some are the result of terrible accidents or disease, and some involve old age and dementia. In many cases, we will be talking about progressive decline, a process of loss, with profound disability as an endpoint. What are we to say about the application of our ideals to these members of the human family — people of the species human who seem to lack the distinctive characteristics that I have been saying are the basis of human equality or for whom a distinctively human story is difficult to tell?

Some philosophers seize on these cases as an opportunity to deny there is anything special about human life as such, compared (say) to the life of other animals. For the profoundly disabled are certainly humans, and they are, it is said, no more rational than apes or dogs. The human range may have some outstanding members (like you and me), but the human range as such, when its *whole* membership is taken into account, is not particularly distinguished. That is what some philosophers say. In this final lecture I am going to take an approach opposite to that. I want to explore ways of thinking that allow us to maintain the principle of human equality even in contemplation of these hard and heartbreaking cases.

2.

"Disability" is a broad and problematic term. Because it raises issues of great sensitivity (particularly for those to whom it applies), we need to be careful in its use.[1] It is important, as Martha Nussbaum has

---

1. In the disability rights movement, those who champion "the dignity of being differentially abled" voice concerns about the tyranny of "normal" modes of flourishing and the social construction of disability. There are concerns too about what commonalities exist between inequalities focused on disability and those focused on the differential abilities allegedly associated with gender and race. See Lennard Davis, "Introduction: Normality, Power, and Culture," in *The Disability Studies Reader*, 4th ed., ed. Lennard Davis (Routledge, 2013), 2.

argued, to note the many varieties of impairment.[2] In this section, I want to give an account of what distinguishes the particular range of cases that this lecture focuses on from the broader range of disabilities as that term is ordinarily used.

I shall use the term *"profound* disability" to focus on a relatively narrow range of cases involving radical failure of one or more of the very capacities—reason, moral agency, personal autonomy, and the capacity to love—that are supposed to underlie basic human equality and that might otherwise have dignity-conferring significance.[3] I have followed John Rawls in referring to these as range properties,[4] though (as before) they may include relations, complex and interlocking capabilities, and prospects and structures for narrative. As in earlier lectures, I will sometimes use the term "range properties" as shorthand for this more complex account. The condition that I am calling "profound disability" may be understood as one that blocks or damages or supersedes the range property that in other cases is supposed to make sense of human equality. Or it may be an instance of the property that cannot plausibly be regarded as within the scope of the relevant range. Or it may be understood just as the absence of the key range property—though we are never talking simply about *sheer* absence, for in cases of profound human disability there are always present the organic rudiments or remnants of the capacity.

Let me elaborate that. The properties we are considering do not exist independently of our embodiment; they have material and biological infrastructure. The capacity for language, for example, depends on morphological and structural features like tongue and larynx and

2. Martha Nussbaum, *Frontiers of Justice: Disability, Nationality, Species Membership* (Harvard University Press, 2006), 99.

3. Inasmuch as different accounts of human equality emphasize different capacities, their understanding of this problem of profound disability will differ also.

4. John Rawls, *A Theory of Justice*, rev. ed. (Harvard University Press, 1999), 444.

also on the functioning of certain areas of the brain. Those areas and those features are not simply absent in the case of profound disability; they are sort of there, but damaged or not functioning for some reason. Evidence of this infrastructure entitles us to say the person concerned has or had a potential to speak, which heartbreakingly has not been realized. This will turn out to be quite important in our discussion (Section 9). So, when I talk about profound disability, I do not want it to be understood as a case in which a superficial human appearance is belied by the utter absence of the capacities in question, as though we were dealing with a fundamentally different organism that just happened to look like a human being. The tragedy of profound disability is that these familiar capacities might have been present but are not, and that sense of possibility is not just modal, but material. It is not merely that their presence is imaginable; it is that there is a material story to be told about the causes and contingency of their absence.

Profound disability understood in this way needs to be distinguished from other situations where we might use the term "disability." For many people who are regarded as disabled, there is no question but that they fit within the ordinary range of human functioning. I mean "disabilities" (with or without quotation marks) like deafness, dwarfism, and Down syndrome. For those cases, there is no question that the relevant capabilities fall within the range of the properties that equality is supposed to be based on. The young adults with Down syndrome whom I have met live distinctively human lives; people with dwarfism may celebrate difference, which may or may not correspond to other ways people use the term "difference" (or "différence"); those born deaf may strive to accommodate themselves with the way life is lived by others who surround them, or they may immerse themselves in deaf communities and live human lives

in that way.[5] It is up to them. My point is that these lives *are* characterized by the capabilities on which equality is based. These lives too
sparkle with unique human importance and sometimes with greatness. (The case of Stephen Hawking comes to mind.) But lives with
profound disability are lives for which, try as we may, a convincing
case of difference along these lines just cannot be made. And those
are the cases this lecture addresses.

Does this require a bright-line distinction between profound and
ordinary disability? I don't think so. Of course there is an array of
cases: totally nonfunctioning, barely functioning, largely impaired,
partly impaired, and so on, in all sorts of dimensions. And there are
borderline cases where we are not sure what approach to take. My
view is that, if we are anywhere near a borderline, we should resolve
to try applying in turn both the approaches suggested here. We
should think in terms of a layered two-track approach in which we do
our best to locate the case under the auspices of difference, and we
reserve what is said in this lecture about profound disability for cases
where that track proves unavailing.

The issue of profound disability is increasingly recognized as
important in moral and political philosophy.[6] Peter Singer says that
"moral philosophy can and ought to challenge how we think about

5. Indeed, what is known as the social model of disability takes the surrounding social
environment, constructed as it is for the advantage of the rest of us, as a key factor in the
predicament of the disabled. For a good, albeit critical discussion of the social model, see
Adam Samaha, "What Good Is the Social Model of Disability?," *University of Chicago Law
Review* 74 (2007): 1251–1308.

6. Lawrence Becker has observed "that every theory of justice must be tested with respect
to the issues of providing care for the profoundly disabled and of compensating those who
care for them." See Lawrence Becker, "Reciprocity, Justice, and Disability," *Ethics* 116 (2005):
9, citing Eva Kittay, *Love's Labor: Essays on Women, Equality, and Dependency* (Routledge,
1999).

people with cognitive disabilities."[7] I believe also that our thinking about cognitive disabilities ought on occasion to challenge the way we do moral philosophy.[8] That is what I shall try to show.

3.

The main thing I want to do is confront and refute an approach taken by a distinguished Australian philosopher, Peter Singer, the author of *Animal Liberation*, who teaches at Princeton University. I said a moment ago that the existence of profound disability among humans is treated by some ethicists as a basis for denying the thesis—which we have called "distinctive equality"—that humans are equal on a basis that distinguishes them from all of the non-human animals we know. That is more or less Singer's position. The approach that Singer takes is sometimes called "the argument from marginal cases." It may seem offensive to someone unfamiliar with the way philosophers argue, but I assure you it is necessary to set the position out clearly in order to refute it. So, here goes. Considering "the claim that self-awareness, or autonomy or some similar characteristic, can serve to distinguish human from non-human animals," Professor Singer invites us to "recall that there are intellectually disabled humans who have less claim to be regarded as self-aware or autonomous than many nonhuman animals. If we use these characteristics to place a gulf between humans and other animals, we place these less able humans on the other side of the gulf; and if the gulf is taken to mark a difference in

---

7. Peter Singer, "Speciesism and Moral Status," *Metaphilosophy* 40 (2009): 567.

8. Cf. Carolyn Ells, "Lessons about Autonomy from the Experience of Disability," *Social Theory and Practice* 27 (2001): 599, for a claim that "the experience of disability [can be] a means to inform and critique philosophical theory, in particular, theories of autonomy."

moral status, then these humans would have the moral status of animals rather than humans."[9]

But, says Singer, this may have consequences few of us would be willing to accept. In a rather blunt passage he writes, "None of us would want to use profoundly intellectually disabled humans in painful experiments, or fatten them to satisfy some gourmets' interests in tasting a new kind of meat."[10] Which is what we do with animals. Singer mitigates the bluntness, however, by insisting that the aim of his argument is "to elevate the status of animals rather than to lower the status of any humans. . . . I would like our conviction that it would be wrong to treat intellectually disabled humans in this way to be transferred to nonhuman animals at similar levels of self-awareness and with similar capacities for suffering."[11]

Fair enough. Still, as I said, the argument from marginal cases might be described as opportunistic. The idea is that if we follow through on our intuition that profoundly disabled people nevertheless have human status, we will find we have no basis for excluding certain non-human animals from that status. If we are to be consistent, we must either include the animals or exclude what Singer calls their profoundly disabled human equivalents. That is the argument from marginal cases. I say it could be described as opportunistic. By this I simply mean that it takes the difficulty that theories of human equality face in dealing with profound human disability as an opportunity for rethinking the separate question of the rights of animals.

Singer is surely right to insist that we deal consistently and nonevasively with this issue, extending the benefit of whatever scheme of classification we use to understand cases of human disability to all

9. Peter Singer, *Practical Ethics*, 3rd ed. (Cambridge University Press, 2011), 66.
10. Ibid.
11. Ibid., 67.

other sentient entities as well. Otherwise any thesis of distinctive human equality is going to be arbitrary and in bad faith.

To see in more detail how the argument from marginal cases is supposed to work, consider the account we gave of the properties underpinning basic equality in Lecture 3. I said there that an account of human dignity or equal human worth is going to have to deal with differences of degree among humans anyway. Think of the properties that our moral status might be based on. I mentioned our common capacity to feel affection, but people can feel affection in different ways and to different degrees, and some are hardly capable of love at all. I emphasized reason, but we know that there are differences here too, unequal degrees of intelligence and insight. I mentioned moral agency, but people are notoriously unequal in their moralizing, in the steadfastness of their moral character, and in their adeptness with values and principles, not to mention the uneven quality of their own moral lives. I mentioned personal autonomy, but people vary not only in the kinds of life they lead but in the extent to which their actions over time add up to "the leading of a life." Some people stumble from one decision to another while others lay out the vista of a whole life plan. These are differences of degree, and as long as those differences of degree are admitted, we have to ask: How can equality be predicated on such a variable basis?

To cope with this, I followed John Rawls's lead in invoking the idea of a range property.[12] Surveying the differences in people's moral or rational lives, we might identify a certain range of human functioning, with a bottom threshold, for example, and say that what matters is that one is within the range, not where in the range one happens to be. We do this sometimes in the law. In Lecture 3, Section 1, I gave a Scottish example. The city of Stirling, I said, is more

---

12. Rawls, A Theory of Justice, 444.

or less in the center of Scotland, whereas the little village of Gretna
Green, notoriously, is just over the line from England. But jurisdictionally Stirling and Gretna Green are both *equally in Scotland.* I
can give you a case for the United States as well: Princeton, where
Professor Singer teaches, is near the heart of New Jersey; Hoboken
is just across the river from New York; but jurisdictionally they are
both *equally in New Jersey.* Being in Scotland, being in New Jersey—
these are *range properties.*

Can we also say that scalar differences in the degree of our intelligence or differences in the quality of various individuals' moral decision making are eclipsed by a focus on some underlying range
property of rational or moral capability? I think we can, *provided we
motivate the focus on the range rather than on the detailed differences
of degree.* So, in order to ground human dignity in certain attributes,
we do not have to say that all humans have exactly the same cognitive capability or identical moral abilities. Instead we define a range
of capability—moral or rational, as the case may be—and we explain
why that range is more important (for thinking about dignity) than
an individual's location in the range.

Well, with that device in our pockets, we may be tempted by the
following thought. Perhaps we can take advantage of the flexibility of
a range property, manipulating it in a way that responds to our strong
intuition that the lives of the profoundly disabled are nevertheless
human lives and that their worth is human worth. Just as we use the
idea of a range property to comprehend large ranges of human difference among people who would not normally be regarded as disabled,
so perhaps we can use it to encompass an even wider range, taking in
those I have called profoundly disabled persons as well. Certainly we
should use the flexibility of a range property, if need be, to widen our
sense of the distinctively human lives lived by those who are disabled
in what I have been calling a nonprofound way, to accommodate the

lives they have made for themselves and the way they exercise their distinctive rational, moral, and affective capabilities. And it seems natural to think that the same approach should be taken to include profoundly disabled persons as well if their inclusion is what our intuitions command. True, this may have the consequence of including many beings who would not normally be characterized as humans but whose mental capacities may also fall within this drastically expanded range. A well-functioning chimpanzee may have mental abilities equal or superior to those of a profoundly disabled human being. But that is the price of our determination to accommodate all humans; or, more neutrally, it is the implication of the specification of this range for the relevant range property. We give up the idea of any distinctive human equality. And that, as I said, is Singer's conclusion in the argument from marginal cases. That is what he makes of "the existence of some humans who quite clearly are below the level of awareness, self-consciousness, intelligence, and sentience, of many non-humans."[13] We expand the range of the human to take in the marginal human cases, and the higher animals come trooping into the range as well, two by two.

4.

I left this issue until the end of this series of lectures, not because I thought it was less important than what I was saying in Lectures 1 through 5 but because I did not think I would be in a position to say anything sensible about it until I had the rest of the account in place. I needed the Rawlsian idea of a range property (and the complexities

13. Peter Singer, "All Animals Are Equal," in *Animal Rights: A Historical Anthology*, ed. Andrew Linzey and Paul Clarke (Columbia University Press, 2004), 167.

and difficulties associated with it) to be understood in order to be able to raise the question of whether the best way of approaching the problem of profound disability was to expand the range of the range of properties we were considering.

Rawls himself thought the answer was no. He made it clear in *A Theory of Justice* that the idea of a range property was *not* supposed to solve challenges to the equality posed by humans who are so severely intellectually disabled as to be incapable of the forms of functioning we regard as "human." Those problems are to be addressed in other ways. Thus with respect to "the capacity for moral personality," which is the range property he invokes, Rawls observed: "When someone lacks the requisite potentiality either from birth or accident, this is regarded as a defect or deprivation. There is no race or recognized group of human beings that lacks this attribute. Only scattered individuals are without this capacity, or its realization to the minimum degree, and the failure to realize it is the consequence of unjust and impoverished social circumstances, or fortuitous contingencies."[14] He seemed to imply that once a range property was specified, such scattered cases might be dealt with as tragedies in relation to the broad human range rather than being encompassed by extensions of the outer limits of the range. He implied that the theorizing that deals with these cases must be complex and sensitive, and it will involve special elaborations of moral theory, especially the theory of rights and justice. But arguably it cannot be done until we have specified *independently* (using a range property) the general potentiality of which these cases fall tragically short. So we needed the idea of a range property, even though — as I think — that idea itself is not what we are going to use in solving this issue.

14. Rawls, *A Theory of Justice*, 506.

Rawls has been criticized by some for his indefinite postponement of any full consideration of profound disability.[15] He never returned to it as far as I am aware. But I believe he was right about the order of argument, even if he himself had nothing to say about the second phase. I think it is not fair to say that Rawls evaded the issue, even though Singer is probably right that the challenge posed here is so uncomfortable that brushing it aside is often taken as the easiest way out. So far as Rawls is concerned, there is a kind of *dayenu* point to be made. There are hundreds of good philosophers in the world; someone who already did as much for political philosophy as Rawls did might reasonably have expected others to take up this particular challenge.

5.

I left my discussion of this issue also until after the lecture about religion (Lecture 5). The prescription for the Gifford Lectures has a slightly religious flavor. Lord Gifford set up them up in 1885 for the stated purpose of " 'Promoting, Advancing, Teaching, and Diffusing the study of Natural Theology,' in the widest sense of that term."[16] Some have suggested that we need a religious account to solve this

15. See, for example, Nussbaum, *Frontiers of Justice*, 108ff.; Peter Singer, *Animal Liberation: The Definitive Classic of the Animal Movement* (Harper Perennial, 2009), 240.

16. Lord Gifford set up these lectures for the stated purpose of " 'Promoting, Advancing, Teaching, and Diffusing the study of Natural Theology,' in the widest sense of that term, in other words, 'the Knowledge of God, the Infinite, the All, the First and Only Cause, the One and the Sole Substance, the Sole Being, the Sole Reality, and the Sole Existence, the Knowledge of His Nature and Attributes, the Knowledge of the Relations which men and the whole universe bear to Him, the Knowledge of the Nature and Foundation of Ethics or Morals, and of all Obligations and Duties thence arising.' " See *Trust, Disposition and Settlement of the late Adam Gifford, sometime one of the Senators of the College of Justice, Scotland, dated 21st August 1885,* http://www.giffordlectures.org/lord-gifford/will.

problem.[17] But that feels like a counsel of despair—an appeal to a deus ex machina. My reason for this order of argument was mostly negative. I wanted the religious material in place so we could have it available for *possible* use and so we would not be distracted or enticed by its unavailability. But I believe the problem of profound disability can be solved without drawing on religious material as such, although one of the themes I shall use in this lecture—the idea of a narrative, the idea of the trajectory of a human life—was important in Lecture 5 also.

You must know that I do not mean to disparage religious accounts of profound disability. And I have no doubt that religious people—church folks—can bring a special variety of respect and a special sense of our shared obligation to care for those whom God has called to live life under those conditions of disability. Christian accounts provide a familiar example. People say simply that God loves the profoundly disabled; they say the profoundly disabled are as touched by his love as any of us, and that it is God's freely given grace that consecrates each of us as one another's equal. That is not an evasion; it is a profession of faith, and we should respect it as such. The question is whether we can say a little more about the cases than that.

Actually, it is possible that a simple Christian approach of this kind may reflect badly on other things I have said in these lectures. In his

17. Singer has little patience with anything along these lines. Sometimes—for example, in Peter Singer, "Sanctity of Life or Quality of Life?," *Paediatrics* 72 (1983): 129—he talks about "the religious mumbo-jumbo surrounding the term 'human.'" At other times—in Peter Singer and Helga Kuhse, "Resolving Arguments about the Sanctity of Life," *Journal of Medical Ethics* 14 (1988): 199—he is a tad more accommodating: "Perhaps there are some who take a theological view about the value of human life, and follow through this view consistently. If there are such people, it may be there is no way in which we can refute their position, short of refuting some of their theological premises, such as that there is a God and that this God holds certain views about the value of life. We will rest content if we show that such people are much more rare than is commonly assumed."

encyclical *Evangelium Vitae*—the gospel of life—Pope John Paul II raised the question of whether we should even be considering capacities like rationality, language, moral agency, or personal autonomy, given our knowledge that there are some human beings whose lives cannot possibly be characterized in that manner. In section 19 of the encyclical, the pope criticized "the mentality which tends to *equate personal dignity with the capacity for verbal and explicit, or at least perceptible, communication.*" He said, "It is clear that on the basis of these presuppositions there is no place in the world for anyone who, like the unborn or the dying, is a weak element in the social structure, or for anyone who appears completely at the mercy of others and radically dependent on them, and can only communicate through the silent language of a profound sharing of affection."[18] Pope John Paul II intimated that it would be better if we did not make such capacities key to human equality but rather invested all our philosophical faith in the knowledge of God's love for each person, able or disabled. But one cannot help noticing that elsewhere in the encyclical—presumably where nobody who has read section 19 is looking—the pope seemed happy to insist that humans are distinguished from the other animals by their reason. He says God has endowed us with understanding precisely in order to distinguish us from other animals, and that this is part of the glory of the image of God in us.[19] I do not mean to be catching him out. I just mean that the reasons we have for focusing so strongly on moral agency—rationality, language, the capacity for love, and the capacity for autonomy—cannot be pushed aside in this way. They are part of our egalitarian

18. Pope John Paul II, *Evangelium Vitae*, §19, https://www.ewtn.com/library/encyc/jp2evang.htm. See also the discussion in Jeremy Waldron, *Dignity, Rank and Rights* (Oxford University Press, 2012), 28–29.

19. See, for example, *Evangelium* Vitae, §§34–35.

heritage, including the heritage of Christian approaches to these matters.

It would be wrong also not to mention that some theologians have actually bought into something like Singer's argument. I have seen arguments to the effect that higher animals bear the image of God more convincingly than profoundly disabled humans.[20] Robert Wennberg, who taught philosophical theology at Westmont College for many years, suggests that "the grossly retarded . . . need not be assumed to possess a moral standing as full as that of a normal human adult."[21] As we saw at the beginning of Lecture 5, there is no guarantee that religious arguments will solve our problems for us.

6.

It is important that the account we give should not be or appear to be rigged in favor of distinctive human equality. Frank and peremptory speciesism will not do, although some have taken this line. Stanley Benn (another Australian philosopher) cited the relevant property as *being a member of the human species*. He said, "We respect the interests of men and give them priority over dogs not *insofar* as they are rational, but because rationality is the human norm." Rational capacities, "may provide the point of the distinction between men and other species, [but] they are not in fact the qualifying conditions for membership . . . and this is precisely because a man does not become a member of a different species, with its own standards of normality,

20. See Malcolm Jeeves, "Neuroscience, Evolutionary Psychology, and the Image of God," *Perspectives on Science and Christian Faith* 57 (2005): 170–186, cited in John Kilner, *Dignity and Destiny: Humanity in the Image of God* (Eerdmans, 2015), 187.

21. Robert Wennberg, *Life in the Balance: Exploring the Abortion Controversy* (Eerdmans, 1985), 131.

by reason of not possessing these characteristics."[22] But this really will not do, since (as Singer notices) Benn's position explicitly begs the question in favor of human distinctiveness without justifying that postulate. One could as easily justify racism in this way.[23]

Nor will it do to use a methodology like reflective equilibrium to *rig* a set of range properties to accommodate profoundly disabled humans while excluding animals.[24] (One imagines the unit circle appearing like a large slice of Swiss cheese to ensure that only humans are within its perimeter.) That is the sort of thing that gives reflective equilibrium a bad name. As I emphasized several times in the past few lectures, any range property we come up with must *make sense* as a way of thinking about equality. True, in the discussion of "shapelessness" in Lecture 2, I acknowledged that we should not demand that the emphasis on the range property make sense independently of any concern about equality. But a patently rigged range property will explain nothing, make sense of nothing, do none of the things that a grounding property is supposed to do.

7.

So, is there any respectable way of making sense of the inclusion of profoundly disabled humans and the exclusion of the higher animals within the range of basic equality?

I am going to back into my answer by talking for a little while about an analogy to the case of the profoundly disabled: the case of very small children or babies. Actually I believe Singer thinks it is just an-

22. Stanley Benn, "Egalitarianism and the Equal Consideration of Interests," in *Nomos IX: Equality*, ed. Roland Pennock and John Chapman (Atherton Press, 1967), 69–71.

23. Peter Singer, "All Animals Are Equal," in *Bioethics: An Anthology*, 3rd ed., ed. Helga Kuhse, Udo Schüklenk, and Peter Singer (Blackwell, 2016), 538–539.

24. Rawls, *A Theory of Justice*, 40–46.

other instance of the same difficulty. He sometimes uses language that lumps babies and the profoundly disabled together: he talks of "humans with severe and irreparable brain damage, and also . . . infant humans."[25] Or he says, "Once we ask why it should be that all humans—including infants, mental defectives, psychopaths, Hitler, Stalin, and the rest—have some kind of dignity or worth that no elephant, pig, or chimpanzee can ever achieve, we see that this question is as difficult to answer as our original request for some relevant fact that justifies the inequality of humans and other animals."[26] Hitler, Stalin, mental defectives, and infants—how can we admit them all to the privileged family without admitting the higher animals too? Hitler and Stalin I addressed with my remarks on the back-and-forth between range properties and particular assessments of merit in Lecture 4. Nothing is gained, I think, by lumping all these complexities together into an undifferentiated "problem" for distinctive human equality.

But the approach that it seems sensible to take to the problem of babies will definitely help us with the case of the profoundly disabled. For babies too have profound cognitive, mental, and moral limitations: newborn babies are incapable of any of the various modes of thought or practical reason that we have identified as the ground of human equality. Newborn babies, two-year olds, even five-year olds are profoundly different from us grown-ups. Whatever model we have of basic human equality has to be able to encompass these cases as well. Once again a drastic expansion of the boundaries of the human range may be proposed as a solution: we expand the lower threshold of the relevant range property so that the cognitive capacities of babies are included. But then Singer is standing by to remind us that

---

25. Singer, "All Animals Are Equal," in Linzey and Clarke, *Animal Rights*, 167.
26. Singer, "All Animals Are Equal," in Kuhse et al., *Bioethics*, 537.

if we extend the range to include the newborn human baby, consistency requires us to include the dolphins and the chimpanzees as well.

There are, however, two reasons for thinking that a simple expansion of the relevant range property is inappropriate. One point is about trajectories (of life); the other is about teleology. First, *trajectories*. Singer's argument involves a rather static approach, as though there were simply these different kinds of beings: babies, toddlers, grown-ups, chimpanzees, and so on. So far, for the ontology of these lectures, I have simply used the language of *human beings*, identified as individual entities considered in terms of their current capacities. But the key thing about babies is that they are growing and changing. They exist at points of time, but they are not just individuals existing at points of time. They are early and frenetically developing stages of whole lives that will eventually be lived over a period of some eighty or ninety years. The element of time is inescapable, and our account of the grounding of basic equality is impoverished—especially with regard to infants but actually for all of us—if we think of it in "freeze-frame" terms.

True, we exercise our capacities at particular moments—though even then the exercise itself takes time. We do not just have flashes of rational insight; we think and figure and calculate and revise. We do not just make momentary moral decisions; we ponder moral issues, sometimes for years, and our acting on a particular moral decision is also often a matter of steadfastness—or constant alert and adjustment—over time. We have had hints of this already. In Lecture 5, I introduced the element of time and extension over time, suggesting that religious conceptions of the basis of human equality might proceed not just in terms of capabilities but also in terms of narratives—faith, moral knowledge, sin, consequence, repentance, redemption, salvation, and so on—involving the successive exercise of various capabilities, not to mention the receipt over time of things like judgment, forgiveness, and grace. But whether or not it is religious, any philosophical account of human equality ought to come to terms with the fact that human lives are lived along a trajectory, at various stages of which—infancy, childhood, mature adulthood, senescence—we seem to present ourselves as different kinds of human. This is true of every human life. As Eva Kittay observes, we have all been in the condition of babies at one stage in our lives.[27] Every human life is a developmental trajectory—changing, but changing intelligibly according to a familiar pattern. And what we value when we value human persons is the whole of that trajectory. We value whole human lives, as well as whatever matters to us about particular time slices of them, and even when we value the time slices we do so in reference to the whole human lives of which they are a part.

None of this is incompatible with the idea of range property. But if we were diagramming it, we would need a three-dimensional rather than a two-dimensional presentation of ranges, with ranges at particular times arrayed in a sort of salami shape, from birth to death. On this model, a person's possession of a range property would be conceived not just in terms of a point in a circle but in terms of a line connecting successive points in successive circles (with different diameters, each reflecting the ordinary human range at that time of life).

How does this affect the way we think about babies? Well, the trajectory of every human life comprises phases of development, and at each such phase there will be a range of capacities—a range of baby capacities, a range of toddler capacities, a range of teenage capacities, a range of adult capacities, and a range of octogenarian capacities. For certain purposes we might want to compare a baby's capacities with

27. Eva Kittay, "Taking Dependency Seriously: Family and Medical Leave Act Considered in Light of the Social Organization of Dependency Work and Gender Equality," *Hypatia* 10 (1995): 8.

adult capacities—for the purposes of developmental research, for example. But not for purposes of human dignity or human equality. I believe that dignity is to be accorded to a whole life—developing, flourishing, and declining—rather than to privileged time slices of a life. And the equality claim is made as between the full trajectories of all humans, not as between particular time slices of those trajectories. Even if our attention is riveted on the present, we say, "This human is to be treated now as the equal of all other humans, because of the sort of life it has or will have or could have had." In a sense it is true that the human range has to be wide enough to accommodate each human baby as well as each human adult. Overall that has to be the case. In another sense it is a category mistake to compare a particular baby's location in the baby-capacity space with any particular adult's location in adult-capacity space, at least for ethical purposes.

This temporal dimension—lives lived on a trajectory—is true not just of humans. It is true also of the other mammals that, on Singer's account, we might compare them to. It is true for chimpanzees: they too develop; their capacities too are to be considered in a three-dimensional series. They too have infant stages and adult stages. And if we are making the comparison on which Singer predicates his position, we should surely be making the comparison of whole lives, not comparing adult chimpanzees with human babies. The relevant comparison for any ethical purpose, at this level, is to compare a human life with a chimpanzee life. Or, if we *are* interested in human life slices, a human newborn with a chimpanzee newborn or an adult chimpanzee with an adult human.

This leaves us with a difficult question, which also needs to be addressed: What are the implications of what I have just said for our view about stages of human life before birth? Presumably a fetus is part of this human trajectory as well, and when I say human value and human worth have to be ascribed to a human life as a whole, there does not seem to be any way of denying that this whole will comprise fetal as well as infant and adult stages. It does not follow that there should be laws prohibiting abortion: abortion policy is about what the law should or should not do so far as interfering with the reproductive lives of women is concerned. To sustain a pro-choice position one does not have to deny that the fetus is an early stage of a human life. And certainly it would be a mistake to let our picture of what a human being essentially is to be held hostage to abortion politics; it would be wrong to abandon what I have called the trajectory view of a human life simply because, for political reasons, one wanted to ascribe subhuman status to the fetus. We have to give the best account we can of the trajectory of a human life and also give the best account we can of what the law should do about reproductive rights.

8.

The trajectory of life is one thing I want to stress in our understanding of the position of babies. (Remember we are considering the status of babies, for a few minutes, in relation to other humans and in relation to non-human animals as an analogy to or as proxy for our discussion of the profoundly disabled. I will return to disability shortly.) I said that the second point I wanted to stress about babies is *teleology*. It complements what we have already said about the early stages of a whole human life. But it involves some more complicated intellectual challenges.

Suppose one were to emphasize something like *the capacity for reason* as the relevant range property underpinning basic equality. Then one might deal with the case of infants not by expanding one's notion of reason to include the mental operations of a one-month-old baby but by defining something like a teleological relation between the baby's present capacities and the capacities indicated within the ambit of a range property focused on mature reason. Here I take as my inspiration the philosopher John Locke. Addressing reason as the basis of human equality, Locke said this about children: "Children, I confess, are not born in this full state of Equality, though they are born to it. . . . We are born Free, as we are born Rational; not that we have actually the Exercise of either: Age, that brings one, brings with it the other too."[28] This is a compressed passage, but very important. Human children are not born in the full state of human capacity; they are not born with mature intellectual capability. But they are, as Locke says, *born to it.* They are destined for rationality. Locke uses this to develop a functional account of parental authority and the constraints upon it: "The Power, then, that Parents have over their Children, arises from that Duty which is incumbent on them, to take care of their Off-spring, during the imperfect state of Childhood. To inform the Mind, and govern the Actions of their yet ignorant Nonage, till Reason shall take its place, and ease them of that Trouble, is what . . . the Parents are bound to."[29] It is the job of the parents, he said, to bring the children to the rationality that is their destiny.

Locke had to say this because he was combating prejudices that treated children as the (disposable) property of their fathers and theories that used paternity, so understood, as a conception underlying absolute monarchy. I think modern parents largely accept Locke's developmental account and the understanding of parental responsibility that goes with it. Confronted with a six-month-old baby, they do not just say to each other, "Oh how interesting, a human-looking entity with the intelligence of a chimpanzee." Instead, they take seriously the potential that their child exhibits, and they take themselves

28. John Locke, *Two Treatises of Government* (1689), ed. Peter Laslett (Cambridge University Press, 1988), 322, 326 (II, §§55, 58).

29. Ibid., 324 (§58).

to have the obligation to develop this potential and bring it on, encouraging it and safeguarding it even in its earliest stages against damage. They think about it teleologically.[30]

Where does this leave the comparison with other animals? Well, it means we can say that human babies are different from chimpanzee babies inasmuch as the former are, in Locke's terms, born *to* the status of adult rational humans whereas the latter—infant chimpanzees—are not born to human rationality but (using the same teleological "to") *to* the capacities of adult chimpanzees. The human baby has the potential to become a rational adult human; the chimpanzee does not. Anyone nurturing a baby has no choice but to think in these terms.

I am saying the *telos* of their development is different. Should we be comfortable with this teleology? Singer is not, and he tries as far as possible to avoid any talk of potential.[31] Sue Donaldson and Will Kymlicka claim that arguments based on "species potential" involve "contorted" intellectual gymnastics and "forms of argumentation that are widely discredited in all other areas of moral and political philosophy."[32] And I have heard other philosophers denounce the relevant ideas of potential and telos as superstitions—as though my

30. Singer seems to deny this. He says that "we should give no weight to the potential of the newborn infant." Helga Kuhse and Peter Singer, "Ethics and the Handicapped Newborn Infant," *Social Research* 52 (1985): 531. I suspect he worries that if we acknowledge the significance of the newborn's potential, we will be led to uncongenial positions regarding abortion. See also the discussion of fetal potential in Peter Singer, "Ethics and Disability," *Journal of Disability Policy Studies* (2005), http://www.egs.edu/faculty/peter-singer/articles/ethics-and-disability/. As I indicated at the end of Section 7, this seems to be a case of the tail wagging the dog so far as the priorities of our analyses are concerned.

31. Singer, "All Animals Are Equal," in Kuhse et al., *Bioethics*, 537, says that he wants "to avoid the complication of the relevance of a being's potential" in his analysis.

32. Sue Donaldson and Will Kymlicka, *Zoopolis: A Political Theory of Animal Rights* (Oxford University Press, 2009), 29.

previous few paragraphs were about what God intends for our development. Certainly in Locke's hands, the idea does have a religious flavor. But it need not.

In the first instance the teleology I am invoking here is biological. The child is born with a tongue, a larynx, and a brain that develops in certain ways, and the ways in which they develop are unintelligible except on the assumption that they are developing for speech. The underlying account here is evolutionary, not theological. The tongue, the larynx, and the neural pathways that control them became, in evolutionary terms, what they now are because successive stages of noise making, oral communication, and the external rendering (for self and others) of complex thought processes were advantageous to the organisms that happened to develop structures that made them possible.

The topic of functional explanation in the biological sciences is huge, and I cannot go into it in detail here.[33] As Philip Kitcher puts it, "The organic world is full of functions and biologists' descriptions of that world abound in functional talk."[34] Philosophers continue to debate the precise way to formulate and analyze the workings of functional explanations in biology. Suffice to say that explanations of this kind are neither rigged nor spooky. As you know by now, I am not opposed in principle to religious explanations. But this is *not* a case where religious explanations are needed. Instead the account involves the evolution and growth of organic structures, whose best explanation is the survival and reproductive advantage (to the generations of organisms that possess them) of the ways they will perform and be exercised later in the entities' lives. Capabilities like speech, perception, cognition, and reasoning do not just light upon individuals at

33. See, for example, the essays in Colin Allen, Marc Bekoff, and George Lauder, eds., *Nature's Purposes: Analyses of Function and Design in Biology* (MIT Press, 1998).

34. Philip Kitcher, "Function and Design," in Allen et al., *Nature's Purposes*, 479.

various stages, being utterly absent at others, by God's touch or in the spirit of some sort of Aristotelian mysticism. They have an organic infrastructure and an evolutionary backstory.

Nor is it just a matter of logical possibility.[35] The underlying account is material, not modal. The nature of the potential can be described in material terms and the trajectory of its ordinary development delineated.

It is true that in their early stages, the material infrastructure of these capacities—for speech, say, or cognition—does not support the operation that constitutes their function. The evolutionary advantage of speech and understanding is something that is realized organically over time in the development of each individual. What has evolved, then, in the species is not just a set of structures and mechanisms that enable speech and cognition but processes of individual growth and development for each individual of a set of structures and mechanisms that enable speech and cognition. Understanding them in this way, we can attribute a telos, *in an entirely naturalistic sense*, not only to the structures and mechanisms when they are fully developed but to the earlier stages of their organic development. This is what I am invoking when I say, with Locke, that the individual infant human, unlike the individual infant chimpanzee, has a potential for rationality.

Of course it is one thing to observe and make sense of functional explanation in biology and human development; it is another thing to assign value to the relevant potentialities. I assume that Singer will not deny this naturalistic teleology—how could he?—but I know he wants to deny that it carries any weight in ethical argument. I have not been using teleology here to assign any particular value to anything.

35. Cf. Nathan Nobis, "Carl Cohen's 'Kind' Arguments for Animal Rights and against Human Rights," *Journal of Applied Philosophy* 21 (2004): 49.

But I have used it to discredit Singer's suggestion that there is no difference, ethically speaking, between an adult chimpanzee on the one hand and a human baby (or a profoundly disabled human) on the other hand. There is this teleological difference. What we make of this for the overall account of equality and human dignity remains to be seen.

If there is a difficulty with the teleological account, it is that it seems to privilege just one of the stages in the whole trajectory that I spoke of in Section 7, as though the only thing of importance about being a baby is being brought on to the actual attainment of adult reason. Locke talked about "the imperfect state of Childhood." We by contrast have come to see that undeveloped infancy has its own dignity and value, just as there is dignity and value in old age even when, mentally and organically, these structures are unraveling. I think it is possible to hold these two positions together—admittedly in some tension with each other. We delight in the young child for what she is, even though that delight is entwined also with our delight in her development.

9.

The teleological account helps us think more deeply about disability. Here are some simple examples. Birds have hollow bones, which make it easier to fly; the function of the absence of bone marrow is to make flight possible. But a bird whose wings are clipped nevertheless still has hollow bones, and the state of those bones cannot be explained or understood apart from the potential to fly, even though that potential now will never be realized. Giraffes have long necks to enable them to browse the leaves of very high trees. A giraffe whose legs are crippled and cannot stand up still has a long neck, and the explanation in evolutionary terms of why a crippled giraffe and an able-bodied giraffe both have long necks would be the same. They have long necks because that was the best way to browse the high leaves. We do not have to engage in anything mysterious or intellectually disreputable to understand the idea of potential here even in the midst of disability with regard to that very potential. And, again, it is not just a matter of logical possibility; it is something that can be made sense of structurally and organically.

We may say something along similar lines about disabled humans. The injury, disease, or genetic failure that they suffer from has prevented certain organic structures and features from developing in the way they evolved to develop or, when developed, from fulfilling the function for which they evolved. So they had this potential, which is something they share with the rest of us. But in their case, as not in ours, the potential has been damaged or frustrated. My point is that one cannot understand the nature or significance of profound disability without seeing it in this functional context.

I remember that Peter Singer was once giving a presentation at Columbia University in which he was pursuing his line about disabled persons and well-functioning chimpanzees. A woman in the audience raised her hand to ask a question. She said something like this:

> I have a profoundly disabled daughter, and you cannot understand the disability she suffers without understanding that this is a girl made for speech who can't speak. This is a being made for thought that can't think clearly. This is a person made for neural control of movement who can barely control motor functions. You can't understand the situation she is in except for her being, in a sense, *wired* for speech, for reason, for neural control of movement and the wiring not working. You can't understand her predicament unless you understand the potential that has

been frustrated in her case. She is not like a well-functioning chimpanzee.

I do not remember Singer's answer. In a subsequent personal communication, Professor Singer said he did not recall the incident, but questioned the ethical significance of the point I said the woman had made. "What difference does it make to the subjective experience of this woman's daughter that she is, in this sense, 'wired for' speech, reason, etc.?" I still think the woman had something important to say. Notice that her invocation of potential and function and of what her daughter was made for did not need to involve anything superstitious or theological. I forget whether she actually mentioned religious ideas. Certainly, if we want to, we can say God created her daughter to speak but her daughter cannot speak. I do not want to disparage that way of talking. But there is no need to introduce God into the picture in order to make sense of the potential Singer's interlocutor was referring to. This is a *human* potential, a potential of the (evolved) human organism, present in rudimentary form in the daughter, but effaced, blocked, or damaged. The profoundly disabled were human in their potential and they are human in their disability.

Our capacities and our potential are in the first instance material and biological facts, even if they have spiritual and metaphysical significance (as in Kant's account or as in the religious account). This means that their growth is to be understood in the first instance as a biological process. They grow, they are nurtured, and they develop. What is true of the growth of these capacities is true also of their decline and decay. The trajectory of our lives has a downside to it: aging and the decline of our faculties is a significant part of the human trajectory and thus of the overall lives to which we egalitarians attribute a distinctive worth and dignity.

Together these conceptions of the trajectory of a life and its potential give us some background context for disability. Think back to our model of the trajectory of a human life. We may complicate what we have already said about it by imagining that each stage in the trajectory is shadowed by a variety of ways in which things may go wrong, ways in which the organism, developed so far, may be harmed or disabled or fail to develop further. This is what we humans are like. All of us are subject to the contingencies of illness, dementia, genetic failure, and consequent, more or less profound disability. The possibility of these failures and disabilities is part of the human condition. Other species have their own equivalents — their vulnerabilities, their possible impairments. And so we should not think of the profoundly disabled human as belonging, ethically speaking, to a species that just happens to look like our own. Each one of them is one of us; *like us* they had potentials and, *just as in our case*, those potentials were fragile and vulnerable.

Some say we can't understand the value of anything human without understanding the prospect of fragility, failure, and decay. That can be a quasi-aesthetic point.[36] (In the words of the Richard Griffiths character (Uncle Monty) in the movie *Withnail and I*, "There is no true beauty without decay.") But whether or not we cherish fragility in a romantic sense, it is definitely part of what we are. We saw something of its importance already in Lecture 3 in Thomas Hobbes's invitation to consider "how brittle the frame of our humane body is."[37]

36. Martha Nussbaum, "Disabled Lives: Who Cares?," *New York Review of Books*, January 11, 2001: "Our dignity is that of a certain sort of animal; it is a dignity that could not be possessed by a being who was not mortal and vulnerable, just as the beauty of a cherry tree in bloom could not be possessed by a diamond."

37. Thomas Hobbes, *De Cive: The English Version*, ed. Howard Warrender (Oxford University Press, 1984), 45 (bk. 1, chap. 3).

The appropriate inference is to a view of the human person which unites us with rather than differentiating us from those who are not just fragile like us but broken.

It is not just a matter of potentials being unfulfilled, though of course that is also true. It is about the bases of our potentials being there and being damaged. This vulnerability to damage is a vicissitude of the human species, the species to which you and I belong. As Singer himself has put it, "At the start of someone's life, we can never know how that life will turn out."[38] Accordingly, the appropriate reflection on this fragility in the context of any given example of a person who is profoundly disabled must include the content *that could have been me*. In entertaining this possibility I am not imagining that I might have been a different sort of animal but rather that the structure and organic character of *my* capacities—*my* flesh, blood, bone, neural pathways, genes—could have been damaged, could have atrophied, could have failed to unfold and develop. It is part of the human condition—*our* material condition—that we are vulnerable in these ways. And matched with this sense of contingency for us all, there is an obvious inference: this person, for all her or his disability, is *one of us*.

10.

I said a little while ago that there is a difference between noticing organic functions in nature and assigning value to them. One value-laden way of talking in this context is the discourse of *misfortune*. We say it is unfortunate that an individual with the potential for speech and thought cannot speak or think clearly. I don't think this is inap-

38. Peter Singer, "Ethics and Disability: A Reply to Koch," *Journal of Disability Policy Studies* 16 (2005): 130, http://www.utilitarian.net/singer/by/2005----.pdf.

propriate.[39] We may even use the language of *tragedy*: organically there was a prospect of flourishing, but like all prospects for human flourishing, it was fragile, and in fact it was overtaken by disease or genetic failure. The good sense of these ways of talking again distinguishes our view of the profoundly disabled human from our view of the well-functioning non-human animal. As Benn observed, "We do not see the irrationality of the dog as a deficiency or a handicap, but as normal for the species."[40]

And we can take this further. Martha Nussbaum makes the point that, whatever is to be said for the Singer position, it must not efface the sense that the profoundly disabled person is one of us. We should not allow the analogy between members of other species and profoundly disabled humans to suggest (however slyly) that the profoundly disabled human may be thought of belonging, even as an honorary member, "to a species that has a normal form of life that is her own; that she has fellow species members with similar capacities with whom to form sexual and family relationships; that she is surrounded by species members with similar abilities, with whom she can play and live."[41]

Socially as well as genetically, potentially, and vulnerably, the disabled human is one of us. As Nussbaum points out, she lives surrounded by humans who lack her impairments.[42] Not that it is a misfortune for her to be surrounded by people whose capacities are different from hers. It is respect, concern, and love from other humans

---

39. We do have to be very careful with this vocabulary. Many people in the disability rights movement protest being analyzed through the lens of tragedy or misfortune. I respect that. For the *profoundly* disabled, however, the language of misfortune is not inappropriate.

40. Benn, "Egalitarianism and the Equal Consideration of Interests," 71.

41. Nussbaum, *Frontiers of Justice*, 192.

42. Ibid.

that sustains people with profound disabilities. Every disabled person
who suffers impairment of the range properties relevant to human
equality is related to someone who has those properties, and in that
sense the profoundly disabled person belongs to the human community. There is *no other* community of carers for the profoundly disabled person, no other community except the human community to
which they belong. The profoundly disabled human is not going to
be cared for by the chimpanzees whom Singer compares her to,
nor—to put it brutally—is she capable of a life among them or like
theirs. Moreover, the relatedness the disabled person relies on par-
takes of the importance of human relatedness in ordinary cases: a
parent says of her disabled daughter, "This is my child *too*," just like
her other, nondisabled offspring. Often it is a matter of love. We talk
of tragedy here, and it is important to note that whatever tragedy
we attribute to this situation is *felt*, and it is important to see also that
we have human ways, including loving ways, of responding to these
misfortunes.[43]

43. Jeff McMahan, "Cognitive Disability, Misfortune, and Justice," *Philosophy and
Public Affairs* 25 (1996): 34–35, whose position is in other respects quite close to Singer's,
acknowledges the point about those who care for the disabled when he writes:

> The cognitively impaired do stand in important special relations to some people.
> Their impairments do not cancel the significance of the relations that their parents
> and siblings bear to them. These people have special reasons to protect and care for
> them and are typically strongly and appropriately motivated by love and compassion
> to do so. And the rest of us are morally bound to respect these people's feelings and
> commitments. We therefore have indirect or derivative moral reasons to be specially
> solicitous about the well-being of the cognitively impaired that we do not have in the
> case of animals.

Actually I think McMahan is willing to consider a more direct position as well: maybe "the
relation we bear to the cognitively impaired gives us reason to give their interests priority
over the similar interests of comparably endowed animals" (34).

11.

I believe these considerations are sufficient to dispose of Singer's contention that any embrace of the profoundly disabled under the auspices of a theory of basic equality and equal concern and respect must lead to an embrace of the higher animals under those auspices too. There are all sorts of reasons for enhancing the concern and respect we show to non-human animals. But an analogy with the human disabled is not a good way of pursuing that agenda.

Still, establishing this is not the same as establishing that the profoundly disabled are in fact the full equals of other human beings, or at least we have to explicate that further step. What I have done so far is to complicate our sense of the range property or properties that underpin human equality. The relevant property should not be conceived of as just the trait of being rational or being a moral agent. It should be understood as a potential, and this means, *first*, that it is something represented organically (if only as organic infrastructure) in the life of every human. It means, *second*, that it is to be understood as something unfolding in time, presenting itself in different ways at different stages of the human life whose dignity is being considered. And *third*, that it is to be understood as something fragile, whose unfolding will in every instance be shadowed from beginning to end by the possibility of organic or genetic failure or damage. In these three respects, the profoundly disabled person and the person who is not profoundly disabled are on a par. They both have this heritage of a fragile potential that is supposed to unfold over time. Understood thus far, possession of the property need not involve the full realization and exercise of the relevant capacities.

Some may be willing to say that this by itself is sufficient to make sense of human equality. It is human potential that is the key, they will say. And just as it matters little, within the boundaries of a range property, the extent to which it is realized, so it may not matter, they will say, whether the potential is actually realized in a particular life at all. After all, "not just the disabled but every human being has potentials which through circumstances remain unrealized."[44] On this account, human equality embraces all humans, even those who are profoundly disabled. But it does not embrace the higher animals, for whatever potential they have or have realized, it is not the potential of human rationality or human agency.

I think it is possible to take this position. There is nothing arbitrary about the exclusion of animals on this account—nothing that their advocates could complain about as inconsistency or unfairness—and nothing question-begging about the inclusion of profoundly disabled humans. But is there a strong enough connection here between the range property so conceived and the prescriptive force of basic equality?

This is a difficult question to answer. We said in Lecture 2, in our discussion of supervenience, that there is no question of finding a property shared by all humans whose presence would *entail* that those who bear it ought to be treated as one another's equals. The search for an underlying property was not supposed to be a search for a way of bridging the "is"/"ought" gap, the gulf between fact and value. We are talking about factual predicates that make sense of an inclusive understanding of human equality rather than factual predicates that reach across the gap and drag us across. (I said this, in Lecture 2, in response to the view of Margaret MacDonald and Hannah Arendt, who both maintained that one could simply *opt* for basic human equality, simply *decide* to uphold such a principle, without treating it as a response to any factual property. I acknowledged their

44. Anita Silvers, "Reconciling Equality to Difference: Caring (f)or Justice for People with Disabilities," in *Feminist Communication Theory: Selections in Context*, ed. Lana Rakow and Laura Wackwitz (Sage, 2004), 57.

point that no such property could compel acceptance of the principle, but I said that the identification of such a property was necessary anyway to make the opting or the decision intelligible.) The point of looking for an underlying property was to find a way of *making sense* of the relevant principle or principles and providing a well-organized basis for their application. I admit that neither of these constitutes a clearly defined criterion. People may disagree about what makes sense of what, and they may disagree too about whether the application of a given principle is clear and well-organized. On the latter point, Singer and his followers may complain that, if mere human potential is treated as sufficient for basic equality and the rights it generates, then it is not clear whether that will extend to a right to be born or even a right to be conceived, for in both these cases, we are dealing with the prescriptive implications of some sort of human potential.[45] It is just not clear how basic equality, grounded as it is in this idea of human potential, is supposed to apply in these cases.

Moreover, it may be controversial whether the potential really does make sense of the prescriptive implications of basic equality. No doubt, to a certain extent this is in the eye of the beholder. But here is the difficulty as I see it. Inasmuch as we associate basic equality with certain fundamental rights, there may seem to be an insufficient nexus between what we are supposed to be making sense of (the rights) and what is supposed to make sense of it (the potential). In the ordinary course of things, we say that a person has human rights like free speech, personal liberty, freedom of religion—all this on account of capabilities like reasoning, reflection, personal autonomy, and moral agency. But the application of such rights to a being who has human potential but for whom the unfolding of that potential is

45. Cf. Peter Singer, "The Concept of Moral Standing," in *Ethics in Hard Times*, ed. A. Caplan and D. Callahan (Plenum, 1981), 43: "So far as the argument from potential is concerned, the non sentient fetus is on a par with unconceived potential human beings."

blocked or curtailed makes little sense. In ordinary cases, it is, after all, the *exercise* of these capabilities that rights-based respect is oriented toward. A potential for choice that is not realized, let alone exercised may make little sense of the relevant duty of respect. The same applies to the more abstract idea of respect, considered as a general requirement rather than as fixed on particular rights. True, if we define "respect" in the bland way Joseph Raz offers — where respect equals acknowledging the value of something and acting on that acknowledgment[46] — we may have little difficulty. We just acknowledge the importance of the potential. But if respect is defined more substantively, as a form of deference and accommodation, if it is defined to include recognition and acknowledgment of someone as an intellect with a point of view and opinions of her own, then again we may be hard put to say that we can make sense of such a requirement just by pointing to a mere potential for reason and agency in the being to whom it is supposedly accorded.

12.

The alternative is to understand the relevant property — the property that is supposed to underpin basic equality — in terms of the *actual* presence of capacities like rationality or moral agency within the human range as ordinarily defined. It is understood as a range property, as before, with different kinds and manifestations in the lives of different people. Also it can be understood in the complicated terms of narrative that we discussed in Lecture 5 (even if the specifically Christian version of that is not accepted). But on this alternative the primary understanding of the range property is not of a potential as

46. See Raz, *Value, Respect and Attachment* (Cambridge University Press, 2001), 160–170.

such. The underpinning of equality is understood first and foremost in terms of the capacities and their exercise. Nevertheless, what we understand as the relevant property is still seen as the realization of a potential. And all three points mentioned at the beginning of Section 11 remain important. The capacity is understood as a realized potential. Its realization is understood to have happened or to be happening organically; that is, it is something that has unfolded or is unfolding in time. And it is understood, as before, as a fragile process, whose unfolding will in every instance be shadowed from beginning to end by a possibility of organic or genetic failure, damage, and decline. Understanding its actuality in this complex way enables us to define a number of different relations an individual may have to the realization and exercise of this capability: (a) The individual may be at the early stages of its unfolding, as a newborn baby is, but we are to treat the newborn baby as though the unfolding of this capacity were of the utmost importance. Or (b) the individual may have suffered the misfortune of the unfolding of this capacity going badly wrong, leading to profound disability, in which case the individual concerned bears a tragic relation to the capability. Or (c) the individual may be at the end of a life, in which the capacities that underlie human dignity begin, more or less quickly, to undergo their inevitable decline—a process too that is shadowed by the possibility of the failures associated with conditions like Alzheimer's disease. These are stages, vicissitudes, or prospects that are or have been or will be pertinent to the condition of us all. On this account, those whose lives are lived within the ordinary range of human functioning have a basis for also recognizing as their brothers and sisters in human dignity those who have these more complicated features of consummated fragility and human misfortune.

So the second approach is more complicated than the first—the first being the pure potentiality approach. The second approach maps out different modes of participation in the basis of human dignity: full possession of the capacity, growing into the capacity, or growing out of it, or tragic consummation of the possibility of brokenness that exists or existed as a possibility in everybody's case. On both accounts we recognize the profoundly disabled person as one of us, but on the second account, the basis of human dignity is understood in a complex way, which may make sense of nuanced application of its normative implications.

What, then, are the normative implications of the second approach? For those who are within the ambit of the relevant range property, we give the individual the full benefit of human dignity, rights, and equality. Are we compelled to draw the same normative conclusions for the profoundly disabled persons, related to the human range in the ways I have just outlined? My answer is complicated.

First, we are not compelled to do anything. I already pointed out that there is not going to be a property that compels us to say anything. There is no intellectual property whose obtaining requires us to recognize others as our equals. There are properties and ranges of properties, clusters of properties, capabilities, and narratives that help make sense of our recognizing one another as equals. So the question becomes: What is the appropriate response to this sort of delicate and complicated situation?

When we deal with the profoundly disabled, we are determined to include them as humans and as our equals—grimly determined as a tribute to the nature they have so tragically failed to fulfill. I think we bend over backwards to give to those who are profoundly disabled as much of the benefit of basic equality, equal worth, and human dignity as we possibly can. No doubt there will be normative implications that cannot apply. There will be a need for continued guardianship and intense care; there will be less concern about independence. There will be choices that are normally privileged by rights that become problematic in the case of the profoundly disabled. A profoundly disabled person may not have or be able to conceive a view or a preference to express as a vote in an election, for example, though of course that does not mean that a vote to protect or advance his interests could not be cast in his behalf by a guardian.[47] Other normative implications of basic equality stand firm: equal consideration of interests, for example—pursued directly rather than through voting—and other forms of equal concern. And issues of justice and fairness are important, too, because of the great vulnerability of the profoundly disabled and the danger of their being neglected, exploited, or taken advantage of.

13.

Some writers, concerned for the disabled, describe approaches like this as patronizing. Anita Silvers denounces a comment by Charles Taylor, who, in his book *Multiculturalism and "The Politics of Recognition"* talks about our extension of the protections of equal dignity "even to people who through some circumstance that has befallen them are incapable of realizing their potential in the normal way— handicapped people . . . for instance."[48] This, says Professor Silvers, "suggests that it is only in virtue of an intervening fiction that such 'defective' agents have equitable access to the categorical principles on which humans generally are accorded dignity or respect."[49] She denounces what she sees as the intimation "that 'handicapped' people are equal only by extension or derivation or fiction because they really

47. For this point, I am most grateful to an anonymous reader for Harvard University Press.

48. Charles Taylor, *Multiculturalism and "The Politics of Recognition"* (Princeton University Press, 1992), 41–42.

49. Silvers, "Reconciling Equality to Difference," 57.

don't possess the essentially humanizing capacity to fulfill their potential normally."[50]

But talk of fiction here presupposes that there is some better account of the status of the profoundly disabled that we are covering up or compromising. That is not the case. I think one of the two accounts I have mentioned in Sections 11 and 12 makes the best sense that it is possible to make of the human dignity of the profoundly disabled. And I believe the second, more complicated account makes better sense. Whether the first account—the account based on sheer potential—would be any more acceptable to Silvers (and whether she could overcome its difficulties), I wouldn't care to say.

Bear in mind, too, the point I made at the beginning. This account is intended to apply only to *profound* disability. It is complemented by the determination that many forms of what we call "disability" are to be understood as the living of human lives within the ordinary range, even if these lives are distinctive or different. As always, we pursue that two-track model. We apply the track I have just mentioned to nonprofound disabilities and to borderline cases (as far as we can), and then in cases where, through misfortune and contingency, a person is profoundly disabled, we fall back on one or the other of the two accounts set out in Sections 11 and 12, underpinned in both cases by the considerations of trajectory, teleology, and fragility that I outlined in Sections 7 through 10.

Series Conclusion

The conclusion to almost everything I write is that *it is all very complicated.* And that applies here too. Will Kymlicka and Sue Don-

<hr>

50. Ibid.

aldson adverted to the increasingly contorted intellectual gymnastics that people like me have to resort to in order to sustain these points about basic equality.[51] But one man's contortion is another man's analytic complexity. I don't know if this is a satisfactory or unsatisfactory note to end on. Going in, one might have thought that the challenge of human equality would be met by finding some little nugget of humanity—some unitary soul within, some amulet or highly polished *je ne sais quoi* that would be the host of our dignity and the explanation of our worth.

In our exploration, we have found nothing so simple. Instead there has been complexity at every turn: distinctions between basic and surface-level equality; distributive and relational equality; continuous and distinctive equality; Rashdall-discontinuities; dignity and status; description as well as prescription; supervenience; multiple normative dimensions; range properties; range capabilities; clusters of range capabilities; range narratives composed of range capabilities; dynamic accounts versus static accounts; religious and metaphysical theories; trajectories and teleology; vicissitudes and vulnerability.

Is this what we should have expected? I believe it is. We humans are exasperatingly complex creatures. Our relations to ourselves and each other, as well as to God, are complicated. We are challengingly different from one another too, and these differences have been credited in a bewildering variety of hierarchies of subordination over the ages in religion and ethical and philosophical thought. And yet in the midst of all this, the idea of equal worth has shone insistently. "We hold these truths to be self-evident, that all men are created equal." I think the power of this insistence is compatible with the

---

51. Donaldson and Kymlicka, *Zoopolis*, 29.

principle's complexity, and I don't think we should throw up our hands in despair whenever things get difficult. We use the talents we have to make sense of these complexities, exploring them, keeping track of them, and seeing what we can make of them. Nothing less is expected of us. I hope in these lectures I have been able to provide an illustration so that we see how far this approach can be taken.

Index